JOSIAH TUCKER

ECONOMIST

A STUDY IN THE HISTORY OF ECONOMICS

BY

WALTER ERNEST CLARK

AMS PRESS
NEW YORK

COLUMBIA UNIVERSITY
STUDIES IN THE
SOCIAL SCIENCES

49

The Series was formerly known as
Studies in History, Economics and Public Law.

Reprinted with the permission of Columbia University Press
From the edition of 1903, New York
First AMS EDITION published 1968
Manufactured in the United States of America

Library of Congress Catalogue Card Number: 77-76670

AMS PRESS, INC.
NEW YORK, N. Y. 10003

INTRODUCTION

It is an unfortunate fact that we have as yet no history of political economy worthy of the name. The development of economic thought in Germany has indeed been well treated in the monumental work of Roscher, but we still lack any account of the far more important literature of economic thought in England. For the period before Adam Smith, so rich that a contemporary writer collected no less than fifteen hundred works on economic topics, we have virtually nothing but a few short essays. Even the separate writers, with the exception of Petty, Mun, Locke and Cantillon, have found little, if any, recognition. The absence of an historical school of economics in England and the glamour of a few great names which have thrown everything else into the shade explain, but do not excuse, this neglect. Careful students of Adam Smith who are at the same time acquainted with the earlier literature, are well aware of how much he owes to his predecessors; but the ordinary manuals of the history of economics lay but little emphasis on this debt.

In the course of many years of lectures on the development of economic thought before Adam Smith, it has long been apparent to me that before an adequate history of economics can be written, two things above all are needed. The one is a series of studies, each of which should take up by decades the controversial pamphlet literature on current economic problems in England, from the middle or end of the seventeenth century. The second need is a careful and detailed study of each of the more important writers.

The present monograph by Mr. Clark is the first of what it is hoped will be a series of such studies to be issued under the auspices of Columbia. It is not an easy thing for a young man to make a successful contribution to the history of economic thought. Exposition is indeed simple, but an exposition that is at once sympathetic and critical presupposes a fund of knowledge and poise of judgment that are not easily found united in scholars of less than middle age. Mr. Clark, however, has had unusual opportunities in the way of general preparation and has devoted a considerable time both in America and in England to research work on the subject.

The author that he has selected for his monograph is one whose importance has in modern times been much underrated. Tucker is one of those men whose considerable contemporary reputation has subsequently been unduly dimmed by the lustre of his more famous successors. Mr. Clark's exhaustive and interesting study speaks for itself, and will without doubt succeed in re-establishing Tucker in the estimation of his countrymen. The monograph is a painstaking, thorough and scholarly piece of work. It ought certainly to embolden others to take up the task of dealing in a similar way with the remaining important figures in the economic science of the eighteenth century; and when once this preliminary work has been accomplished, we may expect to be able to have some one undertake a real history of economic thought in England.

EDWIN R. A. SELIGMAN.

COLUMBIA UNIVERSITY, JULY, 1903.

PREFACE

THE economic writings of Josiah Tucker are scattered through four thousand pages, printed and manuscript, and are, in part, in very rare volumes. This statement suggests three of the aims of this monograph: (1) To collect and to arrange systematically the scattered writings; (2) To condense the voluminous writings; (3) To make striking passages of the very rare volumes easily accessible.

Part I. sketches, in outline, the man and his day, and gives a bird's-eye view of all of his writings. This is purely preparatory, that the reader may the better interpret the economic writings of which Part II. aims to make a convincing presentation. Tucker has been allowed to speak freely, for himself, that the reader may eliminate any interpretative bias which, much as the writer has striven against it, may have here crept into his comments.

The illustrative quotations, as far as possible, have been drawn from either the *Elements of Commerce,* or the *Instructions for Travellers,* that important parts, at least, of these works may be accessible. These two works are Tucker's most important, least known, and rarest, economic works. So far as the writer can learn, upon careful inquiry, only three copies of each of them are known to be in existence. Few, even among students of the history of economics, have ever seen them, and no one has ever made their complete contents known.

In making quotations no attempt has been made to preserve the orthography of an eighteenth century writer;

superfluous capital letters have been lower-cased, and quaint " ye " has been modernized to commonplace " the."

It is the writer's hope that this volume may be instrumental in making Josiah Tucker's economic writings better known; it is his belief that, when these writings are better known, their very considerable merit will place their author in the fore rank of English economists prior to Adam Smith.

To Professor Edwin R. A. Seligman, of Columbia University, who suggested this monograph, who advised wisely during its preparation, and who read it critically, in manuscript and in proof, especial acknowledgments are due, and are here gratefully tendered.

NEW YORK CITY, *June 22d, 1903.*

TABLE OF CONTENTS

PAGE
INTRODUCTORY NOTE. By Edwin R. A. Seligman 5
PREFACE 7
TABLE OF CONTENTS 9

PART I

THE DAY, THE LIFE, THE MAN, THE WRITINGS

INTRODUCTION 15

CHAPTER I

ENVIRONMENT

I Eighteenth Century Great Britain 17
II Bristol 18

CHAPTER II

TUCKER'S LIFE

Early Life 22
Clerical Preferments 23
Clerical Friends: Butler, Forster, Birch, Secker, Seward, Warburton. 27
An Active Politician 29
Relations to Turgot, Hume, Kames and Townshend 32
Family Relations 34
Personal Appearance 35
Epitaph. 36

CHAPTER III

CHARACTERIZATION

I Tucker a Thinker 37
II Tucker an Observer 40
III Tucker Independent 42

PAGE
IV Tucker Sincere 43
V Tucker Practical 44
VI Tucker Tolerant 45
VII Tucker Controversial 46
VIII Summary 46

CHAPTER IV

Tucker's Writings

I Classified by Decades 48
II Classified by Topics 50
a. Religious 51
b. Political 55
c. Economic 59

PART II

TUCKER'S ECONOMIC THOUGHT

Introduction 71

CHAPTER I

Fundamental Notions

Commerce as a Science 73
Analysis of Human Wants 74
Analysis of Self Interest 75
I Tucker on Wants 77
Wants in General 77
a. Luxury 79
b. Spirituous Liquors 82
II Tucker on Self Interest 84
III Tucker on Relation of Ethics to Economics 87
IV Tucker's Theory of National Prosperity 91
V Tucker's Historic Sense 95

CHAPTER II

Population

Tucker Advocates Needed Increase in Great Britain's Population . 104
Desirability of Large Population in General 105
Desirability of Large Population in Great Britain 107

PAGE
Polity to Increase Population in Great Britain 108
I Tucker on Immigration and Emigration 110
II Tucker on Rural Exodus 114
III Tucker on the Poor 115
a. Describes Condition of Poor. 115
b. Presents Claims of Poor 116
c. Criticizes Poor House System 117
d. Proposes a Poor House System 119

CHAPTER III

Agriculture

Relation of Agriculture to Manufacture 121
I Polity for Subdividing Great Estates 122
II Polity for Enclosing Commons 123
III Polity for Changing Tithes to Glebes 125
IV Polity for Increasing Buildings on Marshy Ground 125
V Polity for Increasing Amount of Timber 126
VI Polity for Registering Landed Titles 126
Tucker on Rent. 127

CHAPTER IV

Manufactures

Tucker's Economic Freedom Thesis 129
Manufactures, and Freedom of Trade Defined 130
Arguments Against Claims of Exclusive Companies 131
Against Standard Manufactures 131
Against Company's Claim to Develop Industries 131
I. Competition and Monopoly 132
Opposes Apprenticeship Act 134
Opposes Navigation Act 135
II. Labor and Wages. 135
a. Competition in the Labor Market 136
b. Piece vs. Time Wages 136
c. Division of Labor 137
d. Domestic vs. Factory System 141
e. Danger of High Wages and Holidays 144
f. Unproductive Classes 145
g. Opposition to Fixed Wages 145
h. Opposition to Apprenticeship and Settlement Acts . . 146
i. Opposition to Slave Labor. 148

PAGE

III Capital and Interest 149
a. Capital 149
b. Interest. 150
Rate of Loan Interest 150
Distinguishes Interest from Profits 151
Condemns Usury Law 151
IV. Machinery—Tucker Advocates its Use 152

CHAPTER V

Commerce—Foreign Trade

Tucker a Mercantilist 156
Glimpses of Full Freedom of Trade 158
Attack upon Chartered Trading Companies 161
I Philosophy of Exchange 167
II Jealousy of Trade 168
Opposes War 172
III Mercantilism 174
a. Tucker a Mercantilist 175
b. Tucker a Neo-Mercantilist 178
Gold not Riches 178
Favors Export of Bullion. 179
Distinguishes Merchant's Balance of Trade from Nation's 180
In Exchange both Nations Gain 180
IV. Bounties, ... 181
Infant Industry Argument 183
V. Colonies 184
VI. Statistics. 190

CHAPTER VI

Money

Summary of Tucker's Thought upon Money 193
I Functions of Money 194
II Standard of Value 194
III Market Price 195
Formula for Market Price 195
Opposition to Government Standards for Marketable Goods. 196
IV Philosophy of Exchange 197
V A Circulating Government Bond Scheme 197

PAGE

CHAPTER VII

Taxation

In General 198
I Tax Criterion 199
II Application of this Criterion to British System of Taxes . . . 201
Tucker's Summary of his Theory of Taxes 207
III Taxation Miscellany 209
a. Ability to Pay 209
b. Incidence 209
c. Collection of Taxes 209
d. High vs. Heavy Tax 210
e. Smuggling 210
f. Lottery Scheme 211
g. The National Debt 211

PART III

SOURCES, INFLUENCE AND CONCLUSIONS

CHAPTER I

Sources

I Debt to Other Writers: Petty, Child, Gee, Harrington, Mandeville, Berkeley, Ustariz, Montesquieu, Hume, Turgot, Stewart, Smith 213
II Reports, Statutes, etc. 219
III Personal Observations 220

CHAPTER II

Influence

I Tucker's Controversial Pamphlets. 221
II Tucker's Scientific Works Unknown 222
III Influence on the English School 224
IV Influence on the Physiocrats 226

CHAPTER III

Conclusions

I Tucker Deserves Higher Rank than he has Received. 229
II Tucker's Works Contain Much Thought Similar to that of the Wealth of Nations 230

PAGE
Appendix—The Skeleton of Tucker's Great Work 233
Bibliography of Tucker's Works 241
Bibliography of Replies to Tucker's Works 252
Bibliography of Tucker's Correspondence 254
Bibliography of Tucker's Life 256

PART I

THE DAY, THE LIFE, THE MAN, THE WRITINGS

INTRODUCTION

JOSIAH TUCKER (1713-1799) was an English clergyman who wrote many volumes and pamphlets upon theological, upon political, and upon economic subjects. This study aims to analyze his economic writings and to estimate their worth. To understand a writer or fairly to interpret his works, it is necessary to know his social environment, his life and his personality. The three chapters which immediately follow suggest the main economic problems with which eighteenth century Great Britain was concerned, give in outline the commercial and industrial conditions in Bristol, Tucker's city of residence during his productive half century, state the salient facts in Tucker's life, and present his leading traits of character.

CHAPTER I

THE ENVIRONMENT

I. Eighteenth Century Great Britain

During the eighteenth century Great Britain prepared herself to win and to maintain her supremacy in the nineteenth century. It was a martial century for Britain. Seven wars and two rebellions blared the red trumpet during thirty-eight of the hundred years. It was a century of territorial aggrandizement. The late seventeenth century's naval victories had made Britain mistress of the seas, and this contributed largely to the increase of the national domain during the eighteenth century. An island gained dominion over continents. In the east, British sovereignty began to extend over India, and Australia became a British colony. In the west, the Seven Years' War made North America, from pole to gulf, bend the knee to the British sovereign.

The possession of vast and far distant territories called for an able colonial policy. Perhaps the most important lesson in colonial policy which the century taught Britain, was that Anglo-Saxon colonies may be controlled best by being controlled least—the lesson of the protracted, but vain effort to retain the American colonies. Owing in part to sea control, and in part to growing colonies, British commerce in the eighteenth century greatly increased.

Thus wars, widening territory, developing colonies, and rapidly expanding foreign commerce were the large factors in British international relations in the eighteenth century.

Within Britain's own island territory, a new life, reflective of her widening world life, was everywhere in evidence.

Roads were made, canals were dug, wastes were redeemed, commons were inclosed, and harbors were improved. In her manufacturing life, the great change from the domestic to the factory system occurred, with its concomitants of labor and machinery problems, and its consequent development of manufacturing centers. To sustain the wars and colonial enterprises, and to further the large internal improvements, greater revenue was demanded.

The great problems, then, which would naturally attract the attention of a British student of politics and economics in the eighteenth century, were those concerning wars, colonies, population movements, machinery, trade relations, internal improvements, and taxation.

II. Bristol

Second city of the kingdom, Bristol, in the eighteenth century, was the busiest of the outports. It was naturally fitted to become a great commercial center; it swam upon the waters and "had its streets full of ships." [1] In the fourteenth century docks had been built, and from time to time they had been improved and extended. Its naturally excellent harbor, thus improved by art, attracted the world's shipping. The rivers Avon, Severn, Wye, Usk, Parrett, and Tone afforded natural water connections with the inland district about Bristol. A system of canals, built during the eighteenth century, connected the upper waters of these streams and perfected the means for inexpensive transport of domestic commerce. This brought all of South Wales and of West England into intimate market relations with the city by the sea.

Bristol also entered early upon a manufacturing career. Woollen manufacture began there about 1340. Thomas

[1] A statement credited to Alexander Pope.

Blanket, whose name still clings to a class of woollen fabrics, was among the Bristolians who early distinguished themselves in this branch of manufactures. The manufacture of soap began, at Bristol, in the first quarter of the sixteenth century, and the manufacture of pins and of stockings began there in the last quarter of the same century.

Eighteenth century Bristol made good use of her manufacturing and commercial legacy. By the close of this century Bristol shot had a reputation; crown, flint, and bottle glass, soap, hats, tanned and dressed leather, shoes and saddlery, brass, copper and zinc goods were being made, and there was a considerable tobacco and an extensive snuff manufacture. The domestic commerce had become large, Bristol foreign imports and local manufactures supplying a wide inland districtc. This district in turn sent its products to the seaport city for sale or for shipment. The most important sea traffic was being carried on with the West Indies. They took Bristol building materials, clothing, bottled liquors and sugar-making implements, in exchange for their products, sugar, rum, coffee and cotton. From Spain there came annually 4,000 bags of Spanish wool. In order of further importance, ranked the city's trade with Ireland, with Newfoundland, and with British America, in all of which a considerable capital was invested.

Thus the commercial and the manufacturing problems of eighteenth century Great Britain were Bristol's problems. Its merchants were sending their vessels laden with its manufactures to far lands, whence they returned with cargoes ranging from timber and tar to human beings.[1] If there were outport grievances against London, Bristol would have them. If national trade restrictions unfavorably

[1] It was to the Bristol slave mart that Rev. Thomas Clarkson came, in June of 1788, when he began his study of the slave trade. *Annals of Bristol*, by John Latimer, p. 473.

affected commerce, Bristol merchants would suffer. If frequent and prolonged wars interfered with commercial prosperity, British merchantmen would lie idle in Bristol's harbor. Bristol coffee-houses would discuss colonial relations, for had not that city been foremost in equipping early exploring expeditions,[1] and was not its commercial intercourse with Newfoundland, the Americas and the West Indies most active throughout the eighteenth century, excepting only when war checked it?

Again, Bristol's manufacturers were patenting and were introducing new machinery and were developing a factory system. If statutes preventing the free movement of laborers to their points of greatest productivity curtailed the supply of labor needed by the rising manufactures, the leather manufacturers, the sugar refiners, and the foundrymen of Bristol would have their complaints to make. If British jealousy of foreigners checked their immigration by refusal to give them full naturalization privileges, there were in Bristol evidences of contributions toward British prosperity made by the capital of rich immigrants and by the skilled labor of artisan foreigners. Since the manufacturers of the city were beginning to use patented machinery, the anti-machinery agitation would be certainly thrust upon even the least thoughtful observer of Bristol business life. Itself a historic slave mart, and in close touch with the slave-using colonies of the kingdom, Bristol's news records and current tales of slaves and of slavery would stimulate an analytic mind, in the presence of developing manufactures, to question the relative economic efficiency of slave and of free labor.

Sufficient illustration has been given to make it evident that eighteenth century Bristol epitomized eighteenth century Great Britain in manufactures and in commerce.

[1] Sebastian Cabot was a native of Bristol and voyaged from that port.

Perhaps no other place in the empire would have furnished environment more apt to lead an inquiring mind to analyze the economic life of the day. The very prominence, politically and commercially, of London would lead the outport student to familiarize himself with its industrial and commercial conditions. The capital's attempt to monopolize foreign trade, through the wide reach of privileges granted to its chartered companies, would certainly arouse in the outport a spirit of self-preservative criticism and opposition. This was conducive to a study of underlying principles of trade. Thus, a Londoner, studying the manufactures and commerce of the day, would tend to favor customs, for the customs favored London; a Bristolian would advocate an examination of customary privileges, in the hope that new thought might destroy old tradition, and give the growing smaller cities a chance to obtain, in rivalry with London, a larger share of the nation's business. London environment made for the advocacy of stereotyped ideas; Bristol environment made for that critical re-examination of these same stereotyped ideas, in the light of new conditions, which is so essential to progress in any realm of thought. The constructive critic is the potent factor in all thought progress; the apologist for existing conditions is, at worst, a complete check to any advance, and, at best, he has the negative virtue of preventing rash experiment. London was environment for an apologist, Bristol for a critic, of economic conditions. Out of Bristol, then, one conversant with eighteenth century Britain might rationally expect a teacher to come, who would teach as nearly the truth concerning the nation's economic life as any one of his generation.

CHAPTER II

THE LIFE

IN 1737 Josiah Tucker, a young churchman, came to the busy, manufacturing outport, Bristol, as a curate of St. Stephen's.

The twenty-four years of his life had recorded no unusual event. He was born in Langharne, Carmarthenshire, in 1713.[1] His father, Josiah Tucker, was a farmer who, not long after his son's birth, moved to a small estate which he had inherited, near Aberystwith, in Cardiganshire. In spite of the father's small means, the lad was sent to Ruthin school, in Denbighshire. Here he attained some proficiency in the classics, and obtained an exhibition at St. John's College,[2] Oxford, which he entered January 26, 1733.

[1] There are no biographies of Josiah Tucker, except the brief accounts given in the various encyclopædias and in the magazines current at the time of his death. With but three exceptions these biographies state 1712 to be Tucker's birth year. These exceptions are the *Penny Cyclopædia* (vol. xxv, p. 338) and the *Annual Register* (vol. xli, p. 350) both of which give 1711 as the birth year, and the *European Magazine* (vol. xxxvi, p. 291) which gives it as 1713. For the following reasons the writer believes that Tucker was born in November or December of 1713: (1) In *Alumni Oxonienses* Tucker is registered as having matriculated "26 Jan., 1732-33, aged 19." (2) The closing line of his obituary tablet on the east wall of the south transept of Gloucester Cathedral reads, "He died November 4th, 1799, in the 86th year of his age." (3) In *Letters to Shelburne* (written 1783), p. 113, he speaks of himself as in his 70th year. (4) In a letter to William Seward, October 29, 1790 (Brit. Mus. Add. Mss., 5419), he speaks of himself as "almost 77 years of age."

[2] Several of the biographical sketches, *e. g.*, *Public Characters of*

He was accustomed to walk from his home to Oxford, a hundred and sixty miles. Owing to the bad roads and to his baggage, carried in a bundle, swung from a stick across his shoulder, this was a full six days' walk. The narrow circumstances of the family are shown by the fact that the horse upon which the young man made one of these journeys, and one only,[1] was the only horse owned at the little farm.

There is no line to tell of the friendships, the difficulties, the successes, and the aspirations of his college life. His whole Oxford story, after matriculation, is summed in the simple line of the *Alumni Oxonienses:* "B. A. 1736, M. A. 1739, B. & D. D. 1755."

Adopting the profession offering the best opportunities for advancement to one, who was entered upon the Oxford rolls as "pleb,"[2] Tucker entered the church, taking holy orders at the age of 22. His preferments may be summarized briefly. In 1735 a Gloucestershire rural parish curacy located him in the region so suggestive, on every side, of the great problems of his land and of his day. This region he never left thereafter, except for brief visits. For sixty-four years he served in the rural curacy, and in Bristol and in Gloucester cities. He saw two generations of local farmers, merchants, traders, manufacturers and politicians, ply their industries and influence the shaping of the business policy of the whole nation.

In 1737 came his first promotion, which gave him a curacy

1798–99, 4th ed., p. 162, and *The Monthly Mag.*, vol. viii, p. 912, state that this exhibition was obtained at Jesus College, Oxford. The *Alumni Oxonienses* registers Tucker at St. John's College.

[1] Young Tucker refused again to inconvenience his father by taking away his only draught animal, and all remaining Oxford journeys were made on foot.

[2] *Alumni Oxonienses*, *v.* Tucker.

of St. Stephen's Church, in Bristol, and in May, 1739, he became rector of All Saints' Church, in the same city. In 1737 a minor canonry of the Bristol Cathedral was conferred upon him.

He attracted the attention of the famous Joseph Butler,[1] Bishop of Bristol, and he was chosen by Bishop Butler to serve as the Bishop's private chaplain. His next promotion came through the influence of the Bishop, when, in 1749, he returned to St. Stephen's as its rector, succeeding Dr. Alexander Catcott.

A prebendal stall was granted to him at St. David's in April, 1752, and one at the Bristol Cathedral in October, 1756. His last preferment came in July, 1758, when he was made Dean of the Cathedral at Gloucester. He thereupon resigned his prebendal stall at Bristol Cathedral, but retained the rectory of St. Stephen's until November, 1793, when he resigned in favor of his curate.[2]

The resignation suggests much in the man's character. Feeling the heavy hand of age, he was willing to lighten his duties some time before he took the final step. His curate, the Rev. Mr. Grenville, appears to have been a worthy

[1] As an instance of Tucker's friendly and intimate intercourse with Bishop Butler an incident related in Tucker's *Humble Address, etc.* (pp. 20 and 21, footnote), may be cited. Tucker states, in this note, that it was the Bishop's custom to walk in his garden for hours even on the darkest night, and that he "frequently had the honor to accompany him." On one such occasion the Bishop asked Tucker what security there was against the insanity of individuals. When Tucker replied that neither physicians nor divines knew of any such security the Bishop continued, "Why might not whole communities and public bodies be seized with fits of insanity, as well as individuals? Nothing else can account for the major part of those transactions which we read in history." Tucker comments that though he had thought little of "the Bishop's odd conceit" at the time, he had "frequently thought of it and applied it to many cases since."

[2] For an account of this see *Gent's Mag.*, vol. lxiii, part ii, p. 1063.

man and was the father of a large family.[1] Tucker desired that Mr. Grenville should succeed him as rector. The appointment was in the power of the Lord Chancellor, who had other plans for a successor to Tucker. On being apprised of this, Tucker decided to retain the rectory unless Mr. Grenville was to receive the appointment. He had a petition, that Mr. Grenville be chosen, circulated among his parishioners, and it received their signatures unanimously. The Lord Chancellor yielded upon the presentation of this evidence to the worthiness of St. Stephen's curate and promised to advance him to the rectory if Tucker resigned. This Tucker promptly did, thus stripping himself of all duties and emoluments except those of the Deanery of Gloucester, which he held at the time of his death.

Stratford states:[2] "A Bishopric was subsequently offered to him [Tucker], but this further preferment was declined." The writer has found no evidence to confirm this assertion. On the contrary, there seems to be evidence against it. In his *Humble Address*, etc. (p. 7), published in 1775, Tucker states:

"I thank God I have no cause to complain of any disappointment; having since my advancement to the Deanery of Gloucester in the year 1758, neither directly nor indirectly made the least or the most distant application for any other or higher station."

In his *Series of Answers*, etc. (p. 97), published in 1776, Tucker says:

"As a clergyman it is often objected to me that I am a mercenary wretch or as Mr. Burke was pleased to call me a 'court vermin' writing for preferment. This is very hard and

[1] This increased Tucker's respect—see his *Population Thesis*, part ii, chap. 2 of this monograph.

[2] *Gloucestershire Biog. Notes* (p. 131), by Joseph Stratford.

cruel after so many solemn declarations to the contrary. Let it therefore be observed that whereas I had often said before that I would never directly nor indirectly seek for preferment, I will here add once for all, that I will never accept of any even tho' offered to and pressed upon me." [1]

This attitude remained unchanged in 1783, when, in his *Letters to Shelburne* (p. 2), Tucker wrote:

"As to my views of preferment . . . . I have none at all; being quite content with my station."

Tucker was an efficient administrator of the church properties under his care, and he was, in all respects, a conscientious clergyman. Despite the many allegations to the contrary, made by those who deemed him too inclined to spend much time in dealing with commercial themes, he put his duty as a clergyman before all others. Tucker's own clear statement of his aim is in one of his letters to Lord Kames. He says:

"The avocations belonging to my new office of Dean are very many and are too important to be omitted. I came into a house which wanted to be almost rebuilt and into a chapter where many disorders required to be rectified; and I have a cathedral and cloisters to examine and repair, which, in some respects, are the finest Gothic structures in the world, and which are now perhaps the best kept. . . . . There are two resolutions which I cannot depart from: The first is that charity begins at home . . . . and the second that I will not put it in the power of any one to say that I neglected the proper business of my function and station upon any pretences of

[1] This statement was made by Tucker with reference to Burke's attack upon him in the latter's speech of April 19, 1774, when he characterized Tucker as a "court vermin" whose efforts might win for him a Bishopric.

serving the public. I have always kept clear, I thank God, of this imputation, even my adversaries being judge . . . . and I trust I ever shall." [1]

Tucker's epitaph indicates that he carried out this intention to the very end of his life.[2] This life rule, and the unimpeached testimony that he followed it to the last, are a sufficient reply to the slur against Tucker's loyalty to his duty as a clergyman implied in Dr. Warburton's acid fling that the Dean " made a religion of trade." [3]

Tucker appears to have been upon good terms with many leading clergyman of his day, and the strained relations existing between him and Warburton were at least as much due to the latter's overbearing intolerance of any opposition, as to Tucker's lack of due respect for his official superior. Bishop Thomas Newton testifies to Tucker's faithfulness

[1] *Memoirs of Life and Writings of Lord Kames* (Alex. Fraser Tytler), vol. iii, pp. 174-175. This letter is dated Feb. 15, 1764.

[2] See end of this chapter where epitaph is given in full,

[3] John Selby Watson in his *Life of William Warburton* (p. 496) relates that a Dr. Squires and Dr. Tucker were both candidates for the deanery of Bristol. A Mr. Allen, who had spent much money in repairing this deanery for Warburton, was willing to complete his planned repairs if he knew that an acceptable man would succeed the retiring Dean. He asked Warburton about the two candidates and Warburton, with characteristic epigrammatic rudeness, replied: "One makes a trade of religion; the other [Tucker] a religion of trade." Tucker's own reply was: "The Bishop affects to consider me with contempt; to which I say nothing. He has sometimes spoken coarsely of me; to which I replied nothing. He has said that religion is my trade and trade my religion. Commerce and its connections have, it is true, been favorite objects of my attention, and where is the crime? And as for religion I have attended carefully to the duties of my parish, nor have I neglected my cathedral. The world knows something of me as a writer on religious subjects, and I will add, which the world does not know, that I have written near 300 sermons and preached them all again and again." *Gent's Mag.*, vol. lxxxvi (1799), p. 1003.

in his clerical labors, and laments the lack of harmony between the Bishop and the Dean. Of Tucker he says:

"He was too, an excellent parish priest, an exemplary dean, in keeping his residence and performing his duty, in managing the chapter estates, in living hospitably, in repairing and improving his house and in adorning and beautifying the church and churchyard. In these things he merited well and had many good qualities, but it is to be lamented that he had not the respect for the bishop (Warburton) which was really due to his personal character as well as to his high station. . . . . They were both men of great virtues but they were both also men of strong passions. Both were irascible but the Bishop was more placable and forgiving; the Dean longer bore resentment." [1]

Bishop Butler's friendship for Tucker has already been mentioned. It had further illustration in the fact that he selected Tucker, in 1741, to write an account of Methodism desired by the Lord Primate of Ireland.

With the Rev. Dr. C. N. Foster, Tucker was in continuous correspondence [2] from 1752 until the untimely death of Dr. Forster. With the Rev. Dr. Birch, Tucker corresponded for many years.[3] Archbishop Secker, of Canterbury, was enough interested in Tucker and his work to read carefully and to annotate one of the proof copies of Tucker's *Elements*.[4]

Of Tucker's sermons and theological contributions something will be said later in the chapter of this Part I. upon his writings. The evidence cited here seems to show that

[1] Bishop Newton's *Life by Himself* in vol. 2 of *Lives of Eminent English Divines* (London, 1816), pp. 107–108.

[2] See Forster *Mss.* Brit. Mus. Library *Add. Mss.*, 11275.

[3] See Birch *Mss.* Brit. Mus. Library *Mss.*, 4319, vol. xx, 818.

[4] The copy now in the New York Public Library, Astor Division.

Tucker was a capable and zealous clergyman, helpful throughout his parish, and respected by the clergymen of his day.

But although Tucker was a faithful clergyman, he found time to write much upon political and upon commercial themes, and for a number of years before his appointment as the Dean of Gloucester he took an active part in Bristol politics.

When bills for the naturalization of foreign Protestants and of Jews were before Parliament in 1751 to 1753, Tucker strongly advocated naturalization. The Bristol populace were violently opposed to naturalization. When news reached Bristol that the consideration of one of these bills had been postponed, a great demonstration was held, placards denounced supporters of the bill, and the exulting, intolerant mob, gathered in the public square, even burned Tucker in effigy, dressed in full canonicals.[1]

In 1753 Tucker's tract, *Reflections on Turkey Trade,* aroused a storm of opposition against the privileged Turkey trading monopoly, which culminated in action by Parliament in June, 1754, when the trade to Turkey was opened to all British citizens upon the payment of £20.[2]

From 1754 to 1757 Tucker was a political mentor of the Bristol Whigs. He advised setting up only one candidate in 1754, and they did so; he advised the compromise of 1756, and it prevailed. The event in each case justified his political sagacity. In 1754, when Mr. Robert Nugent (afterward Earl) was the Whig candidate for Parliament from Bristol, Tucker actively espoused his cause. He wrote letters, tracts,[3] and newspaper articles in Nugent's behalf,

[1] *Gent's Mag.* (April, 1751), vol. xxi, p. 186.

[2] See *Preface Reflect, Turkey Trade, 2nd Ed.*, 1755.

[3] Such tracts were *Great News from Rome*, *Reasons for Chusing Mr.*

took part in committee work, kept in regular communication with Nugent, whom he advised as to the local political conditions, and even planned the order of march and invented part of the banner mottoes for a political parade of Nugent supporters.[1] Many of his parishioners opposed Nugent's return. Some of these were influential in church affairs, and threatened that "if he voted against the vestry they would not collect him a single shilling." His reply was characteristic: "Gentlemen, do whatever is right in your own eyes. I shall certainly vote for Lord Clare, consequently against you, and I shall certainly do my duty towards you as your minister, whether you collect for me or not."[2]

In brief, all of this evidence seems to show that Tucker was a practical politician, a man manager and a successful local diplomat, on occasion and in good cause (the country's or his own). The practical outcome of the Bristol election was that Nugent was returned, and he secured clerical preferments for Tucker, a prebendal stall in the Bistol Cathedral (October 28, 1756) and the Deanery of Gloucester, July 13, 1758.

After his appointment as Dean, Tucker was not so active in local politics. Indeed, for a decade he did little more than attend to his increased clerical duties. His deanship had devolved new and heavy duties upon him, and he had wearied of being misunderstood and calumniated as a self-seeking, commercial, clergyman. The reputation given to him by slanderous attacks of political opponents is illustrated by his statement in a letter to Lord Hardwicke, Dec. 6th, 1760:

Nugent, etc. (See Bibliography of Tucker's works, 1754). In a letter to Dr. Birch (see Birch *Mss.*) on Apr. 29, 1754, he encloses "the eighth paper" he had written during the contest.

[1] These facts are attested to in Tucker's correspondence with Forster, Birch and Nugent. See British Mus. Library *Mss.*

[2] A tale of Stratford's *Gloucestershire Biographical Notes*, p. 131.

"Before my coming to Gloucester the people were made to believe that I was a monster of the vilest parts of Whiggism and Judaism." [1]

The war with the American colonies aroused Tucker again in the seventies, and he wrote a series of tracts. His separation policy drew down upon him the wrath both of those for the government and of those against it. Such men as Burke and Dr. Johnson saw fit to oppose Tucker's views, Burke attacking [2] him from the floor of the House of Commons. The very opposition with which he met proves that his tracts had influence, an influence which probably had weight in bringing about the final settlement of the war.

Tucker had favored the union of Ireland and Great Britain from his earliest economic essays, and was convinced it would ultimately be made. In his last tract upon this subject, *Reflections upon Present Matters in Dispute between Great Britain and Ireland* (1785), he opposed an immediate union, arguing, from the Irish standpoint, that until Great Britain abolished her trading monopolies the Irish would be losers by the incorporation.

During his years of political activity, Tucker made a reputation for himself as an able political writer and thinker, and had won notice from leading active politicians and political organs.[3] Even the king himself had taken personal

Brit. Mus. Library *Mss.*, 35692 f. 130–134–143.

[2] The vehemence and abusiveness of Burke's attack was at least partially due to the fact that Tucker, satisfied with Lord Clare's representation of Bristol, had opposed Burke when he sought election from Bristol in 1774.

[3] The bitterness of some attacks almost drove him to institute criminal suit. In a letter of May 13, 1754, to Dr. Birch (Brit. Mus. *Mss.*) he asks that inquiry be made from Mr. C. Yorkes, an attorney friend, if he would be justified in instituting a suit for libel against the *London Evening Post*, for its virulent attack upon him in its issue of May 11th.

interest [1] in the advancement of the clergyman-politician, because of his effective, loyal, writings and personal influence in the Bristol elections.

Outside of clerical and political friends and enemies, Tucker did not have an extended acquaintance or correspondence. He traveled but little, and so had small opportunity to meet leading men. He was on the continent for a short time, some time prior to 1757.[2] On this journey he did not meet Turgot, although he later carried on a correspondence, to which reference will be made in the consideration of Tucker's writings.

Despite his little travel and few famous acquaintances or correspondents, Tucker strove to be a citizen of the world. The passage in his *Cui Bono?* in which he is addressing himself to M. Necker, is one of many such confessions of aim scattered throughout his works:

"My aim is the good of mankind. Endeavoring to divest myself of national partialities and local prejudices to the utmost of my power, I now enter on the work proposed, not as an Englishman, but as a citizen of the world; not as having an inbred antipathy to France but as a friend of the whole human species." [3]

He offers to give all damages to a charity but says he cannot afford the costs of a non-suit. Birch's reply was that altho' "the insults were gross and scurrilous," a libel suit would be uncertain, both because of the law and of a London jury partial to a London paper.

[1] Letter from Dr. Birch, May 18, 1754, states, "His Majesty himself, I am well assured, mentioned you to my Lord Chancellor for Mr. James Yorke's prebend at Bristol," etc.

[2] In *Instruct. for Trav.* (p. 28) Tucker mentions a brief journey abroad. In a letter to Tucker dated Sept. 12, 1770, Turgot regrets that he did not meet Tucker on this visit. *Oevres de Turgot* (Paris, 1810), vol. ix, p. 367.

[3] *Cui Bono?* pp. 4 and 5.

But so far as Tucker really attained his ideal of being a "citizen of the world," he attained it largely through books and through acute observations of human nature, and of commercial and political life in his home environment. His only traveling, besides his journey to France, mentioned above, and occasional journeys to London and to Oxford, was a journey to Ireland in 1762[1] and one to Scotland in 1782. Both of these journeys he mentions in letters to Lord Kames, with whom he carried on a long correspondence. This correspondence was begun in 1757, at Tucker's request, and was carried on, with mutual satisfaction, until the death of Lord Kames. Tucker, with a customary frankness, and in the language of the economist, admits that "self-interest alone prompts this desire (for correspondence with Lord Kames)—the knowledge and instruction to be gained by it."[2]

The correspondence with David Hume was of a similarly strenuous nature. It began through Lord Kames, in 1758, and continued for many years. In 1752, with Lord Townshend, Tucker interchanged a number of argumentative letters,[3] dealing with bounties on corn, monopolies and freedom of trade, the relation of national morality to national commerce, and taxation.

There is no evidence in Tucker's letters or works that he had an acquaintance with Adam Smith, or even that he knew of him at all. Nor is there any indication that he knew James Steuart or Bishop Berkeley, except through the

[1] See *Memoirs of Lord Kames* (By Alex. Fraser Tytler), vol. iii, pp. 168 and 178. It was probably upon this visit that Tucker was admitted to the degree of D. D. at the Univ. of Dublin, and was made an honorary member of the Dublin Society. See *Europ. Mag.*, vol. xxvii, p. 18.

[2] *Memoirs of Lord Kames*, vol. ii, p. 6.

[3] *Hist. Mss. Commission* 11th Annual Rep., Append. Part iv, Sessional Reports, vol. xlvii, pp. 371 to 379 and 382.

Querist. His correspondences which bear upon economic themes appear to have been limited to those with Kames, Turgot, Hume and Townshend.

Tucker's family relations can be briefly stated. He was twice married. His first wife, the widow of Mr. Francis Woodward, of Grimsbury, Gloucestershire, died in 1771. January 17, 1781, he married Mrs. Frances Crowe, of Gloucester. She survived him, and it was his will to "bestow all of my worldly goods of every kind and nature to [sic] my beloved wife, Frances Tucker, as my sole executrix and only legatee." [1]

No children were born in either marriage. Mrs. Woodward had a son by her first marriage, and this young man Tucker educated and aided in various ways.[2]

Although Tucker had no children of his own, he had a large family for which to provide. Writing to Lord Kames, in 1764, he says: "Though I have no children of my own, I have no less than eight of an only sister, all thrown upon me, whom I must breed up to get their living in some shape or other." [3]

The charity of the man went beyond his family and relatives. He is recorded[4] to have been a liberal benefactor of several public institutions and a patron of merit. The "celebrated John Henderson, of Pembroke College, Oxford, was sent to the University and supported there at the Dean's

[1] This will was drawn Sept. 15th, 1797, and was probated Nov. 12, 1799. It is recorded at Somerset House, London. It is a very brief document, simply prefacing the above quotation with a commendation of the testator's soul to God.

[2] Tucker secured letters of introduction in 1755 to persons of consequence upon the continent, for Mr. Woodward and a young nobleman friend who were to travel and whom Tucker calls his pupils. See Birch *Mss.* Letter of May 11, 1755.

[3] *Memoirs of Kames*, vol. iii, p. 174.

[4] *The Monthly Mag.*, vol. viii, p. 914.

expense when he had no means whatever to gratify his ardent desire for study." [1] The instance of his resignation in favor of his curate has been cited above. In 1784 he proposed a plan for competitive theses on commercial and political subjects by students in the English and Scotch universities, and he offered to pledge personally £20 per year for life towards the £200 necessary to the plan.[2] Speaking of himself in 1782, he says:

"The Dean is a man who, with a very moderate income, which many people would think rather scanty, can truly say that he has all that he wishes and more than sufficient to satisfy his wants." [3]

The illustrations given above are sufficient to show that he did manage, even out of his scanty income, to liberally aid deserving persons and plans. Others were probably also liberal in their gifts to him. At least one considerable gift was made to him by a parishioner. When Mary Ann Peloquin died, in 1778, she bequeathed to Tucker, rector of St. Stephen's church, her residence in Queen's Square and £5 per annum.[4]

If one may trust a painting [5] to give accurate impressions of a man, Tucker was a person of rather heavy build, with

[1] *The Monthly Mag.*, vol. viii, p. 914.

[2] *Europ. Mag.*, vol. xxvii, pp. 29 sqq.

[3] *Treatise on Gov't*, p. 364.

[4] *Annals of Bristol* (John Latimer), p. 284.

[5] In a dusty corner of one of the little-used rooms of the Gloucester Cathedral there hangs an oil painting of Tucker. It is unsigned and undated. It gives a front view of Tucker's face and is a much more satisfactory portrait than the one from which the print portraits have been made. The portrait painted by G. Russell was twice engraved. See *Bromley*, p. 472. A print portrait from this painting appears in the *Europ. Mag.*, vol. xxvi, p. 290, and in *Literary Anecdotes* (John Nichols), vol. ix, p. 295.

ruddy face, blue eyes and dark hair. Strong features accent the firmness of expression, which is that of the very determined man, whom an opponent calls obstinate. Tucker's habits were simple and his health was vigorous. The peasant strength coming to him by heredity, and perpetuated by outdoor exercise and plain diet, endured to the end of his active eighty-six years, when a stroke of paralysis brought on death. He was buried in the Gloucester Cathedral. In the east wall of the south transept is erected a memorial tablet. The inscription briefly characterizes the Dean, the man, and his writings:

" Sacred to the memory of the Revd Josiah Tucker, D. D., Dean of this Cathedral, who in the long period of forty-two years during which he filled that station, was never once obliged by sickness or induced by inclination to omit or abridge a single residence; and the state of the fabric at the time of his death bore ample testimony to the conscientious and liberal interest which he always took in the preservation and improvement of it.

" Distinguished by a vigorous comprehensive and independent mind, whilst his theological writings acquired him a high rank among the ablest divines, he was eminently conspicuous for political discernment on the important subject of national commerce; for the free spirit of which, unrestrained by monopoly and colonial preference, he firmly contended against prepossessions long and generally entertained; and he lived to see his opinions established on the sure basis of experience.

" His publications were numerous and of a nature not soon to be forgotten. By them 'being dead he yet speaketh' and will not speak in vain, as long as an earnest but well tempered zeal for the established church, an enlarged policy, the true principles of commerce and their alliance with the benign spirit of religion, shall be understood, respected and maintained.

" He died November the 4th, 1799, in the 86th year of his age."

CHAPTER III

A CHARACTERIZATION

No more is known of the ancestry of Josiah Tucker than that his father was a Welsh peasant of small property. No hereditary tendencies can be suggested, therefore; but a brief characterization [1] of the man may be drawn from his life, and especially from his writings. Since interest in his life, and especially from his writings. Since interest centers in his authorship, emphasis will be laid upon those traits that give individuality to his writings.

I. Tucker a Thinker

Tucker was, first of all, an able thinker. His mind was clear and logical. This made him systematic in his treatment of every subject, a characteristic attested to by nearly every one of his writings. It also led him to desire consistency [2] with all the passion of the philosopher. Again, his mind was actively inquisitive. It raised questions and proposed problems. This made him critical. He accepted nothing upon faith which he could test by reason.[3] Still,

[1] The characterization which follows is no eulogy; it is a simple statement of the impressions made upon the writer in his reading of Tucker's works.

[2] "Tho I make no pretensions to infallibility . . . yet I would willingly support the general character of a consistent writer . . . This hath been my aim thro' life and wherever I have failed it was thro' ignorance and not by design." *Letters to Dr. Kippis*, pp. 4 and 5.

[3] This is well illustrated (remembering that Tucker was an 18th century clergyman) by his assertion of "the inalienable right of private judgment" in his *Letter to Dr. Kippis* (p. 18) where he says: "Christ

again, his mind was progressive. It moved on persistently until it had reached answers to its questions and solutions to its own problems, which answers and solutions satisfied its own logical tests. This made him constructive and creative. He never left a subject satisfied with mere destructive criticism. His writings abound with "polities" and remedies.[1] After criticising the existing poor system, he gave a detailed plan for bettering it;[2] when he discussed American affairs, he offered his own solution of the problem;[3] he criticized Locke and Hobbes, and then offered his own system of political thought;[4] and so on, almost every criticism of his being followed by a constructive program. The most striking and comprehensive illustration of his tendency to invent ways and means is to be found in the "skeleton" of his great work.[5] A large part of this great

himself expects that we should use our reason and our judgment in understanding His laws and applying His general instructions to particular times and circumstances."

[1] To those who might regard him as a political and commercial nostrum peddler, because of his many schemes for betterment, Tucker says, in justification of the theorist reformer: "I am also aware that there is a customary prepossession entertained against projects of all kinds and that projectors are looked upon as a race of beings who have something very singular and whimsical in their composition. And yet I think it must be allowed, that notwithstanding all the prejudice which some chimerical gentlemen of this stamp have drawn upon themselves, there must be both projects and projectors, when things are bad and wanting mending; otherwise they never could be better nor the faults corrected." This is but a paragraph of a three page defense of the theorist-reformer. See *Essay on Trade, 3rd Ed.*, pp. 141-144.

[2] See *Manifold Causes of Increase of Poor.*

[3] Viz., Complete voluntary separation from the colonies, the central thesis of all of his American tracts.

[4] See his *Treatise on Civil Government.*

[5] See *Appendix* of this monograph, where the "skeleton" is printed in full.

work, as therein outlined, would have consisted in "politics" for reforms in commerce and in government.

A logical, inquiring, creative mind is the mind of a theorist, and Tucker was a bold and original theorist. Two tests of the well-grounded theorist were fully met by him:

(1) He did not lose faith in his conclusions because passing events did not immediately justify them, or because men did not at once accept them and act upon them.

An example of his confidence in his own conclusions, even when events seemed to argue against them, occurs in a postscript to one of his American tracts,[1] in which he forcefully presented his conviction that separation was inevitable. In the postscript he stated that news of a victory over the American rebels had just come. This was early in the war (1776), but so far from doubting his thesis and withholding his tract from publication, or qualifying his conclusions so as to save his reputation in case the British should ultimately retain the colonies, he boldly issued the tract, and commented:

"Arguing from mere contingencies and the chance of war is at best but the *chance of war,* and is the more fatally delusive, as it is so flattering to human vanity. Indeed it has no weight at all in the balance against the natural and therefore, in the end the necessary, course of things."[2]

His faith in the ultimate triumph of right reason and his belief that his own conclusions were products of right reason, despite the rejection of them by others, is well illustrated in his argument for the union of England and Ireland. He closed a compact, forceful plea thus:

"Nevertheless, strong and convincing as these reasons for

[1] *Series of Answers, etc.* (1776).

[2] See *Postscript of Series of Answers.*

union are, I do not depend on them for success in the present [1] case. For that man must be very ignorant of human nature, who expects to subdue deeprooted prejudice merely by the force of reasoning. But there is a tide in human affairs to which prejudice itself must yield, because it cannot resist it." [2]

(2) Depending upon his reasoning, he made a number of prophecies, which were amply justified by events. For examples, he prophesied the separation from the American colonies, the union with Ireland, the ultimate abolition of special chartered privileges, and the rise of a great American nation. In every case his prophecy was a logical conclusion from his knowledge of men and of conditions.

II. Tucker an Observer

Tucker was, secondly, a careful observer of the world about him and a close student of recorded facts. Although he was so confidently logical a theorist, he was not a mere dialectical visionary. A study of his writings amply confirms his own clear statement[3] that he was not content with mere formal beauty or accuracy.

That he was no cave-hermit philosopher is abundantly proven by his works. They evidence his instinct for personal observation and for original research. His earliest work, *The History of Methodism*, was the result of his study of this sect, as its votaries lived and preached in his own city. For his treatises upon trade, he drew his materials, in part, from conversations with merchant parishioners, from observations in and about Bristol's wharves and harbors and places of manufacture, and from personal

[1] The tract is dated October 19, 1785.

[2] *Union or Separation*, p. 29.

[3] "I have ever made it a rule to prefer things to words, ideas to sounds, and sense to language." See *Letter to Dr. Kippis*, p. 117.

knowledge of English pastures, marshes and rivers. When he wrote of the poor system, he quoted the poor laws; when he condemned monopoly, he examined the grants of privilege under Elizabeth and James I.; when he discoursed upon politics, he first traced out the historic Gothic system of England. These are but illustrations.[1] One of the clearest impressions left upon a reader of his works, is that he was a close observer of men and of things and a thoughtful student of history.

To say that Tucker studied facts, and either directly induced his theories, or corrected his theories to accord with his fact findings, is not to say that he made no use of other men's writings. He appears to have been well acquainted with what previous writers upon economics, politics and religion had written, and was, doubtless, in some measure influenced by them, but he did not give much weight to mere authority.[2]

His knowledge and thought emboldened him to criticize commonly accepted ideas, if his own independent conclusions were antagonistic to them. He says:

> "One would not willingly run counter to the settled notions of mankind and yet one ought not to make a sacrifice of truth to mere numbers and the authority of opinion, especially if it should appear that these are truths of great moment to the welfare of society." [3]

[1] See the section treating of Tucker's *Historical Sense* in Chapter I, Part II, of this monograph for a fuller treatment of this idea.

[2] "When other arguments are equal the weight of authority ought to turn the scale, and this maxim I venture to apply to all cases whatsoever, in church or in state, and to all arts, sciences and professions." *Letters to Dr. Kippis*, pp. 68 and 69. For a similar statement see *Treatise on Government*, p. 378.

[3] *Four Tracts*, p. 20.

III. Tucker Independent

Tucker was independent. His confidence in his own conclusions, and his light estimate of mere authority or of public opinion, are bases for an independence in thought. The fact that he did not servilely seek preferment has already been developed in treating of his life. Perhaps the most marked illustration that he was a truth-seeker rather than a place-seeker, was his resignation of the commission to write a treatise of commerce for the instruction of the Prince of Wales.[1] Such a commission might have contributed both to his fame and to his fortune, but when he found that his conclusions were very variant from popular ideas, and would, therefore, be accounted unsuitable for the instruction of the Prince, he yielded the opportunity rather than that he should present a treatise whose teachings should be acceptably altered from the conclusions to which his study had led him. This act alone is ample proof that his frequent declarations[2] of independence are not empty words.

Tucker struggled for a still higher form of independence. He endeavored to free himself from the insular prejudices of a British citizen, and he strove consciously to become a citizen of the world.[3] Although not a widely traveled man, he lived, observantly and thoughtfully, in a world's trading port and preached a world-embracing religion, so that from speculations upon international commerce and upon the uni-

[1] *Four Tracts preface*, pp. ix and x.

[2] Typical of them is: "The writer of the following pages professes himself to be of no party; he disdains the idea of bigotry in behalf of any set of men whatever; he owes no particular service either to those in power or to those in opposition; he aspires to the character of an independent man, a friend of his country, etc." *Dispassionate Tho'ts on Amer. War*, pp. 6 and 7.

[3] This thought is further developed in the section on *Jealousy of Trade* in part ii, chap. iv. of this monograph.

versal brotherhood of man, his thought passed the confines of island narrowness and sought world relations. His advocacy of the naturalization bills, and his condemnations of war and of jealousy of trade, are all, in large part, the fruits of his cosmopolitanism.

IV. Tucker Sincere

Tucker was a sincere man. Faith in his own thought and contentment with his moderate preferment consort naturally with sincerity. He sought the truth, and expressed it boldly when he thought that he had found it. Neither the contumely of a derisive mob [1] nor the gilded promises of powerful politicians [2] induced him to write other than he believed. His style as a writer, in its directness and utter lack of affectation, reflects this spirit of sincerity. He testified frequently to the intent of being an honest seeker after truth. To Dr. Kippis he wrote:

"You are, on the whole, a candid and impartial seeker after truth; and I solemnly promise to follow you in the same pursuit . . . let what will be the consequence . . . . If I am mistaken few persons have taken more pains to be rightly informed than I have." [3]

He relied upon reason and honesty, and desired his works to be accepted solely upon their merits. As to any errors he may have made, he says:

"Should anything appear which convinces me that I have been essentially mistaken in what I have asserted, I here assure the public that I will immediately retract it; thinking it no disgrace for a fallible man to confess himself mistaken." [4]

[1] *Gent's Mag.*, vol. xxi, p. 186.

[2] See *Letters to Shelburne*, pp. 2 and 3.

[3] *Letters to Dr. Kippis*, pp. 5 and 132.

[4] *Preface to Six Sermons*, p. iv.

This honest desire to get at the truth was further evidenced by Tucker's custom of submitting his more important manuscripts to friends for criticisms. This was neither perfunctory, nor merely complimentary to the friends. He sought real criticism. In his letters to Dr. Birch and to Dr. Forster, he insisted that they should point out every error which they detected. The best evidence that he really sought the critical judgment of friends is the fact that he sometimes acted upon their expressed judgment. He entirely suppressed[1] a lengthy preliminary discourse citing errors of Locke, because advised by his friends that this might carry readers aside from the central point of the *Treatise on Government*. Two of his most important works[2] survive only because of this practise of seeking honest pre-publication criticism. Only a few of the quasi-manuscript copies, which he had privately printed to distribute among friends for criticism, remain.

V. Tucker Practical

Tucker was a practical man. He managed the church property, under his care, successfully. He was an effective politician, influential in Bristol politics. He aimed always to focus his thought upon any subject into a "polity" to better conditions. These "polities" he endeavored to keep as free as possible from chances for political jobbery.[3] He aims to formulate such programs as will be practicable, and not such as satisfy a visionary ideal. Compromises of this kind he frequently comments upon, for example:

"The author has the following proposals humbly to offer, not as what he himself can recommend as the wisest and best

[1] See *Treatise on Government, Preface*, p. i.

[2] *Elements of Commerce*, 1755, and *Instructions for Travellers*, 1757.

[3] See *Appendix of Essay on Trade*, pp. 118–119.

but as the most feasible, the least repugnant to the obstinate prejudices of mankind and therefore the likeliest to be accepted by the contending parties." [1]

He makes one sweeping declaration, which pledges him to offer nothing impracticable for publication. This is his parting word in the *Elements* :

" But tho' the general nature of the subject is so very plain and intelligible and tho' the application of it would be extremely easy to a state *now* in *forming*, yet it requires the nicest and coolest judgment, to adapt the several parts of it to a state *already formed*. Nothing should be offered to the regard of the public but what is really practicable and may be introduced without throwing the body politic into unnatural and dangerous convulsions." [2]

VI. Tucker Tolerant

Tucker was tolerant. He championed the right of the dissenter to dissent.[3] He says that

" Persecution is popery and the worst of popery, come from whatever quarter it may." [4]

He favors keeping the Catholics under disabilities,

" not as a sect in religion but as a faction against the state . . . . not surely to harass and oppress the papists, but to secure ourselves." [5]

No better proof can be given that Tucker was tolerant in

[1] *Proposals for General Pacification*, *Gent's Mag.*, vol. l, p. 221. Similar statement in *Cui Bono*, pp. 128–129, and in *Four Tracts*, p. 220.

[2] *Elements*, p. 170.

[3] *Letters to Dr. Kippis*, pp. 61–66.

[4] *Ibid.*, p. 33.

[5] *Reflect. Nat. For. Prot.*, part ii, pp. xiv and xv.

spirit as well as theory, than his strong pleas for the bills for the naturalization of foreigners, and especially of foreign Jews. His persistent advocacy of these bills brought upon him stinging reproach from his fellow citizens.

VII. Tucker Controversial

Tucker was a controversialist. It would have been strange if he had not been one. His logical acumen, his abundant knowledge of facts, and his direct style, fitted him to be strong in debate. He took a great interest in current affairs. His exercise of the clergyman's prerogative of giving advice had doubtless cultivated a proneness to present his opinions upon subjects which interested him. Finally, his life was almost coincident with the controversial, pamphleteering, eighteenth century.

His fondness for controversy is reflected in his works, and largely explains some of the inconsistencies to be found in them. The *Essay on Trade* arranges the material advantages and disadvantages of France and Great Britain in trade, as if it were a source book for debate upon the relative commercial strength of the two nations. The naturalization papers, the treatise upon the trade to Turkey, the papers upon the subscription controversy, the American tracts, and the criticism of Locke are all avowedly controversial. Indeed, with the exception of a few didactic sermons, the *History of Methodism,* and large parts of the *Elements* and the *Instructions for Travellers,* his works are of uniformly controversial cast. His sincerity, tolerance and independence save his works from the extremes of partisanship and the wide bias of advocacy all too common in controversial literature.

VIII. Summary

Josiah Tucker was an independent, sincere, practical, and

tolerant, thinker and writer, well read in the literatures of theology, politics and economics, but more widely versed in the facts of historic and current religious, political and commercial life. In energy and industry, in intellectual power and poise, and in moral stamina, he was eminently fitted to be the creator of an influential system of thought. Tastes and environment led him to study political and economic life. Economic problems were the more immediately pressing for solution, and his environment spoke to him most clearly in economic terms. It would, therefore, have been most natural that his great work should have been a science of economics. Such a work he did plan and partially execute; but, through the increasing burden of clerical duties, through deflection of energy in active participation in current controversy, and, not least of all, through a growing conviction that his generation was not prepared to receive the truth as he saw it, he at first deferred, and finally abandoned, the execution of the great work which would have won him high place in the history of English economics. Although this monumental work was never completed, the rough casts of parts of it, and the lesser works he has left, make possible a presentation of almost his entire system of thought.

CHAPTER IV

THE WRITINGS

BEFORE entering upon a detailed topical analysis of the economic thought in Tucker's writings, an outline survey of them will afford an idea of their extent, of their general nature and of the impelling reasons for their production.

I. BY DECADES

The first published product of Tucker's pen was given to the world in 1739; the last, in 1787. This fifty years of authorship subdivides interestingly. The first decade, 1739-1749, brings but four brief publications upon religious subjects or addressed to religious persons. But during this decade, so apparently unfruitful, Tucker was mastering a wide range of commercial facts and was making the most of an opportunity to understand the busy industrial and trading life of Bristol. He was reading and observing and thinking. The second decade proves this for it is the most fruitful of the five.

During the ten years, 1749-1759, Tucker produced his greatest works. It is plainly his economic decade as an author. It opened with a strong essay in 1749, comparing the trade advantages of Great Britain and France and closed with his most extensive economic work, *Instructions for Travellers,* published in 1757. In 1752 occurred the thoughtful correspondence with Lord Townshend and in 1758 Hume was converted to an economic view of Tucker, in a correspondence with Lord Kames acting as letter-box.

The naturalization essays, clear and tolerant, came in 1751 to 1753. The strong attack upon the privileged Turkish Company was made in 1753. The first two of the Four Tracts were developed in the later fifties tho' not published until later. The crowning economic work of the man, his *Elements of Commerce* appeared in 1755.

Tucker was thirty-six years old at the opening of this decade and forty-six at its close, the very prime of his initiative vigor. Again he entered this period fresh from twelve years of active, observant, inquiring life, in the busy second trade center of great Britain, and he continued to reside and to study the trafficking life there, throughout the decade. These two facts go far to explain (1) that the decade was the most fruitful of his life and (2) that the productions were largely economic in character.

At the same time that this was Tucker's master decade as an economic writer it was his period of greatest activity in practical politics. In both of the Parliamentary contests of 1754 and 1756 when Mr. Nugent was returned for Bristol Tucker was his active supporter. A series of his tracts advocating Nugent's cause were published and his correspondences at this time are almost wholly concerned with election matters. As a reward for his effective political aid to Nugent, the latter secured for him the Gloucester Deanery and the economic decade ended. The scientific economist, who might have produced a master work, was lost in the Dean.

The years from 1759 to 1772 gave the press little from Tucker's hand. A sermon, an essay treating the effect of war upon trade, a study of the poorhouse system and a brief report on improvements in the navigation of the Stroud river, are all that twelve years record from the man who filled the preceding decade with works that entitle him to high rank among early English economists.

Another burst of author power came in the ten years from 1772 to 1782. This may well be styled his political decade. The American controversy papers, by which alone, some know Tucker, came at almost regular intervals from 1774 to 1781. While the economist is everywhere in evidence in these productions and the theories of the fifties are applied to the practical commercial problems of the seventies, discussion of governmental rights is prominent. The questions started by the political topics involved in the discussion led Tucker to examine closely the thought bases of governmental systems. The best of evidence that this decade of authorship is rightly characterized as the political decade, is the fact that in its closing year 1781, he issued his ambitious attack upon Locke, his most extensive work, a theory of government.

The clerical subscription controversy called forth from Tucker during this decade his leading religious controversial papers and in 1776 he published a volume of sermons; but these religious writings are of subordinate importance when compared with his political essays during this decade, just as his activity in practical politics was subordinate to his economic achievements in the mid century decade.

After 1781, there were five brief publications and an author's day was done.

II. The Writings by Topics

Tucker was a philosopher. He sought the fundamental unity of life. He attempted to show that the principles of theology, politics and economics are in ultimate harmony. To these three subjects he gave all of his life as an author, emphasizing now one, now the other, according to the varying stimulus of the day. The widest generalization in all the range of his work, is this often repeated thought that the true principles of religion, government and commerce, not only are not in contradiction, but fully complement one another. Perhaps the clearest expression of this idea is in the Introduction to his *Elements of Commerce:*

"Let us therefore enter upon the ensuing work, with the following maxim strongly upon our minds viz.: That universal commerce, good government and true religion are nearly, are inseparably, connected. For the directions and regulations of each of these are no other than to make private coincide with public, present with future happiness. And whoever is conversant with the affairs of the world cannot fail to observe, that, whenever the parts of this extensive system have been separated by the arts or folly of men, religion has sunk into superstition or enthusiasm, government has been turned into tyranny and Machiavelian policy, and commerce has degenerated into knavery and monopoly." [1]

In accord with this "system" of Tucker's thought, the obvious topical classification of Tucker's writings is threefold: Works upon religion, upon government and upon commerce. Under such a grouping they will now be classed with brief comments upon the occasion inspiring them.

a. RELIGIOUS WRITINGS

From life choice Tucker was first of all a clergyman. It is fitting therefore that a number of his works should be upon religious and theological themes. It is noteworthy that all the publications of his first author decade are of a religious nature or addressed to religious parties.

In 1739 he published *Queries and Arguments, addressed to Mr. Whitefield concerning Methodism.*[2] Bristol was a

[1] *Elements*, p. 8. A similar statement in *Instruct. for Trav.*, p. 48, where he closes with; "Those men, therefore, who would represent the principles of religion and the principles of commerce as at variance . . . are in reality friends of neither."

[2] *London Mag.*, vol. viii, pp. 340-343.

stronghold of this growing sect of Dissenters and Tucker made a first hand study of their methods and of their development and he expressed his skepticism of the validity of such of their doctrines as were variant from those of the established church.

A Brief History of the Principles of Methodism was published by Tucker in 1742. The author's title page summary of this work is that the rise and progress, together with the causes of the several variations, divisions and present inconsistencies of this sect are attempted to be traced out and accounted for. The Lord Archbishop of Armagh, Primate of all Ireland, had written to Bishop Butler in June of 1741 requesting an account of the " divisions and the quarrels of the Methodists," and Bishop Butler chose Tucker, one of his minor canons, " as being a person well acquainted with their principles and proceedings." The Archbishop was so pleased with the report that he desired that it be published.[1]

The third of these early publications was an occasional sermon upon *Hospitals and Infirmaries Considered as Schools of Christian Education for the Adult Poor and as Means conducive toward a National Reformation in the Common People.* It was preached in the parish church of St. James before the contributors to the support of the Bristol infirmary at their anniversary meeting, held the 18th of March, 1745. It was published by subscription.

The last of these early publications was *A Calm Address to All Parties in Religion Concerning Disaffection to the Present Government.* As the title indicates, it is a churchman's political address. It properly classifies with Tucker's

[1] The facts and quotations here are taken from the preface of the *Brief Hist. of Methodism.* John Wesley himself answered this in his *The Principles of a Methodist,* 1746. In his pages *To the Reader* Wesley states that this is his first controversy directed to a particular person.

political writings. It foreshadowed the active politician of the next decade and prophesied his Whig leanings.

In the opening year of the next decade, 1749, appeared *Two Dissertations on Certain Passages of Holy Scripture,* etc. These dissertations are criticisms of the first volume of the posthumous work of Mr. Thomas Chubb,[1] entitled *Remarks on Scriptures,* etc. The second *Dissertation* is properly to be classed with Tucker's political writings.

In 1753, or earlier,[2] Tucker's *Earnest and Affectionate Address to the Common People of England Concerning Their Usual Recreations on Shrove Tuesday* was published. A new edition appeared in 1787.

In 1757 Tucker issued his first theoretical religious work, *A Short and Familiar Way of Explaining the Important Doctrine of Justification,* etc. This brief tract was addressed "To the inhabitants of the parish of St. Stephen's, in the city of Bristol . . . . by their faithful pastor."

These three tracts are the only publications by Tucker upon religious topics during this whole decade in which his pen was so busy with economic treatises, and with correspondences and pamphlets bearing upon practical local politics.

The fifteen lean years of authorship that followed Tucker's elevation to the Deanship in 1758 record but one religious publication. This was an occasional *Sermon* preached in the parish church of Christ Church, London, May 6th, 1766, at the time of the yearly meeting of the children educated in the charity schools in and about the cities of London and Westminster. Tucker had been for twenty years[3] a mem-

[1] Mr. Thomas Chubb (1697-1747), deist.

[2] This tract is advertised in the back of *Reflect. on Turkey Trade,* 1753.

[3] See *Appendix* of this sermon, which gives a brief history of the Society for Promoting Christian Knowledge.

ber of the "Society for Promoting Christian Knowledge," under whose auspices the sermon was published.

But if the churchman had been less active than the economist and the practical politician in the preceding decades, amends were made in that from 1772 to 1782.

Tucker's first volume of religious discourses, *Six Sermons,* appeared in 1772. The first five sermons are of no unusual type; the sixth is a reprint of the Bristol Infirmary sermon.

In the same year, he entered the lists of the subscription controversy with *An Apology for the Present Church of England,* a letter addressed to those about to petition for the abolition of subscriptions. The argument is firmly for the maintenance of subscriptions, and yet it is fair and tolerant, upholding the perfect right of dissenters to withdraw from the Church of England and to worship as they choose, and favoring the abolition of subscription among such university students as were not to take orders. It is admitted to have been the clearest and most convincing presentation of the side of the controversy espoused by the established church. A second edition was published within the year. The *Letters to Dr. Kippis,* in 1773, continue the same line of argument.

In 1774 Tucker published *Religious Intolerance No Part of the General Plan Either of a Mosaic or Christian Dispensation,* a well-sustained projection of his general freedom theory into the realm of religion; *A Brief and Dispassionate View of the Difficulties Attending the Trinitarian, Arian and Socinian Systems,* a fearless confession that human reason cannot resolve the mystery of the Trinity; and *Two Sermons,* issued with the *Four Tracts.* These two sermons were on commercial themes, the first emphasizing one of Tucker's favorite thoughts, the harmony of the principles of religion, government and commerce, and the second an excellent and most suggestive discussion of luxury.

In 1776 a new volume of *Seventeen Sermons* came from Tucker's pen. It contained all of the nine sermons previously published and seven new ones, among them one on patriotism (xv) and one on the right of revolution, an occasional sermon on the anniversary of the execution of Charles I. (Number xvii).

b. POLITICAL WRITINGS

Tucker wrote extensively upon political subjects. As was true of most of his works, these political writings were largely stimulated by current events, and were therefore mainly controversial. No attempt will be here made, more than to catalogue these writings, to state the occasions that called them forth, and to outline very briefly the contents of the most important of them.

Three political subjects especially interested Tucker: the right of the reigning line to the throne, the policy of Great Britain towards her American colonies, and the relations of Great Britain to Ireland. His further important political theories concerning war and colonies in general, can be very properly treated under his applied economics, since his arguments relating to these subjects are largely commercial and financial.

The first of his political writings was his *Calm Address,* etc., in 1745, an exhortation for the support of the ruling house in that year of rebellion.

The second of the *Two Dissertations* (1749) is a clear and well-analyzed outline theory of government. His theory can be suggested in a few quoted sentences from this *Dissertation:*

" God gave men inclinations, he gave them the use of reason; and, whenever such an application is made of both, as answers the general end of government, He gives a sanction and authority to it; and constitutes the magistrate his minister and representative to the people for good. The authority therefore of government is derived solely from God, but . . . . forms of government are the workmanship of men, and may be as various as we please, provided they answer the great end for which all government was ordained of God, viz., the good of the people . . . . The people have a *perpetual* and *inalienable* relation to the ends of government i. e., they have *always* a *right* to be governed *well,* be the governors who they *will.* But their relation to the means, to the particular governors subsists no longer than while they are means i. e., during the time they can properly protect and defend their subjects . . . . That as government was designed for the good of the people, the body of the nation or their representatives are the best judges when and how far this end is answered," . . . . As to the English Revolution his position, an application of the principle above quoted, is indicated in a single sentence: "They (persons engaged in the Revolution) allowed that he (King James) had a good title to govern; but not to govern wrong." [1]

During the Bristol parliamentary election of 1754, Tucker wrote a number of pamphlets [2] in support of Mr. Nugent. These sharpwitted appeals to the voters materially aided towards Nugent's election, and incidentally contributed to Tucker's later preferment to the Gloucester Deanery. They evidence a practical shrewdness and a persuasive insight into human nature.

The war with the American colonies combined with the subscription controversy to bring Tucker again into the publication arena, after twelve years of almost complete inac-

[1] *Two Dissertations*, pp. 43, 47. 52, 53 and 54.

[2] See Bibliography of Tucker's works for 1754, for the titles of these tracts.

tivity. His thirteen American tracts [1] were written from 1774 to 1783. Their central thesis is thus stated by Tucker himself:

" The grand principle which runs through all of my treatises on the subject of America viz., that the colonists in quarreling with the mother country are essentially hurting themselves and greatly, tho' not intentionally benefiting us by obliging us to see and pursue our own true and lasting interest." [2] [viz. separation.]

These tracts comprise the most noteworthy series of pamphlets that was written upon the subjects brought forward by the American war.

In 1775, at the close of Lord Clare's (Mr. Nugent) twenty years' representation of Bristol in Parliament, Tucker published a eulogistic *Review of Lord Clare's Conduct as a Representative of Bristol.*

In 1779 Dean Tucker's *Reflections on the Terrors of Invasions* first appeared. This tract, which argues the practical impossibility that there could be landed upon English shores any continental army sufficiently strong and well-

[1] See Bibliography of Tucker's works at close of this volume for the titles of these tracts. Because legislators were heedless of his plea for separation from the colonies, Tucker signed a number of these pamphlets "Cassandra," *e. g., The Dean of Gloucester's Tho'ts, etc., Further Tho'ts, etc.*, and *Proposals for General Pacification.*

[2] *Series of Answers*, p. 40. A comment Tucker makes upon Locke in one of these American tracts will interest students in politics: "As a man I have no ill will against Mr. Locke. When I was inexperienced twenty years of age, I thought him an oracle in metaphysics and politics. At the age of 30 I discovered he was not so original as I had supposed. At 40, 50, 60 and up I saw the tendencies of his writings, that his works had done more harm than good; . . . a mixture of error in the best of them . . . Constant commotions and rebellions would be the fruit of following his works." *Four Letters to Shelburne*, pp. 109–112.

subsisted to conquer England, was reprinted in 1806, to allay popular fear of a French invasion.

The study of the American colony question led Tucker to inquire more deeply into the theory of government, and this inquiry culminated in his most ambitious political work and his most extensive single volume, *A Treatise Concerning Civil Government.* In this volume he examines and attempts to confute the "notions of Mr. Locke and his followers concerning the origin, extent, and end of civil government;" he constructs his own theory of civil government; he compares the forms of civil government; and he censures England's former Gothic Constitution. Worthy of especial mention is the clearness with which he states the political biped thesis in his objection to Locke's idea that government originates in contract. A single sentence from his two-page exposition of this thought will evidence his insight:

> "The instincts and propensities of mankind towards social life are in a manner so irresistible that I might almost say men will as naturally seek to enjoy the blessings of society as they do to obtain their daily food." [1]

Even a meager outline of this four-hundred-page volume would require more space than can be allotted here. The opinion may be hazarded that students of the history of English political theories will find in this *Treatise,* and in the second of the *Two Dissertations,* suggestive thought about government, worthy ampler notice than it has received.

In 1783 Tucker published his *Four Letters to the Earl of Shelburne.* The first letter belongs to the American tracts, and argues that those colonies had ever been a millstone hanging about the nation's neck, and that they at last had themselves cut the rope which the nation was too blind to

[1] *Treatise on Gov't,* p. 50.

do voluntarily. The remaining three letters praise the British "mixt" form of government and further criticize Locke.

In 1784 *Dean Tucker's Opinion on the Present Most Interesting Dispute* appeared in two of the current magazines.[1] The dispute concerned the influence which the House of Commons should exert upon the selection of ministers by the King. Tucker argued that the royal appointing power is constitutionally wholly independent of preferences of either of the Houses of Parliament.

A Sequel to Sir William Jones' Pamphlet, etc., in the same year, continued Tucker's discussion of the principles of government.

Tucker had argued a number of times[2] for the union of Great Britain and Ireland. In 1785 he published a complete tract[3] upon this subject, arguing the inevitableness of union at some time, but declaring that, from Ireland's standpoint, that time had not yet come. In 1799 Dr. Clarke published[4] a number of answers made by Tucker, in 1785, to queries concerning the advisability of the union of Great Britain and Ireland, submitted to him by Tucker.

c. THE ECONOMIC WRITINGS

There are but few of the theological and political writings, mentioned above, which do not give frequent evidences that their author was an economist. A number of them,

[1] *Europ. Mag.*, vol. v, pp. 220–221; *Gent's Mag.*, vol. liv, pp. 202–203.

[2] *Four Lett. to Shelburne*, p. 15; *Essay on Trade, 3d Ed.*, p. 59; *Manifold Causes Increase of Poor. Advertisement;* Section ix of Book ii, chap. ii of the *Elements* was to contain a "Polity for the Perfect Incorporation of Ireland."

[3] *Reflections on Present Matt. in Disp. Bet. G. B. and Ireland, etc.*

[4] *Union or Separation.*

whose titles classify them clearly with religious or political works are in content economic.[1]

The first of the strictly economic writings opened the ten years of Tucker's authorship characterized as his economic decade. It was *A Brief Essay on the Advantages and Disadvantages which Respectively Attend France and Great Britain with Regard to Trade.* This *Essay* was first published in 1749, a second edition appearing in 1750, and a third, with large additions in the form of "proposals" of ways and means to enlarge Britain's commerce, in 1753. France was looked upon as Britain's peculiar rival in trade and in colonization. It was, therefore, a natural choice that Tucker, for twelve years a resident of seaport Bristol, made, when he began his career as a writer upon commercial themes, with a careful factual comparison of the strong and weak points of his own nation and its most powerful opponent in the struggle for world commerce and conquest. To this comparison the body of the original essay is devoted. The proposals in the appendix to the edition of 1753 foreshadow Tucker's later, more complete expositions of his theories of freedom in trade, of monopolies, of bounties, of warehousing, of canals, of colonies, and of immigration. They close with a twenty-page explanation of a tax system for Great Britain. The introduction to the whole essay is noteworthy for its suggestions as to (1) the possibility of a science of economics, (2) the basic importance of self-interest in the new science, (3) the relations of individual and of social interest, (4) a philosophy of exchange, and (5) a theory of prosperity. All of these themes are elaborated in Tucker's later works, especially in the *Elements of Commerce* and the *Instructions for Travellers.*

The English people had quite consistently opposed the in-

[1] *E. g.* Sermons vii and viii of *Seventeen Sermons.*

coming of foreigners throughout their history. The entrance permitted to immigrants under Edward III. and under Elizabeth was exceptional. Under Anne, in 1709,[1] an act was passed for the naturalization of foreign Protestants; but British aversion to foreigners was so great that this act was repealed in 1712.

In the middle of the eighteenth century a vain attempt was made to pass again such an act. Mr. Nugent, afterwards Bristol's representative in Parliament, and a friend of Tucker, early in the session of 1751, brought forward a bill for the naturalization of foreign Protestants who fled to England to escape Rome's power on the Continent. The great trading corporations opposed it; but the Bristol common council and the Merchants' Society of Bristol favored it.[2] Tucker championed the immigrant. In his *Reflections on the Expediency of a Law for the Naturalization of Foreign Protestants*, published in two parts (one in 1751 and one in 1752), he clearly stated the arguments for naturalization and refuted the claims of the opposition.

Although Parliament refused naturalization privileges to foreign Protestants in 1751, it is curious to find that in 1753 it passed an act for the naturalization of foreign Jews. Tucker favored this act in his two *Letters to a Friend Concerning Naturalization* (1753). In the *General Evening Post*, in September of 1753, he answered the charges made by the *London Evening Post* that the Jews were guilty of such practises as crucifying infants. This answer was in a tract entitled, *A Full and True Account of Many Barbarous, Bloody, Cruel and Inhuman Murders.* These naturalization papers were very able pleas, but were not strong enough to overcome the blind avesrion of the nation for foreigners. Prejudice, inflamed by such charges as those made

[1] 7 Anne, ch. v.

[2] *Annals of Bristol*, p. 289, by John Latimer.

by the *London Evening Post,* again prevailed, and in 1754 the act permitting Jews to naturalize was repealed, leaving the naturalization laws substantially as they were at the opening of the mid-century controversy concerning them.

Tucker's opposition to chartered exclusive companies was suggested first in his *Essay on Trade,* and was amplified somewhat in the *Proposals* added to the *3d edition* of the *Essay,* in 1753. In this same year he specifically applied this theory, in a well-sustained attack upon the privileges of the company chartered to carry on a trade with Turkey.[1] This attack was more immediately effective than that of the naturalization papers; it was largely instrumental in causing the opening of the Turkey trade in 1754.

This same thesis of opposition to privileged trading companies is further maintained in Tucker's greatest economic work, *The Elements of Commerce and Theory of Taxes.* This treatise was printed, in 1755, for private distribution, that friends might give the author the benefit of their criticisms. About sixty copies of it were sent to various friends,[2] with the injunction that they should be returned to

[1] *Reflections on Exped. of Opening Trade to Turkey,* 1753. A second edition, with an Appendix in 1755.

[2] The copy of the *Elements* in the "Ford Collection" of the New York Public Library (Astor Division), has many marginal manuscript suggestions by Archbishop Secker, of Canterbury. As a result of reflection upon one criticism by the Archbishop, Tucker has erased the printed title "The Elements of Commerce and Theory of Taxes," and has written above it "The Moral and Political Theory of Trade and Taxes," which probably would have been the title for his great work had he ever completed it for publication. It is interesting to note, in this connection, that when, two years later, he printed his *Instructions for Travellers* (also for private distribution), he sub-titled it "A Plan for Improving in the Moral and Political Theory of Trade and Taxes by means of Traveling."

The British Museum Library copy of the *Elements* has very few marginal notes and has no indication as to the author of these notes.

the author. This work is very rare now,[1] a fact which probably accounts for so little notice being taken of it. It was looked upon by its author as but part of a great work which he had sketched out as early as 1752.[2] *Tract II.* of his *Four Tracts* appears with its title-page comment, "A Fragment of a Greater Work," and the *Instructions for Travellers* (1757) is also but the development of a single section of the planned great work.

In the preface[1] to the *Four Tracts* occurs Tucker's own account of his plan for this great work:

"The facts set forth that it (Tract I) is a fragment of a greater work. This work was undertaken at the desire of Dr. Hayter, then Lord Bishop of Norwich and preceptor to the Prince of Wales, his present Majesty. His Lordship's design was to put into the hands of his royal pupil such a treatise as would convey both clear and comprehensive ideas on the subject of national commerce, freed from the narrow conceptions of ignorant or the sinister views of crafty and designing men; and my honored friend and reverend Diocesan, the late Lord Bishop of Bristol, Dr. Conybeare, was pleased to recommend me as a person not altogether unqualified to write on such a subject. I therefore entered upon the work with all imaginable alacrity, and intended to entitle my performance 'The Elements of Commerce and the Theory of Taxes.' But I had not made a great progress before I discovered that such a work was by no means proper to be sheltered under the protection of a royal personage, on account of the many jealousies to which it was liable and the cavils which might be raised against it. In fact, I soon found that there was scarcely

McCulloch states (p. 50 of his *Literature of Polit. Econ.*), that the copy of the *Elements* then in his possession had a few inconsequential notes by Earl Shelburne, afterwards First Marquis of Lansdowne.

[1] See note on this work in Bibliography.

[2] See letter of June 1st, 1752, to Lord Townshend in *Hist. Mss: Com. 11th Report* (1881) *Appendix*, Part IV, p. 378.

a step I could take but would bring to light some glaring absurdity which length of time had rendered sacred, and which the multitude would have been taught to contend for as if their all was at stake; scarce a proposal could I make for introducing a free, generous and impartial system of commerce, but it had such numbers of popular errors to combat as would have excited loud clamors and fierce opposition; and therefore as the herd of mock patriots are ever on the watch to seize all opportunities of inflaming the populace by misrepresentations and false alarms; and as the people are too apt to swallow every idle tale of this sort I determined to give no occasion to those who continually seek occasion. In short, as I perceived I could not serve my Prince by a liberal and unrestrained discussion of the points relative to these matters, I deemed it the better part to decline the undertaking rather than do anything, under the sanction of his patronage, which might disserve him in the eyes of others. For these reasons I laid the scheme aside; and if ever I should resume and complete it, the work shall appear without any patronage, protection, or dedication whatever." [1]

In his correspondence with Lord Kames, Tucker referred several times to his great work, and defended himself against the charge evidently pressed by Lord Kames, that he was unduly delaying its publication.[2] In 1761 his plea was that it would be useless to publish such a work then:

" War, conquests and colonies are our present system, and mine is just the opposite. Were I to publish at this juncture, the best treatment I could expect is to be taken for a knave or

[1] *Preface* to *Four Tracts*, pp. ix to xi.

[2] This delay is explained in the passages given. In the *Advertisement* to the *Manifold Causes for Incr. of Poor*, Tucker expressly denies that the delay was due to failure to secure subscriptions; that there had been no attempt to get a list of subscribers. The explanation of the delay, as given in Palgrave's *Dictionary of P. Econ.*, appears then to be erroneous.

a madman . . . . I look upon the nation at present to be frantic with military glory and therefore no more to be argued with than a person in a raving fit of a high fever." [1]

Again he gives reasons for abandoning his "political children:"

"I have been too forward in my publications already and those who think most favorably of my performance, consider them as the flights of a well meaning visionary . . . . In the second place there is nothing in the present disposition of the times to encourage one to hope he can do good . . . . the popular jury tears down everything before it and nothing is read or regarded but as it suits the fashionable frenzy.[2] . . . If I should ever publish this work it shall be . . . . to give orders for the publication of it after my decease [3] . . . . . But with regard to my great work, the fact is, that I am not ready for publication, were I ever so willing; nor can I say when I shall be, for the avocations belonging to my new office of Dean are too many and too important to be omitted etc." [4]

These other duties seem to have continued to monopolize his time, for the comprehensive plan was never carried out. And so it came about that only fragments are left; but these fragments are important, for they give a very good idea of the whole.

The *Elements* was intended for the opening of this work. Its preliminary discourse, setting forth the natural disposition or inclination of mankind towards commerce, presenting universal principles in a science of commerce, and

[1] *Memoirs of Lord Kames*, vol. iii, pp. 163–164. Letter of October 18, 1761. The reference to a "frantic nation" shows the influence of Bishop Butler's query as to national insanity.

[2] *Ibid.*, pp. 166–167. Letter of Dec. 10, 1763.

[3] *Ibid.*, p. 172. Letter of Dec. 26, 1763.

[4] *Ibid.*, pp. 173–174. Letter of Feb. 15, 1764.

arguing the fundamental importance of self-interest in the new science—this preliminary discourse alone stamps Tucker as an unusually clear thinker and suggestive writer upon economic subjects. At the close of the *Elements*, Tucker has given a full outline of his tentative plan for a great work. This entire "skeleton," as Tucker calls it, has been printed as an *Appendix* to this monograph for several reasons: (1) It reveals a well-matured plan for an extensive, systematic, master-work. It gives a fuller conception of the wideness of the man's information, of the range of his thought, and of the clearness and completeness of his analyses, in economics, than can be given in any other way. (2) Its subtopics are, in several cases, the only definite statements Tucker has left upon the subjects to which they refer. (3) The whole furnishes a general outline guide for such an arrangement of the later topical presentation of Tucker's contributions to economic thought as will fairly represent his own system. (4) The volume in which it occurs is a very rare one.

Four lesser economic productions belong to this virile decade. In 1751 Tucker made his contribution to the current writings on the liquor problem. He entitled his tract, *An Impartial Inquiry into the Benefits and Damages Arising to the Nation from the Present Very Great Use of Low-priced Spiritous Liquors*, etc.[1]

In 1755, when war was imminent, Tucker published *The Important Question Concerning Invasions, a Sea War, Raising the Militia and Paying Subsidies for Foreign Troops*, etc.

A brief pamphlet upon *The Case of the Importation of Bar Iron from Our Own Colonies of North America* Tucker

[1] See part ii, chap. i, section i, sub-section b, of this monograph, for the argument of this tract.

produced in 1756. It argues, from the standpoint of British manufacturers, for the free importation of American bar iron.

The closing product, fairly attributable to this decade, was not published until 1774, when it appeared as the first of the *Four Tracts*. It was *A Solution of the Important Question whether a Poor Country. . . . Can Supplant the Trade of a Rich Manufacturing Country*. The material in this pamphlet had been developed by Tucker as early as 1758, when he argued at length this very question in the correspondence carried on with Hume through Lord Kames.[1] The tract, as published in 1774, is the most suggestive of all of Tucker's minor works. It evidences his powers in both abstract and concrete presentation of truth, his directness and simplicity of style, and his breadth of view. In it Tucker (1) asserts the possibility of a science of economics, (2) clearly distinguishes *a priori* from *a posteriori* reasoning, (3) declares a harmony between the principles of economics and those of ethics, (4) urges a general naturalization law, (5) notes the importance of capital and of the division of labor, (6) outlines a philosophy of international exchange, (7) develops the thought that all nations may grow rich together, (8) refutes the bullionist error, (9) rejects the parallel between private and national bookkeeping, (10) denies the development-decadence analogy between the individual and the nation, (11) presents a theory of national prosperity, and (12) condemns war—and all this concisely stated within the narrow range of fifty-six octavo pages. No man could have written this tract who was not a theorist of unusual powers in the subject of economics.

[1] See *Memoirs Lord Kames*, vol. iii, pp. 158–161. Letter of July 6, 1758.

In addition to his published works, Tucker carried on at least two correspondences upon economic themes during this decade from 1749-1759. The one with Mr. Hume, in 1758, has already been mentioned above. The other, carried on in 1752-1753 with Lord Townshend, was referred to in the account of Tucker's life. Time will probably reveal to manuscript searchers other such correspondences.

The ten years, from 1749-1759, was the most fruitful decade of Tucker's author life. He was old enough to have insight and good judgment, and yet young enough to have enthusiasm and initiative vigor. A summary of his writing during the ten years will amply justify the characterization of it as his economic decade: He discussed at length the trade relations between Great Britain and France; he took a prominent part in two absorbing national discussions, those upon naturalization and upon the Turkey trade; he interestingly developed a number of minor economic themes, and corresponded upon economic subjects with prominent men of the day, to their frankly acknowledged instruction; and he planned, and partially executed, the first systematic treatise, in the English language, covering the full range of economic thought. It is no wonder, in the presence of such a record for a single ten years, that sarcastic Warburton shot his stinging shaft at Tucker as the clergyman who "made a religion of trade."

During the relatively barren author years that followed Tucker's elevation to the Deanery of Gloucester, he published two pamphlets upon economic subjects, *The Manifold Causes of the Increase of the Poor,*[1] and *Improvements and*

[1] See this monograph, part ii, chap. ii, sect. iii, sub-sect. (c), for an outline of this pamphlet. The Stroud River pamphlet is merely descriptive of attempts to navigate that river with the aid of powerful lifting cranes instead of more expensive locks.

Savings in Inland Navigation Exemplified on the River Stroud. Both of these appeared in 1760, and were thus virtually but an afterglow of the brilliance of the economic decade.

During the fourteen years from 1760 to 1774, Tucker wrote but one economic tract, *The Case of Going to War for the Sake of Trade,* published in 1763, and republished as *Tract II.* of the *Four Tracts.* It was occasioned by reflections upon the Seven Years' War, and it voices Tucker's opposition to war.

In the years from 1774 on, Tucker published a number of minor economic tracts. In 1774 *Four Tracts* and *Two Sermons* appeared. The first two of the tracts have already been mentioned as attributable to an earlier period. The remaining two tracts were political. The *Two Sermons* are his "commercial sermons," one an interesting discussion of luxury,[1] which he intended as models to show that commercial themes could be properly and profitably dealt with by a clergyman. These sermons occur as sermons vii and viii of the *Seventeen Sermons* (1776).

In 1778 he issued *The State of the Nation in 1777 as Compared with . . . 1759,*[2] which foreshadows the modern national census. It is written as a suggestion to legislators, and especially to malcontents, and indicates certain investigations which it would be profitable for them to make.

In the years after 1780 Tucker issued but one pamphlet and one brief magazine article which can be classed with his economic works. The pamphlet appeared in 1782, and is entitled, *Reflections on the Present Low Price of Coarse*

[1] See this monograph, part ii, chap. i, section i, sub-sect. (a), for an outline of his discussion of luxury.

[2] See this monograph, part ii, chap. v, section v, for the contents of this tract.

Wools, etc. It gives his opinion upon the falling prices of this staple product, which occasioned considerable speculation at this time. In 1784 he proposed *Subjects for Dissertations and Premiums to be Offered to University Students.*[1] He was of the opinion that the general tenor of academical studies afforded little instruction in the civil, political, and commercial interests of the nation:

> "A student may excel in that knowledge required for his degree . . . . and yet be very deficient in that knowledge necessary to form the public spirited citizen, the enlightened senator and the real patriot and what is worse, the greater his zeal, without such knowledge, the more liable he will be to pursue wrong measures."

As a partial remedy for this lack in the university curricula, he proposed that prizes be offered in the English and Scotch universities for the best student dissertations upon selected subjects. He proposed subjects canvassing such territory as: The effect of war upon national commercial strength, the relative productiveness of slave and of free labor, and the results of complete abolition of monopoly.

The tract, *Reflections upon the Present Matters in Dispute between Great Britain and Ireland* (1785), was political in intent, and has been classed with his political works, although it is, in main part, an arraignment of monopolies.

[1] This article appeared in *Europ. Mag.*, vol. xxi (Jan., 1792), pp. 17-18. It was first published as *Appendix* to *Reflect. Dispute G. B. and Ireland*, 1785.

PART II

TUCKER'S ECONOMIC THOUGHT

INTRODUCTORY NOTE

This PART II aims to present Tucker's economic thought.

There are a number of important ideas which serve as a background to all of Tucker's economic writings. It will contribute to readier grasp of the more detailed development of his thought if these ideas are first clearly in mind. Therefore, Chapter I has been devoted to a presentation of these *Fundamental Notions*.

In the remaining six chapters of PART II, attempt has been made to give Tucker's entire system of economic thought as concisely as is consistent with conveying a clear conception of the wide range of that thought. The subject-matter has been presented, as nearly as the limitations of the present plan will permit, in the order outlined by Tucker himself, in the plan for his master-work.[1]

Endeavor has been made to set forth, in Tucker's own words, all of his important economic ideas. To effect this, quotations have been made freely; but no quotation has been introduced for the mere sake of quoting. Each has been

[1] See ***Appendix*** for this ***Skeleton***.

carefully chosen as representative of perhaps many similar expressions of Tucker's thought. Further, no quotations have been garbled. Each has been given in sufficient fullness to allow the reader to interpret Tucker for himself. Whenever elisions occur in the body of quotations, they have been made solely for the sake of abbreviation. The part given exactly conveys the complete spirit of the passage.

The present author entered upon his study of Tucker without any bias. He held no thesis which he desired to prove. His aim throughout has been to understand what Tucker has written upon economic subjects and to present fairly the substance of those writings. He has conscientiously striven that the following chapters may convey substantially those impressions which any open-minded student of economics would receive, who should painstakingly study the nearly four thousand printed and manuscript, octavo pages of Josiah Tucker's writings, which are extant.

CHAPTER I

FUNDAMENTAL NOTIONS

TUCKER begins his analysis from the psychologist's point of view. Conceiving the possibility of a science of commerce, and accurately divining the psychological nature of that science, he opens his great work [1] with a "preliminary discourse setting forth the natural disposition or instinctive inclination of mankind towards commerce."

He defines commerce thus:

"Commerce, I mean, in the large and extensive signification of that word; commerce as it implies a general system for the useful employment of our time; as it exercises the particular genius and abilities of mankind in some way or other, either of body or mind in mental or corporeal labor." [2]

This definition obviously widens the term commerce so that it includes the whole range of economic activity, and one who is reading Tucker must keep this sense of the word in mind. A science of commerce so defined is a science of economics.

That Tucker had a clear conviction that commerce was reducible to a science is evidenced by many references in his works. For examples, in 1749 he wrote:

[1] The full synopsis of this great work (partially executed and partially only thus outlined) is printed in the Appendix of this monograph. The order of topical arrangement indicated by this outline of Tucker, has been substantially followed in the following pages, that the impression received in reading them may be as nearly as possible that which Tucker planned.

[2] *Seventeen Sermons*, pp. 138–139.

" Men of a liberal and learned education have disadvantageous ideas of the study of commerce . . . . it has been represented as a dry, unentertaining subject, dark and crabbed, perplexed with endless difficulties, not reducible to any fixed and certain principles. But upon examination it will perhaps appear that this representation is very false and injurious. . . . . . The principles of trade, therefore, being so clear and certain in themselves etc." [1]

and in 1755 he opens his *Elements* with:

" The principles laid down in the ensuing treatise are for the most part general and universal, viz., such as would suit (with very little alteration) any kingdom, state, or climate, whatever and are therefore called *The Elements of Commerce.*" [2]

Preliminary to his attempt to state and to make application of what he conceives to be the principles of the science, he analyzes human nature, concluding:

" Therefore the general and constituent principles of human nature may be summed up: Man hath the appetities of an animal, the temper and affections of a social being, and the understanding of a rational agent." [3]

The analysis proceeds to unfold the relations of this animal appetite, this social benevolence, and this regulative reason. A running abstract will give a clearer notion of the trend and connections of the thought than if the excerpts be given piecemeal and then commented upon.

Tucker observes that as animals, men are more deficient by nature than any other tribe of beings, for they need clothing and shelter. Other animals are quickly able to supply all of their wants, but never progress, *e. g.*,

[1] *Essay on Trade*, pp. viii and ix.

[2] *Elements*, *Advertisement*.

[3] *Elements*, p. 3.

"the first nest is as admirable as the last." Few lower animals "discover any disposition to divide the labor of the community into different branches or assign distinct parts to the respective individuals . . . . Wheresoever any tribe of animals distributes the labor of the community into different parts (as is reported to be the case among beavers, ants and bees, it hath always been observed that those make some advances superior to mere animal life." [1]

"But the social instincts are for the most part, the prerogative of man . . . . mankind therefore being thus under the influence of social and benevolent instincts as naturally seek society in order to gratify these social instincts, as they require food for appeasing the appetite of hunger." In society thus formed there arise artificial needs "to be called social because their first rise and subsequent increase must be ascribed to society. And as our present secular happiness appears to arise from enjoyment of superior wealth, power, honor, pleasure or preferment, self-love, the great mover of created beings, determines each individual to aspire after these social goods and to use the most probable means of obtaining them. Thus, therefore, the passion of self-love operates, with much greater force when excited by such a long train of objects than it possibly could do were men strangers to the artificial wants, the refinements and decorations of social life. And yet were this passion to proceed without direction or control, it would in a great measure defeat its own ends. For self-love is narrow and confined in its views, and admits no sharers or competitors, wherever it can exclude them . . . . and tho' in fact all such mutual exclusions must end in mutual poverty, so that even self-interest is a loser, in the end, by these pernicious schemes, yet the mass of mankind ever did and ever will proceed in this way as far as they have power. They will always regard the present moment and be blind to future consequences . . . . . Indeed I grant that the social instinct of benevolence is some check upon this selfish monopolizing

[1] *Elements*, p. 4.

principle; but it is so very feeble that it would be quite ineffectual to prevent the mischief arising from inordinate self-love, were there no stronger curb to rein it in. For the love of self is implanted in human kind much more strongly than the love of benevolence, according to the English proverb: 'Self knows no fellow.' Therefore reason and reflection must be called in to the aid of the social and benevolent principles. But what is the office of reason? Not surely, to extinguish self love. That is impossible. And it might be questioned whether it would be right even to diminish it, for all the arts and sciences, and the very being of government and commerce, depend upon the right exertion of this vigorous and active principle. And were it once restrained or weakened, human nature would make but feeble efforts towards anything great or good. Nay, in such a case, the social temper itself would want a spur, and all the benevolent affections being destitute of their proper incitement would be very faint and languid in their operations. Consequently the main point to be aimed at is neither to extinguish nor to enfeeble self-love, but to give it such a direction that it may promote the public interest in pursuance of its own; and then, the very spirit of monopoly will operate for the good of the whole. And if this is the proper business of reason, considered in the abstract, the reason or public wisdom of a state or community is particularly called upon to pursue such a law. This politic direction of the pursuits of various individuals towards one common end, the study of philosophies and the aim of every wise legislature, will be found to be nothing more than a strict and scrupulous observance of Christian morality. . . . . Where the auxiliary motives of reason are called in to the aid of social love or diffusive benevolence, the latter become in a good degree a counter agent to inordinate self-love. So that the circulation of commerce may be conceived to proceed from the impulse of two distinct principles of action in society, analogous to the centrifugal and centripetal forces in the planetary system." [1]

[1] *Elements*, pp. 5-8.

Four of the topics suggested by this extended abstract deserve particular notice. They are, 1st, human wants; 2d, self-interest; 3d, the relation of economics to ethics; and 4th, the theory of national prosperity. Tucker develops these four topics somewhat fully, and an attempt is here made to present his complete thought upon the subjects by correlating the partial analyses of them scattered through his various works.

I. Wants

With an insight remarkably prophetic of the economic analysis accepted at the present day, Tucker opens his great work with a study of the wants of man. He sees that man is the important subject for economic analysis. He, therefore, seeks in man's nature for the explanation of the world of commerce which he desires to understand. And, first of all, he sees that there are wants, and that stimulated by these wants men seek to satisfy them.

Considered merely as an animal, "man has animal wants, and is incited to provide for them much the same as animals."[1] But as a social being, man develops other than crude animal wants, and these are to be called artificial wants. This distinction is clearly stated in the opening of his chapter on the polities for the extension of commerce. After defining commerce, he continues:

"And this employment is derived either from the natural or the artificial wants of mankind. The natural wants, as hath been observed, are such as belong to man in common with other animals. But the artificial wants are peculiar to him as a member of civil society. Though, indeed, in another sense, these very artificial wants may be styled natural, because they arise from the peculiar nature of man as distinguished from other

[1] *Elements*, p. 3.

creatures. But this being a less intelligible way of speaking, it would be better to keep to the former division into natural and artificial. . . . If a man is poor, he can supply himself only with necessities;[1] . . . if rich, he can get useful and convenient things." [2]

Natural wants, then, appear to be demands for the most meagre necessities of individual physical life. Any social-born want is artificial. Thus even the Indians of America have developed some artificial wants:

"True, they have not the *same* artificial wants, . . . but they do want beads, etc., . . . and ammunition. . . ." [3]

Tucker believes that the artificial wants may stimulate either social development or social degeneracy. Perhaps his most sweeping generalization in dealing with the subject of want is:

"The support and extension of commerce must result from the multiplication of the artificial needs of man." [4] This same thought is in the query: "Whether the artificial wants of mankind, properly circumstanced and under due regulation, are not the great master-spring of the machine of commerce?" [5]

But Tucker sees the possible evil, as well as the potential good, of artificial wants. This is shown by his query:

[1] Elsewhere he suggests the present time honored classification in a phrase: "Every necessary, every comfort and elegance." See *Four Tracts*, p. 67.

[2] *Elements*, p. 41. For the same thought well stated, see *Reflect. Nat. For. Prot. Part* II, p. 10, *note*.

[3] *Essay on Trade, 3rd Ed.*, p. 80.

[4] *Elements*, p. 41.

[5] *Reflect. Nat. For. Prot. Part* II, p. 10.

"When these (artificial) wants degenerate into vice, intemperance, and extravagance, whether they do not then become a great obstacle to the constant and regular motion of the machine, and indeed have a necessary tendency to stop it at last?" [1]

It is such insight that leads him to criticise Mandeville's famous pamphlet:

"What an absurdity, therefore, was it, in the author of 'The Fable of the Bees,' to say that private vices are public benefits. It is virtue alone that can make a nation flourish, and vice of every kind is either immediately, or in its consequences, injurious to commerce." [2]

An artificial want which Tucker mildly criticises, and to which he often refers, is the desire for foreign wares—the desire that led French women to wear English silks and jewelry, and that induced the English to use French wines. He explains this thirst for foreign goods as due to a craving for distinction. Of this desire for distinction he writes:

"The passion of wishing to be distinguished is, indeed, universally implanted in human nature, and may be made subservient to both good and bad purposes." [3]

But the two wants which Tucker emphasizes as degenerating, and which he treats at length, are desires (a) for luxury and (b) for spirituous liquors.

a. LUXURY

To the discussion of luxury he devotes an entire sermon, one of the two which he called his "commercial sermons." In it he defines luxury, traces its fatal effect upon public

[1] *Reflect. Nat. For. Prot. Part* II, p. 11.

[2] *Essay on Trade, 3rd Ed.*, p. 130.

[3] *Cui Bono*, p. 43.

welfare, and gives test rules to determine the proper expenditure of private incomes. In opening the discourse, he confines his thought to the use or abuse of the world so far as it affects

"the more costly ornaments of life and those embellishments which belong to the higher ranks of society. For if it can be proved that luxury retards even grandeur and magnificence, then surely it will be quite superfluous to descend to inferior matters." [1]

He defines the form of luxury with which he deals:

"The first characteristic of luxury is when expense exceeds ability, that is, when men figure away in the great world for a time and then either sink into poverty or obscurity, or else take bad courses to support their extravagance. The second is when persons live after such a manner as, though it may last for their own time, will, nevertheless, prevent them from making a provision, or at least an adequate provision, for the succeeding generation. This, indeed, is little more than a removal of the former evil to a more distant period." [2]

He expressly omits from the discussion the forms of luxury that connote "indulgence of the carnal appetites," and undertakes to prove that

"Luxury, even in high life, and even in the most favorable view of it, is not that useful thing to society which moralists themselves have incautiously granted, and which advocates for vice have pretended to demonstrate." [3]

He assumes the case of a capital city whose inhabitants live luxuriously, as he defines the term, and pictures how,

[1] *Seventeen Sermons*, p. 152.

[2] *Ibid.*, p. 153.

[3] *Ibid.*, p. 154.

from a transient splendor, the city inevitably sinks to ruins. Beyond the third generation

"by a natural transition, the few wretched descendants of the first prodigals would be glad to inhabit some corner of the mouldering palaces of their ancestors, fitted up as huts or hovels for their reception." [1]

The only remedy is

"to substitute a more virtuous, frugal and industrious set of men [2] . . . . if we are to imagine that the inhabitants of this metropolis did begin from the lowest stages, then we must allow that the necessaries of life must have been the first objects of their care. . . . After these had been sufficiently provided for, and a growing fund of wealth established, mankind would naturally expand their ideas and extend their thought to the comforts and conveniences of their respective condition . . . . Very likely the first generation would here terminate their views; . . . . but the second generation, still persevering in the same plan of good economy, would be enabled, without detriment to their circumstances, to advance higher, so that the works of genius would begin to appear. . . . . From such elegancies and refinements the gradation is easy and natural to that which is grand and magnificent, and thus the affairs might be carried on . . . throughout an almost endless progression and variety." [3]

These latter men, Tucker says, are the real "patrons of the arts." He concludes the discussion by noting (1) the fundamental harmony of ethics and economics, and (2) that

"Temperance and excess are relative terms whose significa-

[1] *Seventeen Sermons*, p. 155.

[2] *Ibid.*, p. 155.

[3] *Ibid.*, pp. 156–157.

tion must be ascertained by the circumstances of the case, . . . the respective constitution, circumstances, age and condition, of this or that particular individual." [1]

This thought of the temperate man leads him to frame rules for wise expenditure:

" Thus, for example, he who uses this world properly . . . is he who adjusts his enjoyment to the following standard, viz.: 1st, when his expenses are brought within his income; 2dly, when he makes a decent and adequate provision for his family and dependents; 3dly, when he lays by for contingencies; 4thly, when he obliges himself to be a good economist, in order the better to be able to provide for the necessities of the poor; 5thly, when he indulges himself in no gratification which may injure either the health of his body or the faculties of his mind; 6thly, when in all his enjoyments he has regard to the influence he may have over others, so as to set them no bad or dangerous example."

" Now whosoever will limit his . . . expenses by these regulations, he is not a luxurious, but a temperate man. . . . Nay, were he to do less, were he to deny himself such gratifications as can be enjoyed, compatibly with these rules, he would not fill the station nor live up to the rank and character allotted for him. In short, he would be the covetous man, ... injurious to society by defect as the other was by excess." [2]

b. SPIRITUOUS LIQUORS

The other artificial want which Tucker treats at some length, is the desire for spirituous liquors. [3] Instead of giving a full and pathetic description of the miseries and

[1] *Seventeen Sermons*, pp. 160–161.

[2] *Ibid.*, pp. 161–162.

[3] See *An Impartial Inquiry into . . . Use of . . . Spiritous Liquors, etc.*, a 33 page pamphlet, written in 1751, devoted to this subject and from which the following digest and quotations are taken.

destructive consequences occasioned by spirituous liquors, he prefers to impartially set forth "such facts as seem necessary to be insisted upon." He answers a number of objections to the movement against the use of spirituous liquors already begun by the chief magistrate in London. He argues that revenue deficiency resulting from lessened liquor consumption can be made up, beneficially,[1] in other ways; that funds spent for liquor may be turned into better trade channels, and that foreign liquors can be made so expensive by high duties that little will be used. To the contention that the legislature has no right to ruin the business of the British distillery, he queries:

> "Is it reasonable that a very great part of the common people of Great Britain should be permitted, ... encouraged in practicing a vice enfeebling and enervating, shortening lives and making victims public burdens, or that a few suffer inconveniences?"[2]

He classifies consumers of spirituous liquors, and discusses the probable effect of his proposed liquor legislation upon each class. The first class includes those "obstinately addicted to" the use of liquors. If the price is made higher, "they can get less, and thus prolong their lives and hinder the corruption of their example." The second class includes those who have "no unconquerable attachment, but who cannot withstand temptation when in their way." These people can be saved, because "there is a difference between being tempted and seeking temptation." The third class includes "the young children . . . who can be entirely reclaimed."

[1] It was a hobby of Tucker's, as will be shown later, that taxes could be laid so as to stimulate industry.

[2] *Spirit. Liq.*, pp. 8 and 9.

In the appendix to this pamphlet on liquors, Tucker estimates the loss to Great Britain through the use of gin and of spirituous liquors. He estimates that there are 400,000 drinkers of both sexes. They consume less of bread, meat, groceries, furniture, and apparel, do less work, die prematurely, commit thefts and robberies, are sick oftener and longer, and increase the poor rates, all of which loss side of the account sums, annually, £5,214,285 14s. $3\frac{8}{7}$d.[1] On the other hand, the annual profit at 2d. per day per drinker on the English spirits they drink sums £1,216,666 13s. 4d. yearly. This leaves a net loss of £3,997,619 $11\frac{8}{7}$ d. Tucker then criticises his own estimate, declaring that, if anything, it underestimates the loss.

The pamphlet closes with an argument that an idle drinker is a " double loss to the community," being weaker both as producer and as consumer, whereas a sober worker is a " double advantage " to his community.

II. Self-interest

The second of the topics suggested by the lengthy quotation, and deserving of further treatment, is self-interest. In his discussion of this subject, Tucker again places himself abreast of modern economic thought. He discovers in his searching analysis of human nature that self-interest is the ruling economic motive. He, therefore, makes it basic in his system of commerce. In the lengthy quotation from the *Elements,* it is made certain that in 1755 he saw clearly that in economic life self-interest is the supreme motive. To this analysis he adhered consistently in all of his later works.

He applied his knowledge of the power of self-interest

[1] **This affectation of mathematical nicety is possibly pardonable in a writer of the eighteenth century, but similar perfection pretense is not unknown to-day.**

again and again. It was the basis for his prophecy that trade relations would be resumed after the war with the American colonies, even though the colonies were granted independence. The ample fulfillment of this prophecy illustrates the practical insight which Tucker developed, through intelligent deductions, from this fundamental motive. As illustrations of Tucker's applications of self-interest, these American trade prophecies will serve well:

"Americans will buy our goods when it is to their interest and they are able to, notwithstanding the bitterest antipathy, . . . and I defy any man to prove that they ever did buy our goods contrary to their own interest."[1] "It is impossible to compel distant settlements to trade with a parent state, to any great degree, beyond what their own interest would prompt them to; and self-interest needs no compulsion."[2] "Let it be observed as the universal rule with merchants and traders of all countries, religions and languages, that self-interest needs no reconciliation. For trade is carried on not for the sake of friendship, but of interest."[3]

Other applications of this same self-interest principle are made in his treatment of population, of trade in general, of manufactures, and of taxation. In short, recognition of this powerful motive to economic activity is so frequent in his works, that it is clearly established that he made self-interest, in vital reasoning, as well as in early formal analysis, a central principle in his system of economic thought.

He recognized the self-seeking motive to be too powerful to be overcome, and that therefore sane systems of legislation should so appeal to this motive that its splendid incen-

[1] *Cui Bono*, p. 75. A similar idea in *Letters to Shelburne*, p. 9.

[2] *Treatise on Gov't*, p. 253. A similar application to trade with Ireland is made in *Union or Separation*, p. 37.

[3] *Series of Answers*, p. 28.

tives should direct individual energies towards promotion of the public welfare. This idea he applies in his system of taxation.

A comparison of the *Appendix* to the *Essay on Trade* [edition of 1753], and the *Elements*, written in 1755, seems to show that Tucker had, within the two years between these writings, developed his idea that self-interest can be made conducive to public good. In the *Appendix*, he refers to "self-interest, the bane of all public good," [1] "that watchful dragon, self-interest," [2] and "the baleful spirit of self-interest," [3] consistently using condemnatory adjective and metaphor. But while this *seems* to indicate that he had not yet reached the advanced position that this primal motive may be appealed to for good as well as for ill, it does not, as can readily be shown. In the *Appendix*, Tucker is attacking the privileges of the chartered companies, and when he uses "dragon" and "baleful" he is but characterizing the evils that result when self-interest is unbridled. That he had noted even before 1753 the possibility of good through self-interest, is evident from a paragraph he wrote in 1752:

"The great view of the divinely-inspired legislator, Moses, seems to have been to turn this principle of self-love into such a channel that it should always operate for the public good. And, indeed, this ought to be the sole aim of every government, if either good morals or national prosperity are expected." [4]

All of the many references made to self-interest in his works published after the *Elements*, recognize it as a powerful motive which may be appealed to for good or for ill. There are many such pasages as:

[1] *Essay on Trade, 3rd Ed.*, p. 61.

[2] *Ibid.*, p. 66. [3] *Ibid.*, p. 84.

[4] *2nd Letter on Naturalization, Note*, p. 37.

"whether they make the passion of self-love, that ruling principle of human nature, subservient to the public good or detrimental,"[1] etc.

In logical consistency with the above thought, it is notable that Tucker, at no time, advocated the complete ultimate harmony of public and private interests. Here, again, he agrees with the modern thought, and is opposed to the Manchester school of economists. He did not trust individual self-interest, free-reined, to labor always for the public good. On the contrary, he pointed out cases in which public and private interest are at variance, as, for example:

"The general interest of trade and the interest of particular traders are very distinct things; nay, are often quite opposite. . . . General interests of trade are interests of industry, and therefore of peace. . . . Many dealers in exports and imports encourage war and oppose peace. . . . Jobbers and contractors for our fleets and armies, clerks, paymasters, &c., are . . . . vultures who fatten on human gore. They keep up the American warwhoop and object to peace measures so long as personal gain may come to them."[2]

III. Relation of Economics to Ethics

The third topic, worthy of somewhat fuller treatment than is given to it in the long extract from the *Elements* at the opening of this chapter, is the relation of economics to ethics. This subject is fully developed by Tucker, and the conclusion he reaches becomes one of his working principles, frequently applied by him in the consideration of varied problems. His position is an *a priori* one. It is the position of

[1] *Instruct. for Trav.*, p. 10. For similar references see *ibid.*, pp. 20 and 32; *Cui Bono*, p. 60; *Humble Address, etc.*, p. 19.

[2] *Four Tracts*, pp. 90-91.

the philosopher enamoured of his ultimate unity. It is, none the less, the position of the present day economist, if that individual see fit to deal with the subject at all. A clergyman, Tucker states his *a priori* position in the churchman's language. Its substance is that there cannot be fundamental disharmony between good moral and wise industrial living. He frequently attributes the harmony between rightly understood moral and commercial relations to a design of the world Creator:

" Providence never designed us to be beasts of prey, to bite and devour one another; but, on the contrary, that whatever is a social duty in a moral sense, was likewise intended by our wise and gracious Creator to be a real, lasting and national interest in a commercial." [1]

That this conception was one of Tucker's working principles is apparent from a number of applications of it which he makes. When arguing the unwisdom of war between nations, and the opposing the current thought that a nation could rise only as it crushed down its rivals, he said that he was

" firmly persuaded that, in His plan of government, the political interests of nations cannot be repugnant to those moral duties of humanity and love which He has so universally prescribed." [2]

In closing his discussion of luxury, he again stated and applied this principle:

" It clearly appears . . . that there can be no real and last-

[1] *Cui Bono*, p. 46. Similar thought in *Seventeen Sermons*, pp. 138–39; *Elements*, p. 8; and *Reflect. Nat. For. Prot. Part* II, p. 10.

[2] *Four Tracts*, p. 63.

ing opposition between the laws of sound morality and those of sound policy, whatever crude opinions may be entertained to the contrary. For even in these cases where it was heretofore usually imagined that strict morality had the disadvantage, it is now evident that the fact itself is far otherwise, and all the claims which luxury, in the most favorable view of it, can possibly make, amount to no more than that, for a short time, it doth promote a greater demand for the ornamental parts of furniture, dress and equipage than, in prudence, there ought to have been. A mighty advantage! . . . . Indeed, there is something extravagant, if not impious, in the supposition that morality and policy, when rightly defined and properly understood, should be at variance with each other. For what an idea must this give us of the Divine Being? What a strange constitution of the world would that have been had it been necessary that our duty and our interest should always clash! . . . . . Nor was He that shortsighted, or improvident, or malicious Being as [sic] to make that to be our duty which is not upon the whole, even as to the affairs of this world, our interest likewise." [1]

A further application of this same principle occurs in his modern-toned discussion of the relative efficiency of slave and of free labor. From an implied premise that ethics clearly condemns slavery, Tucker argues that, according to the fundamental harmony-principle, slave labor should be uneconomic, and asserts that it is so in fact. This is in his open letter to Edmund Burke:

" For my part, I am thoroughly convinced that the laws of commerce, when rightly understood, do perfectly coincide with the laws of morality: [2] both originating from the same Being,

[1] *Seventeen Sermons*, pp. 159 to 161.

[2] This principle is frequently stated in his works. See *Elements*, pp. 40, 42 and 81; *Four Tracts*, p. 20; *Reflect. Nat. For. Prot.*, Part II, p. 10.

whose mercies are over all His works. Nay, I think it is demonstrable that domestic or predial slavery would be found, on a fair calculation, to be the most onerous and expensive mode of cultivating land and of raising produce that could be devised, and I defy you, with all your learning and acuteness, to produce a single instance from history, either ancient or modern, of a country, being well cultivated, and at the same time abounding in manufactures, where this species of slavery . . . . is preferred to the method of hiring free persons and paying them wages." [1]

From the nature of his chosen profession, and from his firm belief in the final harmony of ethical and economic interests, it is to be expected that there should be not infrequent ethical comments in his economic works, just as, owing to his belief in the wholesomeness of thought upon economic life, there is a distinctly commercial flavor to some of his sermons. One of these ethico-economic passages is as applicable to this day as to the mid-eighteenth century:

" For crimes against the public are attended with such consequences as spread the contagion of vice much wider, and are more detrimental to virtue and to good morals, than the like crimes . . . . against private persons. And yet, how differently do most people think of these matters! How light do they make of any injury done to the public! A contraband trade is nothing; nay, it is well if it is not esteemed meritorious. . . . And as to custom house oaths, dealings with the government or with public bodies, and all the other methods whereby society is injured and defrauded, who is there that scruples the repetition of these over and over? . . . . Such facts are too notorious to be denied and too bad to be palliated." [2]

[1] *Letter to Burke*, p. 23.

[2] *Seventeen Sermons*, p. 183.

In summary, Tucker thought that, rightly understood, ethics and economics were closely related, and necessarily in harmony. To him, preaching morality was at the same time inculcating guiding principles for wisest conduct in the commercial world; demonstrating a principle of trade was at the same time pointing out a path to higher levels of national ethical life. The dean and the economist were happily made one by the formula: Sound morality coincides with commercial wisdom.

IV. Theory of National Prosperity

The fourth topic suggested by the opening quotation from the *Elements,* is the theory of the wealth of nations.

Two ideas are the essentials of Tucker's theory of national prosperity: (1) Industry, only, will make a nation rich. (2) State action can, and should, stimulate such industry. Both of the ideas are often expressed, and are almost always implied, in his writings.

Typical expressions of the first idea are:

" This mutual circulation of labor and industry is the grand fundamental truth in politics and commerce, which can never be too much inculcated." [1] "Almost the whole body of the people of Great Britain may be considered either, as customers to, or the manufacturers for, each other—a very happy circumstance this, on which the wealth and prosperity of a nation greatly depends." [2] " Judge also whether a rich country can ever lose its trade while it retains its industry and consequently how absurd must every project be for securing or increasing this trade, which doth not tend to secure or increase the diligence and frugality of the people." [3]

[1] *Cui Bono*, p. 137.

[2] *Instruct. for Trav.*, p. 26.

[3] *Four Tracts*, p, 41.

The second essential of Tucker's prosperity theory is that government action may stimulate this wealth-getting industry. He has very great faith in the efficacy of legislative enactment and of executive enforcement of law. This faith is explicitly avowed in connection with one of his presentations of the idea that nations need not necessarily die as persons must. He argues that not only may "the public body, or political man," by observing "a due regimen" and never deviating "from the paths of virtue," live an unlimited time, but

"what is still more, if, after having injured himself greatly in these respects, he would apply the proper medicines, that is, frame good laws, and see them duly and wisely executed, he would recover from this dangerous disease, etc." [1]

These "good laws," which are to stimulate the industry of individual citizens, must appeal to their self-interest, and so induce them to seek employments which will advance national well-being. This thought is perhaps most clearly expressed in Tucker's very earliest economic work:

"As to the great point of national advantage or disadvantage, this is properly the concern of others, who sit at the helm of government and consequently whose province it is to frame the laws and regulations, relating to trade, in such a manner, as may cause the private interest of the merchant to fall in with the general good of the country . . . . self and social happiness must in this case be made to unite; otherwise it will happen in this, as in most other affairs, that social happiness will not be promoted at all." [2]

This complete confidence that state action can, and conviction that it should, guide individual economic activity, makes Tucker, in a peculiar sense, a political economist.

[1] *Seventeen Sermons*, p. 158.

[2] *Essay on Trade*, p. xiii.

Belief in the need of universal industry among citizens, and in the efficacy of state action to secure this, might lead to socialism. Tucker condemns the class who live upon interest incomes alone, because they are not contributing, by their industry, to the national wealth:

> " Their case being directly opposed to the public good, tho' it may be pitied, should not be provided for by the legislator. On the contrary, make their state uneasy and they must turn to industry." [1]

Again, Tucker favors education of the poor, especially industrial education, and argues that they should have fair opportunity to rise by industry.[2] This is a further advocacy of state action to encourage industry. But although Tucker does so plead the cause of the poor, and although he does condemn the extravagance of the rich, and although he does believe that law-making and law-enforcing powers may do much to right social wrongs, he nowhere takes, or even hints at favoring, the socialistic position. On the contrary, he expressly objects to any levelling schemes. For example, he even objects to restoring the law for the equal distribution of a landed estate among all the children of the deceased owner, because he regards this as

> " running too far into the agrarian scheme of levelling and equality." [3]

[1] This passage was written by Tucker on the margin of the New York Public Library copy of the *Elements*, p. 134. It was a response to Archbishop Secker's marginal note: "I hope you find a place for considering the case of those who can have no other subsistence than the interest of their money."

[2] See *Charity School Sermon*. Some quotations, which bear upon the above topic, are given in treating *population*.

[3] *Instruct. for Trav.*, p. 30.

Elsewhere, he rightly presages the tendency of teaching the equality doctrines of the day, but it is to be noted that he himself condemns the movements "against landlords," etc., as "wild and extravagant conceits:

"The modern doctrines of the perfect equality of mankind . . . . and of the necessity of contending for them even to the death tend to confirm all these wild and extravagant conceits against landlords, etc., ... for they necessarily demolish not only crowns but coronets too, levelling all distinctions with the ground." [1]

When these condemnations of levelling tendencies are coupled with Tucker's anti-republicanism, expressing itself in complete skepticism of the wisdom of the populace,[2] it becomes very evident that no propositions of his may be reasonably given a tinge of socialistic interpretation. All of his pleas that the common people be given opportunity, educational and otherwise, to elevate their standard of living, are but corollaries of his proposition that production should be encouraged by state rewards and penalties. Tucker is an individualist rather than a socialist; but his belief in the importance of state action saves him from being an extreme individualist.

It has been said that the two ideas, (1) that industry should

[1] *Lett. to Shelburne*, pp. 41 and 42. Similar passages against levellers are in *A Sequel to Sir Wm. Jones' Pamphlet, etc.*, pp. 7 and 25.

[2] Clarke in *Survey of Strength and Opulence of Great Britain*, p, 40, says that Tucker once told him that "he hardly ever knew an unpopular measure to be a bad one, or a popular to be truly salutary."

Tucker held that "a democratic government is despotic by nature" and opposed the "universal suffrage of the vile and ignorant." (See *Lett. to Shelburne*, pp. 98 and 114.) In the letter to Dr. Birch, Dec. 20, 1756, Tucker speaks of the "wicked, ungrateful, senseless mob" (see *Birch Mss.* in the Brit. Museum). There are a number of other similar characterizations of the mass of the people who always appear to Tucker as "the mob." See *Four Tracts*, p. 96.

be encouraged, and (2) that the state, by law, should give that encouragement, are the essential components of Tucker's theory of national prosperity. It is now further to be observed that this theory of prosperity is fundamental to his whole economic work. Like that of a greater writer to come after him, his large problem concerns the wealth of nations. The ideas that increased national industry is desirable, and that state action should stimulate it, essentials of his prosperity theory, leaven all of his economic writings. They reenforce him in arguments for the naturalization of industrious foreigners, against the emigration of British citizens, and in favor of plans for increase of population; they are premises to his polities for breaking up great estates, enclosing commons and reclaiming wastes; they background his pleas against the parish settlement and the apprenticeship acts; they lead him to oppose chartered companies and they underlie his mercantilism; they account for his emphasis upon the policing function of taxes. A single thoughtful reading of Tucker's work, as outlined in Chapters II to VII of this Part II, will substantiate the above statements. The two ideas, then, which are elemental in his theory of national prosperity, are presuppositions in his treatment of each of the leading themes of his economic writings, viz., population, agriculture, manufacture, commerce and taxation. Thus, in epitome, Tucker's whole economic work is a theory of national prosperity.

V. Historical Sense

Tucker possessed the historical sense. Since this gave color to all of his writings, it is fitting to show, in this opening chapter of the exposition of his works, that he did possess the historical instinct.

Tucker was never a closet theorist. He put himself in

command of facts. He was the making of an historian. He began his writings, as has been noted, with pamphlets treating current history. In the naturalization controversy, two of his papers traced the history, respectively, of the British attitude towards foreigners in general, and towards Jews in particular. In his attack upon privileged companies, he reviewed the monopoly movement in British history from Elizabeth's day to his own. Frequently throughout his works original sources are quoted, early and later statutes, parliamentary records, and reports of special commissions. His historical researches and his close observation of every-day business in London and Bristol, won for him considerable reputation as one who had a broad knowledge of commercial facts.

A few citations from his works may evidence that Tucker had real historic appreciation. In his *Instructions for Travellers,* he addresses himself to that class of travelers "who will aim to study the effects and consequences of systems of religion, government and commerce." He advises such a traveler that

"He must observe how these systems operate on different people or on the same people at different periods. . . . . For in fact the human mind is in some sense but as clay in the hands of the potters . . . . molded . . . by these different systems. So that the political, the religious and commercial character of any people will be found for the most part to be the result of this threefold combination of religion, government and commerce on their minds." [1]

This same idea of environment's influence he applied years later to an individual case, explaining Locke's leading polit-

[1] *Instruct. for Trav.*, p. 4. Similarly "every nation has its peculiar bias." *Reflect. Nat. For. Prot. Part i*, p. 1.

ical thesis, individual liberty, as an outgrowth of the troublous religious environment in which he matured:

"Locke . . . in his early life was a witness to grievous persecutions inflicted on the score of religion . . . . he saw . . that the interests of the state were not at all concerned in maintaining that rigid, universal, conformity in religion for which bigots of those times so fiercely contended. . . . he inferred, and very justly that every man had a right not only to think but even to act for himself in all such religious mat- as did not oppose or clash with the interests of civil society." Had he stopped here it would have been well "but alas! He extended those ideas which were true only in what concerns religion to matters of a mere civil nature and even to the origin of civil government itself." [1]

A striking generalization upon the influence of the commercial system upon national life occurs in Tucker's treatment of monopolies under Queen Elizabeth. He regarded her as an arbitrary ruler, who granted monopolies, for goodly consideration, partly because she did not want her subjects to grow rich through freedom of trade. She feared that if her subjects became individually more nearly her equals in wealth, they would grow more independent in thought and in speech, according to the general principle that

"Trade and industry naturally create an independent turn of thinking which circumstance necessarily inspires an horror and destestation of arbitrary power. Moreover, freedom of trade brings with it, freedom of debate as well as freedom of thinking." [2]

This puts the emphasis upon commerce, *i. e.*, upon economics, in the interpretation of history.

[1] *Treatise on Gov't*, p. 30.

[2] *Elements*, pp. 151–152.

A caution against rash national analogies reads:

"It doth not follow that that system which might comport well enough with the circumstances of the little state of Geneva would be proper for so large an empire as the British." [1]

His rules for exegetical interpretation indicate the historic imagination:

"Let us place ourselves in the situation of those who heard the speaker or writer himself; and let us endeavor to find out what were the meanings of the words at the time they were spoken, not what they may now imply at times so far distant and among people so very different in their customs and manners." [2]

Although he sometimes speaks of the "natural" order of things and of "natural rights," Tucker does not often use this eighteenth century form of thinking. In one of the following passages he expressly takes exception to it. In 1749 he charged that Mr. Chubb's great deficiency was that he judged that ideas ought to come to others just as they came to him,

"without making the necessary allowance for the difference of times, places, customs, and the faculties of different men. With this fundamental error he went on. He viewed every object through one end of the telescope and thought it necessary for all mankind to do the same. Hence arose his positiveness about fitnesses, relations, etc., which at the bottom amounted to no more than this, that if other men saw things precisely in the same light as he did, without taking in or

[1] *Apology for the Church of England, 1st Ed.*, p. 32.

[2] *Six Sermons*, pp. 23–24. Similar statement in *Two Dissertations*, pp. 4 and 5.

leaving out any other ideas, then the fitness, the relation and the truth of the case was so and so. Which indeed might frequently be allowed him and yet his observations be very impertinent and inconclusive, as arising not from a full, but from a partial view of the subject in debate." [1]

Again, in the American controversy twenty-five years later, he challenged the argument of the colonies because

" they have recourse to what they call immutable truths, the abstract reasoning and eternal fitness of things and in short to such rights of human nature which [sic] they suppose to be inalienable and indefeasible. Former laws and precedents carry little or no conviction to people who argue after this manner. . . . The parent state grounds her present claim . . . on facts and precedents . . . " [2]

Such a paragraph might have been written by Burke.

Tucker condemns a number of the views of his day with reference to history:

(1) He combats Rousseau's concept of the heavenly savage by arguing, from reports of travellers, that the Indians were more subject to disease than the white men, and were lazy, gluttonous and improvident.[3]

(2) In a letter to Lord Kames he criticizes the Saxon system of government in England. He says that " great and glorious things are now said of the Saxon government," and yet he sees " no reason for praise save distance in time and difficulty of disproving heavenly allegations." The Saxon government was " founded on conquest and slavery, and slavery was its staple trade—not exactly a

[1] *Two Dissertations*, p. 58.

[2] *Tract V*, pp. 48–49.

[3] See *Treatise on Gov't*, pp. 182–188.

delectable pattern for modern nations." [1] In another place, speaking of the Gothic government, he becomes ironical in contemplation of the good-old-days idea:

"Doubtless these were very happy times indeed! And what a pity it is that those persons who are so lavish in their praises of Old England and dissatisfied with our present modern constitution, had not lived in these golden days when they might have enjoyed old England to perfection!" [2]

(3) In a critical passage in a letter to Lord Kames he opposes a view of historian David Hume. This passage well illustrates his habit of examining original records, and even of noting folk-lore. It is also notable since Tucker's view here is the one sustained by modern research. He says:

"In Mr. Hume's history of the Anglo Saxons he follows the stream of historians in asserting that they exterminated all the natives; and consequently had no slaves or villians. But I could never find any proof of this; and the appearance of things during the Heptarchy strongly indicates the contrary; the feudal system being as evidently the system among them as among all northern nations. And it is hard to say what could induce them to be so singular in this respect. I am myself a Welshman: we have no tradition in our country of any such measure. On the contrary we suppose that all the slaves remained slaves to their new masters and the gentlemen fled into Wales. Ergo, the Welsh are all gentlemen. Moreover the Danes and Swedes never mention this circumstance when they mention the expedition and victories of the Anglo Saxons, their ancestors, and if Mr. Hume will reflect on the price settled for killing a Welshman in Cambridgeshire, taken out

[1] *Memoirs of Kames* (Alex. Fras. Tytler), vol. iii, p. 183. Letter of June 24, 1782.

[2] *2nd Lett. on Naturalization*, p. 9.

of Hickes, he will conclude that that Welshman must have been a slave."[1]

(4) Tucker also opposed the concept of rhythmic history, the idea that nations must die. He answered to the plea:

"That all human things have the seeds of decay within themselves, great empires, great cities, great commerce, all of them receive check not from accidental events but from necessary principles. . . . . as the ideas and terms used are borrowed from the state of natural bodies and . . . transferred to political constitutions one thing is taken for granted in this argument to which I cannot readily assent. . . . . (i. e.) that as all animals, by having the seeds of decay within themselves must die sooner or later, therefore political or commercial institutions are subject to the like fate and on the same principles. Now this remains to be proved, for the parallel doth not hold in all respects and tho' the body politic may come to an end as well as the body natural there is no physical necessity that it must. . . . . In one word, the constitution of the body natural is so framed that after a certain period of time no remedy in nature can restore it to its pristine health and vigor . . . But diseases of the body politic are not absolutely incurable."[2]

Accurate prophecy is a test of historical insight. Tucker prophesied the inevitable separation of Great Britain and the American colonies when statesmen thought the only question was the terms upon which these should remain under British authority. After the struggle was over and independence had been declared by the colonies, he argued that if the British "would turn over a few pages of authentic his-

[1] *Memoirs of Kames*, vol. iii, pp. 176 and 177.

[2] *Tract I*, pp. 55-56. This thought is suggested in the letter to Hume in 1758. See Clarke's *Survey of Strength and Opulence of Great Britain*, p. 27. See for similar idea *Seventeen Sermons*, p. 158.

tory, either ancient or modern," they would learn that colonies,

"humble and modest in their infant state . . . as they rise in strength become proud and insolent . . . . incessantly aiming at emancipation . . . The Stamp Act, therefore, only hastened that struggle which might otherwise have been deferred a short time longer but which must assuredly have taken place before the expiration of many years." [1]

Another bold prophecy is only now in the course of fulfillment. In 1780, before the colonies had fully achieved their independence, when British public sentiment, British statesmen and British soldiers were yet determined upon subjugation of the rebels, Tucker dreamed a dream of great empire [2] in this western world. It has taken a century and a quarter for Europe to come abreast of this vision:

"Nor is it the least surprising that a country circumstanced like America should so soon have acquired so formidable a share of power. Its natural advantages of climate, soil, extent of territory, both of land and water, are all favorable to agriculture, trade and population; and a spirit of industry, a thirst for gain and an ardent desire of that very independence which has at length been set up, have led the colonists to improve with unremitting application all those means which nature has thrown into their hands. And thus the wise economy of providence diffuses blessings in succession to all the different orders of creation. Learning, Arts and Sciences, Religion, Government, Riches and Power have all been progressive since

[1] *Dispassionate Tho'ts on Amer. War*, p. 26.

[2] Tucker was not a consistent prophet with reference to the American destiny. In *Cui Bono*, p. 119, he says the American colonies will be a "disunited people till the end of time . . . divided and subdivided into little commonwealths." The prophecy given above, however, is the only one he argues out at any length.

the appearance of the present system: and there is nothing chimerical in the hypothesis to suppose, that in a certain period, the American continent will be the principal seat of all these valuable possessions and make a most distinguished figure among the nations of the earth and in the history of the world; while the European states are sinking into weakness, poverty and contempt." [1]

[1] *Dispassionate Tho'ts on Amer. War*, pp. 26-27.

CHAPTER II

POPULATION

THROUGHOUT the whole of his author life Tucker consistently advocated increase of the population of Great Britain. In 1749 he commended the "flocks of children"[1] in the peasant families of France and favored state aid to "those burdened with large families."[2] In 1782 the climax, commendatory result to be achieved by his scheme for placing militiamen upon waste lands, was that it "would considerably increase the human species."[3] In the thirty-three years lying between these dates he repeatedly declared Great Britain's need of a larger population. This was one of his emphasized arguments in the Naturalization papers.[4] It was the central thought of the entire *Book I* of his great work.[5] It had weight in leading him to oppose the settlement acts[6] and to seek a revision of the general system of poor laws.[7] It caused him to lament the emigration to the Americas.[8] It led him to devise burdensome taxes to be laid upon bachelors and corresponding exemptions to be granted to married men.[9] It even induced him to raise a fund to

[1] *Essay on Trade*, p. 41.

[2] *Ibid.*, p. 57.

[3] *Reflections . . . Price . . . Wools*, p. 46.

[4] In *Reflect. Nat. For. Prot. Part II*, p. 17, he quotes approvingly "In the multitude of people is the king's honor." Prov. xiv, 28.

[5] The first draft of this *Book I*, as submitted to his friends for criticism, is contained in the *Elements*, pp. 11 to 41.

[6] *Elements*, p. 21, and *Manifold Causes Increase of Poor*, p. 7.

[7] *Manifold Causes Increase of Poor*, p. 7.

[8] *State of the Nation*.

[9] *Elements*, pp. 16–29. *Manifold Causes Inc. Poor*, pp. 16 and 17.

provide marriage portions for poor young women.[1] Clearly it is his central thesis upon population.

He had reasons for his belief that Great Britain should increase her population, reasons stated in the form of "polities for increasing the numbers of people." Tucker's *Book I* of the *Elements* is headlined as "containing certain polities for increasing the numbers of people." Tucker's theorist instinct asserts itself at once and he endeavors to show "the need for such a polity." A digest[2] of his argument must suffice:

"(1) Where a country is thinly peopled it is impossible to promote a brisk and general circulation of industry and labor by reason of the distance and dispersion of the people . . . . and the consequence of that, their want of rivalship . . . . experience confirms this. In every country extremely thin of inhabitants the people are proportionably poor and miserable and lead such lives as are but a few removes from the brute savages of the woods and mountains. Suppose only 10,000, inhabitants of Great Britain . . . . these few would soon degenerate into British savages . . . ." Division of labor increasing the "quantity of work performed" and bettering the "quality or workmanship" itself is impossible where there is a scarcity of inhabitants.

(2) Where a country is thinly inhabited there is little gain in trade and therefore "country gentlemen are still more prejudiced against it" and against those whom they consider "low born tradesmen and mechanics" and "vie rather with each other in the dangers of chase, pretensions of birth and family and length of pedigree."

(3) Where a country is thinly peopled lands will be the more easily engrossed and entailed in a few families . . . . land-

[1] *Memoirs Kames*, vol. iii, pp. 162–163.

[2] The digests that follow, excepting where special references are given, are taken from the *Elements*, pp. 11 to 41.

holders become more despotic over vassals" . . . . This flatters the pride of the "petty tyrant" but he will have "less comforts than common tradesmen in a populous and industrious country. . . . Commerce as it is cultivated [tends] to extend industry and plenty, equalizes mankind more than any other way of life and at the same time that it connects them together in bonds of mutual interest it renders them free. Trade and vassalage, commerce and slavery are in their natures repugnant to each other."

(4) A thinly peopled country has neither strength nor riches for the numbers of the people are the strength as industy is the riches of a country." [1]

(5) The increase of the people (brings) the increase of rent [2] to the landlord.[1]

(6) A country thinly peopled has no implements for the improvement of husbandry, etc., no good roads, rivers made navigable [3] and canals, etc., etc., no capitals either for husbandry or manufactures.[4]

(7) A country etc., produces no constant supply even of necessaries of life; hence families, etc.[4]

[1] Sections vii, viii and ix (pp. 16–20), of *Reflect. Nat. For. Prot. Part II*, are respectively entitled "The increase of inhabitants the strength of a kingdom," "The increase of people the riches of a country," and ' The increase of people the increase of rent to the landlord."

[2] This is an illustration of the appeal Tucker frequently makes to the landed gentry. He rightly estimated them to be the ruling class in eighteenth century English politics.

[3] Tucker was greatly interested in inland navigation improvements. See his *Improvements and Savings in Inland Navigations Exemplified on the River Stroud, Gent's Mag.*, vol. xxx, pp. 167–168. In the *Essay on Trade, 3rd Ed.*, pp. 116 to 118, he advocates cutting canals "between our great towns of trade for convenience and cheapness of carriage," and "counts canals better than making rivers more navigable."

[4] These two paragraphs just as given above are marginal additions in Tucker's own handwriting, in the New York Public Library (Astor) copy of the *Elements*.

The very depopulation leads others to leave as they cannot secure employment . . . lands lie waste where there are no markets and artificers cannot be employed without customers."

Thus Tucker argues the general proposition that sparse population is detrimental to a country. So far indeed is he from fearing a Malthusian surfeit of population that he says:

" it is impossible there can be a want of labor [i. e. employment for labor] but where there is a previous want of industry on one side or the other. For the more hands there are employed, the more employments they will create for other hands, etc." [1]

He next confines his consideration to Great Britain in particular and contends that something must be wrong in its polity since it is *slowly* gaining in population although well situated and with rich resources:

" Great Britain now has wrong notions of public welfare and national commerce in the following respects (1) The marriage state is loaded with taxes . . . the duties and excises paid by a father on commodities consumed by his family are practically a fine upon marriage." (2) " This inducement to celibacy increases vice " or at best " young people assume no responsibility." (3) By entailing great estates and primogeniture, small farms are destroyed. (4) The nobility remain single and spend their prime in debauchery " so that those of higher rank, who ought to set the example, seldom think of raising a family till they are fitter for a hospital than the bridal bed." (5) The very liberty of the English corrupts their morals; the gallows, electioneering, spirituous liquors and debauchery helping to dispeople the country. (6) " Our distant colonies and navigation, perilous trades and English troops employed by the continent, draw off many " people, while " European nations attract our tradesmen and artificers."

[1] *Spirit. Liquors*, p. 33.

Tucker therefore concludes that Great Britain should adopt a polity that would increase both marriage and immigration. In outline the polity which he suggests for "rendering marriage the foundation of civil society, a matter of the universal choice and aim of both sexes" is:

(1) Let no post or title of honor or emolument be given to a person never married.

(2) Persons to be minors until 25 years of age, unless married before, with the consent of parents; then minors until 21 years.

(3) Statute of 5th Elizabeth requiring seven years apprenticeship should be repealed as to married men but retained as to bachelors.[1]

(4) "Let married men be free to work as journeymen or set up any trade in any town whatsoever."

(5) Let married men reside any where without parish certificates, provided a responsible man gives 5£ security they do not become parish charges within three months.

(6) Let men not work at women's trades unless married.

(7) For twelve months after marriage let a man decline any offices he chooses and be exempt from personal duties and taxes.

(8) Divorce should be granted by lower courts to either party upon proof of the other's adultery.[2]

As consequences of the adoption of his suggested polity Tucker prophesies that:

[1] Tucker comments: "This statute was really meant to serve monopoly and base ends . . . turn it to good."

[2] Pages 23 to 27 of the *Elements* are devoted to a discussion of divorce. Tucker concludes that it should be granted for adultery only, and that the guilty party should be imprisoned for a year. He argues that the lower courts should have jurisdiction instead of, as then obtained, the plan empowering Parliament alone to grant a complete divorce. "It needs friends and money to get this." Archbishop Secker, in a marginal note in the New York Library copy, suggests "Money alone will do."

(1) Marriages, with the honors all to the married, "will become the style."

(2) All will marry and therefore there will be no dissatisfaction in comparing married selves with single blessedness.

(3) Debauchery will be lessened when men of property marry early.

(4) Self-love will prompt the person of family to keep sober in desire to support well their own.

(5) Self-love will prompt them to train their children to sober callings and religious living.

(6) Parents will have more authority in marriage, with the majority at 25 years.

(7) Drinking, crimes and lusts will be lessened.

(8) Divorce will release innocent and punishment threatened will restrain those willing to be guilty.

A fully developed argument for "the admission of wealthy and industrious foreigners," continues Tucker's polity for increasing Great Britain's population. The plan for encouraging this immigration should be, in general:

"(1) To make known to foreigners the true nature of the English Constitution and (2) To enact laws removing all difficulties they labor under but not naturalizing them since the public is too greatly prejudiced." [1]

He closes his presentation of this polity with the statement that later polities which he will present, will co-operate with the one outlined above:

"A set of polities which promote industry and discourage vice . . . puts mankind into a capacity of increasing their species without bringing misery on themselves or entailing it upon their posterity . . . . the several parts of the great com-

[1] An illustration of Tucker's constant aim in his practical programs to offer not what is ideally best, but the best that is likely to be approved.

mercial system do indeed mutually support and strengthen each other inasmuch as populousness hath a natural tendency to promote industry and good morals and these in turn as naturally create populousness."[1]

In close connection with Tucker's treatment of his leading idea concerning population are his suggestions upon three subsidiary but important topics (1) Immigration (2) The rural exodus and (3) The poor.

I. Immigration.

Tucker favors immigration and opposes emigration, even to the British colonies. He asserts that the British have a peculiar and characteristic aversion to foreigners. One of the first pleas in his arguments for the naturalization of incoming foreigners, both Protestant and Jew, is made against this hostility to foreigners. He tells the English that they themselves are "a collection of all races and foreign tongues"[2] and that the common people of Wales are accustomed to call an Englishman who comes amongst them "a little pitiful Saxon who comes one knows not from where."[3] He holds aversion to foreigners to be especially irrational to so motley blooded a people.

He takes up the same topic from the historical point of view[4] and argues that opposition to foreigners is prejudiced

[1] This is another application of Tucker's "fundamental harmony" thesis.

[2] *Reflect. Nat. For. Prot., Part I*, p. 62. [3] *Ibid.*, p. 72.

[4] Part I of *Reflect. Nat. For. Prot.* is an admirable historical critique of the disposition of natives of Great Britain towards foreigners. It traces the history from the time of the conquest, pointing out the periods of development in trade and manufacture as coincident with the periods of freest immigration, and accrediting to foreigners the introduction and development of various manufactures. The *2d Letter to a Friend on Naturalizations* in a similar way traces the historical rights

since much of English prosperity in manufactures and commerce is due to industrious immigrants. These thoughts are all embodied in the queries with which he opens *Part II. of his Reflections upon the Naturalization of Foreign Protestants:*

"Is popular prejudice a test of the truth? Does the word foreigner not carry the idea of contempt and reproach? Have the English any grounds for this? Ought not the native, pursuing aims hostile to the country, be rather regarded as an alien? Do we not owe our knowledge in the manufacture of cloth, stuffs, linens, hats, iron, copper, brass, etc., to the instructions of foreigners?"

But many of those who might acquiesce in his favorable opinion of past immigrant contributions to British prosperity would oppose present immigration on the ground that immigrants displaced British workmen. Tucker therefore presents an argument upon this phase of the subject:

"Let foreigners come to take the bread out of our mouths!! Out of whose mouths? It must be English bread. The corn grew here, was manufactured here, was sold here. And the foreigners who eat it earn it by their labor and pay for it. . . . The more inhabitants there are to consume the produce of our lands, the better can the farmer and the gentleman pay their shopkeepers and tradesman, and the more manufactures will they consume in every respect. Let us see in the next place:

and wrongs of the Jews in Great Britain. Its tolerant theme, for Tucker was a native British, royalist, Protestant advocating the cause of an alien, Jewish, people against the royal, British, oppressors, was: "our princes only used them (the Jews) as sponges to suck up the treasure of the nation, and then when they had a mind to squeeze them dry, they let loose the popular odium and fury upon them. This is the true state of the case and the origin of their sufferings." P. 36 of *2d Lett. on Naturalization*.

Out of what mouths do they take the bread? If they introduce new manufactures, or carry those already established to greater perfection, in that case the public is greatly benefitted and no individual can be injured. If they employ themselves only in such as are already settled and perfected, they will not defraud the mouths of sober, frugal and industrious persons, who may work as cheaply, and can work as well, as foreigners, and therefore should be obliged to do both. . . . But we are told that English tradesmen of every denomination are used to live better than foreigners, and therefore cannot afford to work or to sell so cheap as they. Apply this to foreign trade. . . . If English ask 5 per cent., 10 per cent., etc., more for goods and argue that they live better, other nations will outsell them. . . . The English must trade at least upon an equal footing with other nations, or not trade at all. If not at all, even the most self-interested may be sorry we did not admit industrious foreigners. . . . For example, take Birmingham: It admits freely all; is no exclusive town. Englishmen coming from other towns are practically foreigners to its natives. Yet natives have lost no bread. Property has risen, . . . great accession to its trade, . . . very prosperous, . . . fewer beggars here, and in Leeds and Manchester (both free), than in towns with exclusive charters and trading companies. So true and certain is it that these rights and privileges, as they are called, do multiply the numbers of the poor, because they damp the spirit of industry, frugality and emulation. A manufacturer who knows that no foreigner dares come in to be a competitor against him, thinks himself privileged to be idle."[1] . . . "There must be rivals in commerce at home and abroad. If so, is it not better to have the rivals at home?"[2]

"The immigrants that Great Britain needs are merchant capitalists, artisans and mechanics."[3] Especially desirable are

[1] *Essays on Trade, 3d Ed.*, pp. 84–87.

[2] *Reflect. Nat. For. Prot. Part II*, p. 33.

[3] *Elements*, pp. 30, 31.

those "industrious and ingenious foreigners, men who have their fortunes yet to make," who may "come and enrich the country at the same time that they are enriching themselves." [1] The idle rich are not so desirable. If all the idle rich were to locate in England, it would soon become "a nation of gentlemen and ladies on one side, and footmen and grooms, ladies' women, laundresses, and such like dependents, on the other." [1]

There need be no fear that foreign beggars will come, for they "are too lazy and poor, and cannot speak the language." [2]

As to the alleged danger that foreigners might corrupt the English, Tucker is of the opinion that "there is greater danger that the English should corrupt the foreigners, than *vice versa*." [2]

It is to be expected that one favoring immigration on the general ground that Great Britain needed a larger population, should be opposed to emigration from the British isles. In his American papers, Tucker did oppose such emigration, even to the British colonies.[1] He had accurately noted that:

"The emigrants who lately sailed in such multitudes from the north of Scotland, and more especially from the north of Ireland, were far from being the most indigent or the least capable of subsisting in their own country. No, it was not poverty or necessity which compelled, but ambition which enticed, them to forsake their native soil." [3]

It should be observed that his opposition to emigration to the colonies was expressed after he had arrived at the conclusion that separation from the American colonies was

[1] *Four Tracts*, pp. 26, 27.

[2] *Reflect. Nat. For. Prot. Part II*, p. 40. Tucker had a very low estimate of the moral character of the English people in his day. See *Sermon at Charity School*, pp. 18–20.

[3] See *Humble Address*, etc., pp. 62–65.

inevitable. In closing his earlier argument upon emigration written in 1752 he thought that it would be

"prudent to keep open two doors, one to let in such people as will come to the state, . . . the other to let those go to the colonies who wish; . . . better allow our own people to go to the colonies than to our rivals." [1]

It is only fair to Tucker's logical accuracy to observe that these seemingly contradictory positions are in harmony. After the colonies had declared their independence and were in the attitude of rivals, they were practically a foreign state; and even in his earlier discussion Tucker impliedly opposes emigration to other states. The net result is that he favored immigration into the empire and opposed emigration from it.

II. The Rural Exodus

From his observations of the shiftings of the people within the island territory Tucker is led to remark upon the flow of population towards the cities and its effects:

"As to the continual flux of the lower order of people into towns and cities, and their desertion of their native places, this, alas, may be but too well accounted for: . . . First, it is but natural to suppose that the poor, being of the same flesh and blood with their superiors, and exposed to the same temptations, should be infected with the reigning disorder of the times, viz., a thirst after pleasure and amusements, a taste for gaiety and show, and consequently a desire of supporting their expenses without much industry or application. . . . But, secondly, it is not always true that rustics and peasants come to reside in towns and cities through choice and inclination; on the contrary, they are frequently driven to this expedient of late years, especially

[1] *Reflect. Nat. For. Prot. Part II*, p. 37.

through cruel necessity. For when their narrow-minded landlords pull down their cottages in order to avoid even the contingency of a poor tax, and when they themselves are hunted from one country parish to another for the same reason, and not supposed to fix their abode on any, what can these poor wretches do but flee to great towns and cities?" [1]

The result as Tucker saw it was that

"Great cities are already becoming the bane of mankind in every sense, in their health, their fortunes, their morals, religion, etc., etc., etc., and it is observable of London in particular, that were no fresh recruits, male and female, to come out of the country to supply those devastations which vice, intemperence, brothels and the gallows are continually making, the whole human species in that city would soon be exhausted. For the number of deaths exceeds the number of births by at least 7,000 every year." [2]

III. The Poor

Tucker dealt with the question of the poor at some length. He (a) described their actual condition, (b) suggested their claims upon the nations, (c) criticized the prevailing plan for the maintenance and control of those who became public charges, and (d) constructed a plan of his own for dealing with the public's poor.

a. DESCRIBES CONDITION OF POOR

In describing the condition of the poor he pictures a grievous state of things in England:

"With regard to the morals of the poor, times were never worse. For the lower class of people are at this day so far degenerated from what they were in former times as to become a

[1] *Sermon at Charity School*, pp. 18, 19.

[2] *Treatise on Gov't*, pp. 260–61.

matter of astonishment and a proverb of reproach. And if we take the judgment of strangers and foreigners of every country, who are certainly the most unexceptionable judges in this respect, we shall find them all agreed in pronouncing the common people of our populous cities [1] to be the most abandoned and licentious wretches on earth. Such brutality [2] and insolence, such debauchery and extravagance, such idleness, irreligion, cursing . . . and contempt of all rule and authority, human and divine, do not reign so triumphantly among the poor in any other country as in ours." One reason is, "our people are drunk with the cup of liberty; . . . the lowest of the people are now become the ultimate judges of public affairs; . . . they turn this liberty into licentiousness; . . . they outbrave punishment. . . . Our houses of correction corrupt more than they correct." [3] "And what shall I say of our mariners? . . . What they have been so long in earning, at the hazard of their lives, . . . they profusely and wantonly throw away, as if the whole pleasure of spending their money consisted in doing it as speedily, as foolishly and as wickedly as they could devise." [4]

b. PRESENTS CLAIMS OF POOR

To those who would argue that no attempt should be made to elevate the poor for fear that the "balance of condition which ever ought to exist between rich and poor" be disturbed, Tucker replies:

"If they mean to say that the poor should be treated as so many beasts of burden, without being permitted to enjoy the fruits of their own labor, or to rise gradually in the world by

[1] Previous quotation, see pp. 114, 115, has given Tucker's partial explanation of the crowding of poor people into the cities.

[2] Tucker's *Earnest Address*, etc,, in 1787 argued against cock throwing as unmanly and cruel. It brought reproach upon the country, for "It is on account of such diversions as those that they give us abroad the character of a bloodthirsty and inhuman people," p. 5.

[3] *Six Sermons*, pp. 70-74. [4] *Ibid.*, p. 88.

superior industry or skill, by greater frugality or better economy, this is nothing else but saying, in other words, that the poor ought to be kept in a state of slavery of the most abject kind, . . . and slavery will ever be found as repugnant to the interests of society as it is contradictory to the principles of common justice and humanity. Nay, it is known, experimentally known, to be incompatible with an extensive progress, much less with any great perfection, in manufactures and the mechanic arts. . . . It has been observed . . . that those whose private interest leads them to be industrious and to cultivate everything to the best advantage, succeed the best in making useful discoveries at first, and in prosecuting them afterwards. . . . If any . . . poor . . . exert greater industry, or display superior skill, or practice better economy than others, . . . they ought to be at full liberty . . . to rise in the world. . . . Can we pursue other measures consistently with those ideas of freedom and liberty which now prevail?" [1]

So much for the rights of the poor to an opportunity to rise. As to their claims upon society for charity Tucker says:

" It is a principle of justice and equity . . . that it is fitting and right to return something to the poor, by way of compensation, for the inequality of our possessions, and of making some reparation for the injuries they may have suffered, and the diseases contracted, when drudging on our account." But such charity should be disposed where " most good may be done in the most effectual way; where idleness and imposture may be sure of being detected, ... where industry may be encouraged." [2]

c. CRITICIZES POOR HOUSE SYSTEM

Tucker's criticism of the system of caring for the public

[1] *Sermon Charity School*, pp. 19-22.

[2] *Six Sermons*, p. 86.

poor and his own plan for remedying the defects of the prevailing system are both elaborated in very considerable detail in his *Manifold Causes of the Increase of the Poor.* Only the scantest outline can be given [1] of theme here. In criticism he argued:

1. The present districts are too small (1) to employ the poor effectually, (2) to teach the young Christianity and some particular industry, (3) to have good government of the poor, (4) to secure cheap maintenance and (5) equal taxation, (6) to prevent lawsuits.

2. Annual election of officers is a capital defect. "Little consideration will be given to any plan which cannot be harvested within a year."

3. Because of these defects the poor become desirous of parish pay, "as a pension to support them in laziness and indolence. Therefore they suffer themselves to become the poorer and more miserable in order to move compassion and to be considered as the proper candidates for this desirable state of life, which frees them at once from all labor and care."

4." The taxes for the support of the poor are not founded on a judicious principle; . . . the legislature seems to have had no other end in view than . . . just to raise as much money as the case required. Whereas the first view in laying on taxes for the support of the poor should be to remove or lessen all such causes and temptations as may have contributed towards making people poor, so that these evils may be prevented for the future. . . . Secondly, to raise a sum of money sufficient to maintain those already poor and defray such expenses as cannot now be prevented, and therefore must be submitted to."

5. Poor are daily increasing in numbers; poor rates are becoming intolerable; parishes carry on expensive war, offensive and defensive, with each other; industrious poor are hunted from parish to parish; difficulties are placed in the way of mar-

[1] All that follows, on the subject of the poor, is paraphrased or quoted from *Manifold Causes Increase of Poor*, 1760.

riage amongst the poor; the country is becoming depopulated; labor grows scarce; wages rise, and production of necessities decreases.

6. Due to the fact that the property qualification for voters has not changed since the 8th of Hen. VI, c. vii, which placed it at "40s. by the year at least, above all charges," although the purchasing power of money has changed very considerably, the poorer classes have more power in elections, and this is demoralizing.

d. PROPOSES A POORHOUSE SYSTEM

When he came to propose remedies for the evils outlined above, Tucker first stated the essential characteristics of a sane attempt to reform an ineffective or vicious system:

> "The root of the evil should be reached, but not too precipitately or violently," for "the mass of mankind are more attached to old custom than to truth and reason, or the usefulness of things. . . . To prevent future drunkenness, idleness and extravagance in the rising generation should be the principal object of every proposal made." As nearly as possible the regulations should execute themselves. They should be based upon common principles and applicable throughout the realm. What the official positions lack in profit should be made up in honor to the incumbents.

Tucker then develops in minute detail a plan embodying the principles expressed above and aimed to correct the evils he had detected in the poorhouse system then in use. The details are worked to completeness for levying and collecting the necessary tax and even for the household economy of the poorhouse, the regulations of its workshops and the punishment of offenders among its inmates. A few of the leading features of his scheme deserve mention.

He opposes outrelief in all cases except: (1) infectious

disease; (2) a numerous family of young children;[1] (3) sudden calamity, such as a fire, rendering provident persons temporarily helpless; (4) sickness or casualty, rendering removal dangerous.

He would establish an employment bureau at each poor house.

He would forbid all begging and deal with all cheats and impostors as rogues and vagrants, to be arrested, placed upon a diet of bread and water, at hard labor for ten weeks, whipped twice each week and dismissed with a warning of doubled penalty for a second offense.

He would divide poorhouse inmates into three classes, treating the decrepit and the very young "tenderly," and dealing with those able to labor "according to their productive merits" i. e. at one extreme those producing very little to receive coarsest fare and clothing and scantily furnished rooms; at the other extreme, those producing much to have better food, clothing and rooms, to be permitted to keep a part of their earnings and to be given a certificate of industry and allowed to leave the poorhouse when their savings reached a given sum. He would employ the inmates in gardening, dairy farming, and staple manufacture such as that of coarse woolens. He would pay managers, teachers and others in charge of the poorhouse, in bounties proportioned to the quantity and quality of good produced.

This is but a meager outline of an honest and thoughtful attempt to aid in solving the knotty problem of the pauper in the England of 1760.

[1] Tucker's general thesis for the need of an increased population evidently inspires this exception.

CHAPTER III

AGRICULTURE

Book II. of Tucker's great work was to contain " certain polities for the extension and improvement of commerce." [1] He uses the phrase " commercial employment " [2] to include obtaining food, which is " husbandry," [2] and securing raiment and shelter, which is " manufactures." [2] These two are complementary. They are " mutual consumers of each other's wares and real exaltation or depression of either similarly effects the other."[2] He goes further and classes agriculture under manufactures:

> " Agriculture is nothing else but a distinct phase of manufactures, in relating to which the ground or soil is properly the raw material and the landowner or farmer is the head manufacturer. This being the case, it must necessarily follow that every *general* principle of commerce which tends to establish and promote other manufactures must likewise be productive of good effects in husbandry." [3]

Believing in this close interdependence of husbandry and manufactures, he steers a course midway between the Mercantile and Physiocratic rocks, declaring:

> " How wrong must have been that system of polities which endeavored to set husbandry and manufactures at variance." [4]

[1] See *Skeleton* in *Appendix* of this volume.

[2] *Elements*, p. 42.

[3] *Ibid.*, p. 43.

[4] *Ibid.*, p. 42.

He thus maps out the field of "commerce," embracing all productive activity, broadly into agriculture and manufactures. He turns his attention first to agriculture. Here he carefully distinguishes between the economics and the technology of husbandry for he aims

"not to tell how to cultivate, ... but to show that the universal mover in human nature, self-love, may receive such a direction in this case, as in all others, as to promote the public interest by those efforts it shall make towards pursuing its own." [1]

To accomplish this aim he suggests several polities for the encouragement and improvement of agriculture. These are:

I. "A Polity for Dividing Great Estates"

He objects to the English system of primogeniture and great estates. These great estates are veritable monopolies:

"A farm of four or five hundred, not to mention seven or eight hundred, pounds a year, is certainly a monopoly of its kind, because it would have afforded a comfortable subsistence to three or four families if divided into so many distinct farms. And, indeed, it is attended with all the bad effects which other monopolies are, such as dispeopling a country and preventing the increase of inhabitants, raising one set of persons too high and depressing others too low. All which must be greatly injurious to national industry, good husbandry and extensive commerce." [2]

He objects to a "Gothic baronage landed estate" [3] which

[1] *Elements*, p. 43.

[2] *Ibid.*, p. 62.

[3] Quoted phrases and ideas here are in *Elements*, pp. 43–47.

he believes to be in conflict with the trading interests. The landed lords keep their vassals poor that they may appear the greater by comparison. Such a system also "impedes improvements in husbandry"[1] for it gives no incentives to industry. In the feudal days there may have been a need for these great estates and of primogeniture but now it would be more just, and make more for the public good, to divide say one half[2] of the estate among the younger children. Such a plan would avoid the class of estateless younger sons, Will Wimbles, "too proud to be mechanics and too poor to be high class traders." If the "unwieldly estates" were broken up they "would be far better cultivated."

II. "A Polity for Enclosing Commons and Common Fields"

Tucker was a strong advocate of enclosure. He states[3] that commons originated in the feudal day when common lands attached to every manor and the kings "kept prodigious tracts in almost every county waste and desolate as chase and forests." He thinks that although the British have perpetuated these commons in their original state of desolation "there is not one reason now remaining for their continuance."

To the various objections against enclosure he submits answers, a brief digest of which follows:

To enclosure it is objected: (1) That sheep walks will be

[1] Quoted phrases and ideas here are in *Elements*, pp. 43-47.

[2] Tucker's exact suggestion is that the elder son receive one-half of the landed estate and one child's share of the other half, the personalty to be equally shared by the children. *Elements*, p. 45.

[3] The digest and quotations that follow are from *Elements*, pp. 48-55.

destroyed. But "this assumes that all enclosed lands will be tilled." But the fact is that enclosed lands are pastured frequently, and that "in counties where enclosures have occurred the number of sheep has increased."

(2) That enclosure destroys the fineness of the wool. But "English export woollens are made of coarser wool anyhow." No one knows certainly what does make wools vary. Probably it is the warmer housing of the sheep.

(3) That enclosure will lessen arable lands, for it is so easy to enclose pastures. This is the very reverse of (1) "So long as people want mutton and woollen goods, sheep will be raised, whether lands be in commons or enclosed."

(4) That enclosure deprives many poor people "of their great privileges." "But enclosure is the very means that gives the poor employment and enables the farmer to pay them better wages." . . . "But in regard to their right or privilege of common, that ought not to be taken from them without a full and ample compensation. Nor, on the other hand, ought either poor or rich to be indulged in a petulancy of humor to obstruct the public good, merely because they are resolved to adhere obstinately to the absurd and foolish prejudice of their forefathers." [1]

(5) That enclosure prevents the rearing of young cattle. Rather it should be said that unlimited commons afford "a place for rearing stunted cattle, ... for too many are put there for any to thrive." [1]

Having thus dealt with the argumentative phases of the subject, Tucker, in his usual way, suggests a practical "polity," providing in detail for the methods of determining when a given common should be enclosed and how the claimants to it should adjust their several claims.

[1] *Elements*, p. 52.

III. A Polity for Changing Tithes into Glebe

The tithing plan, instituted by Moses, is suited to a theocracy, in Tucker's judgment. His historical sense is clearly evidenced here when he charges unclear thinking against the church fathers:

"Origen, St. Ambrose, St. Austin, &c., &c., who maintained that tithes were of Divine right under the gospel because they were so under the law, must have had very imperfect notions both of law and of gospel." [1]

He objects to the tithe because it is a tax which burdens industry and involves the clergy in difficulties with their parishioners. He therefore suggests that tithes be exchanged for small pieces of land (glebe) and these re-exchanged until there is a "compact estate in each parish." This will give the clergy a living income which will rise and fall with the prosperity or decline of general business (and is therefore, in his jdugment preferable to a fixed recompense) and will remove all friction between clergy and parishioners. It will be well also to interest men of letters in agriculture for they will improve the science.

IV. A Polity for Reclaiming Marshes, etc

This polity [2] plans for increasing "buildings in low, fenny, marshy grounds and rendering them healthy." It suggests buildings with foundations arched above the ground. The first story is to be used as a store room thus putting the living quarters "sixteen feet above the ground and therefore above the animalcula or poisonous particles in marshy places." He cites the successful experiences of Venice, Marseilles and Bordeaux and closes with an outline of tax

[1] *Elements*, p. 57.

[2] *Ibid.*, pp. 62-68.

exemptions and special privileges to be granted for a decade to those who should so reclaim waste lands.[1]

V. A Polity for Creating Timber

Tucker declares here for compulsory forestry. After a disquisition showing the "vulgar error" of thinking that English oak is the best of all ship-building timbers, he puts the interesting question as to the need of any stimulus to self-interest in the increase of timber land since "timber is a raw material whose demand is increasing and whose uses are multiplying every day." His answer to this query shows that he had noted man's tendency to discount the future:

> "In timber, he who plants cannot expect to reap the benefit. . . . . We must take human nature as we find it, and make the best uses of it we can. . . . If we really expect a growth of timber equal to the demands of maritime, &c., ... we must render it the present and immediate self-interest of every landowner in the kingdom to make plantations."[2]

To compass this end he suggests that the state compel every holder of above 400 acres in one parish to have at least 20 acres of timber under penalty of doubled land, window and poor taxes.

VI. A Polity[3] for Registering Deeds

Tucker asks for registry, hereafter,[4] of the titles involved

[1] In *Reflections upon . . . Causes . . . of Price . . . Wools*, Tucker outlines a plan for placing militiamen upon waste lands to reclaim them in small individual holdings. See pp. 31 to 46. The plan is minutely detailed.

[2] *Elements*, p. 74.

[3] *Ibid.*, p. 77.

[4] An illustration of the sagacity of Tucker the politician, aiming to so shape his plan that it will meet approval.

in marriage settlements, in sales and in mortgages under penalty that such transactions be invalid unless duly registered. Men oppose such a plan only because either they fear their titles are not good or they desire to secure excessive loans by double mortgages. These are the very reasons why a registry should be required.

Tucker on Rent

In connection with his polities for agriculture his treatment of rent may be presented.

Tucker touches incidentally only upon the rent of land. Wherever he offers any explanation of rent it is given in terms of population. The fullest treatment which he gives to this subject occurs in the second part of his *Reflections on Naturalization.* The passage reads:

> "Lands near London rent for 40 times as much as lands of equal goodness in remote parts of England, Wales and Scotland. What is this difference in the rent owing to but to the superior number of inhabitants? And that these distant lands pay any rent at all, is it not (because of) the carrying of the produce of them to distant places? If the city of Bristol could be removed 40 miles off, would not all the estates around it sink in value? . . . . How can tenants pay rent if there is not a market? and what is a market but a number of inhabitants."[1] He sees that "good roads have the same effect as having "the lands contiguous to the towns."[2]

The very few and brief references[3] to rent made by

[1] *Reflect. Nat. For. Prot. Part II*, pp. 21 and 22.

[2] *Elements*, p. 51.

[3] For other references see *Reflect. Nat. For. Prot. Part I*, p. 64, and *Part II*, p. 19, and *Elements*, p. 32. This passage in the *Elements* reads, "The rent of land depends on the number of people, for land is quite useless without a market for its produce."

Tucker seem to indicate that he had given this subject but little consideration. His slight thought upon it, as the above passage shows, had shown him one factor in its explanation, viz., location. He had also noted [1] the relative fertility of different pieces of land but he does not at any time connect this fact with an explanation of rent.

Ideas are contained in passing remarks which show that he had some material which might have led him to a concept of diminishing returns from land, had he but analyzed it. In his frequent appeals to the landed interest he sometimes argues that "every decay in trade must ultimately fall upon the land" [2] and that the development of commerce and manufactures "consumes the produce of lands and raises rent." [3] But nowhere in his writing does he make any attempt to formulate the law of diminishing returns from land nor does he give the slightest evidence that he had any knowledge of the fact of diminishing returns from land.

[1] In *Tract II*, p. 75, he mentions "different soils," and in *Reflect. Nat. For. Prot. Part II*, p. 23, he barely mentions that fertilized lands are more productive.

[2] *Spirit. Liq.*, p. 31.

[3] *Reflect. Nat. For. Prot. Part I*, p. 54.

CHAPTER IV

MANUFACTURE

TUCKER introduces that part of his great work which immediately follows his treatment of the land problems, with a declaration of the aim of all the succeeding portions of the great work:

> "The business and aim of the ensuing sections must be to remove those obstructions which impede the industrious and useful operations of self-love, and to set mankind and nature free. Free, I mean, in that sense in which consists our true liberty. For if self-love is restrained from doing good to society, it will do mischief, and if prevented from doing mischief, it will do good.[1] . . . . Surely nothing can be plainer than that every man hath a right by nature to subsist himself by his own labor and industry in any way that is compatible with the good of the whole; for this is the only limitation that should take place."[2]

This plea for freedom is central to all the thought that follows. The one hundred subsequent pages of the *Elements* have this freedom principle so prominently developed and so persistently applied that they clearly class their author as a strong advocate for economic freedom.

Having dealt with population in general and with land, Tucker elects to consider manufactures as the next subject

[1] *Elements*, p. 78.

[2] *Ibid.*, pp. 81-82.

to be treated in the unfolding of his systematic consideration of economic life. He defines:

"Mechanic trades and manufactures [are] to be understood in the largest signification, including every branch of commercial industry, including shipping and navigation." [1]

As indicated in this definition, manufacture may occur by land industry or it may be accredited to shipping. Tucker treats first the inland division, leaving the carrying trade and its consequent international commerce problems for a succeeding chapter. His freedom principle as he applies it to inland manufacture reads

"Any trade may be said to be free in which every person may engage if he pleases." [2]

This raises with him the inquiry, what trades should be free and what are the means of securing their freedom?

Analyzing the manufacturing life about him he finds that the British have that "liberty of conscience [which] conduces to industry" [3] and that "as to civil liberty, never were a people more free than the English at this juncture." [3] Commercially however he thinks them free only in the sense that they are free from royal control. They are

"slaves in other respects," for, "under foolish and fallacious pretences for supporting their privileges, . . . private parties oppress . . . as would not be tolerated in a king." [4]

These traditional restraints upon commercial freedom he

[1] *Elements*, p. 79.

[2] *Ibid.*, p. 80.

[3] *Ibid.*, p. 81.

[4] *Ibid.*, p. 82.

combats. Two particular claims are put forward by exclusive companies, empowered to enforce these restraints, and he answers these claims at length.

(1) The first claim is that such companies are needed to maintain a standard of manufactured commodities.

He replies (a) That to attempt to set any arbitrary standard is injurious interference with trade and (b) That if exclusive companies are needed to test manufactures in any branch, then they should be given control of every branch; for examples there should be "butter and cheese worshipful companies" and

"on the same wise principle, a law ought to be enacted that for the due and proper exercise of the art and mystery of carrying goods and drawing a load in a carrier-like manner, all horses employed therein shall be duns, blacks or bays!" [1]

(2) The second claim is that exclusive companies aid in developing new industries and induce foreign artisans to immigrate. Tucker's reply is that general bounties will develop new industries more quickly and less expensively to the community than chartered companies and that as to any danger of a mal-adjusted labor supply in industries new or old, perfect freedom to laborers to labor when and where they choose and at what wage they will agree upon, will secure a far more satisfactory adjustment than if exclusive companies attempt an arbitrary settlement. He rounds up his whole argument thus:

"The result of the whole is, . . . that no discouragement ought to be put upon industry and labor; that every trade productive of national commerce, wealth and prosperity ought to be free and unrestrained; that monopolies and exclusions in

[1] *Elements*, p. 84.

the case before us are both foolish and knavish schemes; . . . and, to sum up everything, it hence appears that excellency of work, cheapness of labor, right application of genius, good morals in private life, plenty and prosperity in regard to the public are the sure consequences of universal freedom and emulation." [1]

In connection with manufactures, the theme of this chapter, the topics so developed by Tucker, both here and elsewhere in his works, as to deserve especial consideration are I. Competition and Monopolies; II. Labor and Wages; III. Capital and Interest; and IV. Machinery.

I. Competition and Monopolies

Tucker believed in free competition as the certain stimulator of industrial and commercial activity. He very frequently argues that it makes for society's best interests. His emphasis upon the importance of this principle may be most clearly evidenced by selections from among the many references to its powerful influence, to be found throughout his works:

"What is the public good? Is it not for the most part the result of emulation among the members of the same society? And what would become of industry, temperance, frugality, and the desire for excelling, if there were no emulation?" [2]

"The public good can only be promoted by a free and open trade, and by rival ships and competition." [3]

A corollary of such propositions is that monopoly should be opposed, and Tucker opposed monopoly. Upon no other

[1] *Elements*, p. 92.

[2] *Reflect. Nat. For. Prot. Part II*, p. 33.

[3] *Letter on Naturalization*, p. 5 of Mss. A similar statement was quoted on the previous page from *Elements*, p. 92.

one topic did he write so extensively. The long *Appendix* to the *3d edition* of the *Essay on Trade,* the entire tract on the trade to Turkey, more than one-half of the *Elements* and long passages in other works are devoted to a condemnation of monopoly. Tucker recognizes a tendency to monopoly in every human nature:

"All men, whether natives or foreigners, would be monopolists if they could." [1]

Commercial monopoly is thus defined by him:

"That in a commercial sense, every exclusion from the common benefit of trade due to all men by natural right,[2] is a monopoly. And the degrees of the monopoly are either more or less in proportion to the restraints and abridgements of such natural right." [3]

The spirit of the monopolist he thus characterizes:

"The desire of present gain operates so strongly with every monopolist that he is quite regardless of futurity; hoping that he will have made his fortune before the evil can reach himself; and as to the public, that was never his concern." [4]

He states clearly that the interests of the public and of monopolistic companies clash and he points to free competition as the remedy for monopoly abuses:

"The aims of an exclusive company can never coincide with

[1] *Letter on Naturalization*,, Mss. p. 6.

[2] Natural right is sometimes appealed to by Tucker—the prerogative of an 18th century political writer.

[3] *Elements*, p. 161.

[4] "*Appendix to Turkey Trade*," p. 24.

the welfare of the public, inasmuch as monopolists, established by law, are thereby secured from rivals. So that their particular interests consist in selling as dear as they can; whereas the interest of private adventurers is to sell as cheap as possible, in order to get custom by rivalling one another. Thus the public is benefited by emulation, as it promotes the circulation of labor [1] and universal plenty; but is hurt by monopolists, who are a check to industry, to the circulation of labor [1] at home and the exportation of it abroad, and whose only view, whatever may be pretended, is to sacrifice the general interest of the kingdom to that of a few individuals." [2]

Tucker's chief attacks upon particular monopolies were directed against the great chartered trading companies of Great Britain. His arguments against these privileged companies are considered at some length in the following chapter, upon "Foreign Trade," and will therefore be passed here with the mere mention.

His opposition to monopolies in the concrete did not end with these powerful assaults upon exclusive trading companies. He opposed monopoly in any form in which it appeared to him inimical to the public welfare. For illustrations, *he objects*

(1) "To confining the commission money (from trade in a foreign country) to an English factor. . . . If the trade was free, every man would naturally choose that agent who would serve him best, let his country be what it will," [3]

(2) To the long apprenticeships then required, advising the repeal of "the 5th of Elizabeth, which obliges persons to serve apprenticeships of seven years to several trades which require

[1] Tucker frequently uses the term "labor" when he evidently means by it "products of labor."

[2] *Reflect. on Turkey Trade*, p. 5.

[3] *Letter on Naturalization*, Mss. p. 7.

not seven weeks to learn—a most iniquitous and vexatious law, which gives to dunces and blockheads a power to tyrannize over the most ingenious, useful and industrious members of society." [1]

(3) To the Navigation Act. Of this he says: "By the famous Navigation Act, and other acts still in force, all foreign commanders of foreign-built ships, together with their foreign crews, are in effect excluded from enjoying the benefits and privileges of settling in England were they ever so desirous. Now if this be not a monopoly against the whole trade and manufactures of this country, it is hard to say what it is." [2]

(4) To large estates. The argument upon this subject has already been presented in the preceding chapter.

The only monopoly which Tucker views with tolerance is that afforded by the patent right. Of this he says:

> "The inventor may have a patent to reward his genius, to reimburse his expenses, and to encourage his industry, for fourteen years, if he pleases." [3]

II. Labor and Wages

The second special topic suggested by Tucker's treatment of manufactures is labor and wages.

Tucker presents no distinct theory of wages. He has much, however, to say about labor and its reward. His thought may be given under the following headings: (a) competition in the labor market; (b) piece vs. time wages; (c) division of labor,; (d) factory vs. domestic system; (e) danger of high wages and holidays; (f) the unproductive

[1] *Thoughts on Public Affairs*, *Gent's Mag.*, vol. l, pp. 132–133.

[2] *Further Thoughts*, section VI. A strong and extended attack on the Navigation Act occurs in *Rfleect. on Present Matters in Dispute*, etc., pp. 18–25.

[3] *Tract V*, p. 58. A similar thought is expressed in *Elements*, p. 168.

classes; (g) opposition to fixed wages; (h) opposition to apprenticeship and settlement acts; (i) opposition to slave labor.

a. COMPETITION IN THE LABOR MARKET

A passage in the *Elements* argues that congestions in the labor market will be righted in time better by letting the normal forces of that market play than by attempting corrective interference by state power. It is the application of his freedom thesis to labor. He says:

"Granting that a trade may be accidentally overstocked with numbers; when that is the case the best and safest way is to let the evil alone, and then it will infallibly cure itself. For, in process of time, some of these persons will go off to other trades, and as the trade is out of repute, there will not so many young recruits be bred up to it. Thus the occupation that was once overstocked will soon be reduced to a medium, and may in its turn want hands again, the consequence of which may probably be that it will be again overstocked. For such is the rotation of human affairs, dearness begets cheapness and cheapness, dearness. But if you should take any other course than the one here mentioned, which is in fact the course of nature and of Providence, . . . your attempts will not only be frustrated, but, by endeavoring to remove one seeming evil and temporary inconvenience, you will certainly introduce a thousand real ones, which will grow more dangerous and inveterate by length of time." [1]

b. PIECE WORK VS. TIME WAGES

Tucker develops the advantages of a piece work system. The passage in which he does this closes with an argument against the economy of slave labor which anticipates the

[1] *Elements*, pp. 87–88. A similar passage is in *Reflect. Nat. For. Prot. Part II*, pp. 13 and 14.

order of topic arrangement somewhat; but the passage is given entire that its force may not be lessened:

"Most manufacturers now find it to their interest to pay their people by the piece, or the great, wherever they can, rather than by the day; which circumstance alone is a striking proof that no sufficient check hath yet been invented against loitering away of time when the master was to pay for it; not to mention that the person who works by the day hath scarce any motive to exert an industry, dexterity or skill superior to others, whereas the working by the piece, or the great, calls them all forth, because he himself and none others are to reap the benefit of them. And note well this single remark, were there no others, is sufficient to prove that slaves—who literally work by the day and can have no motive whatever to exert any other industry or dexterity than what is just sufficient to escape the whip of the driver; nay, whose self-interest will naturally teach them to conceal any superior talents from the knowledge of their masters, lest their masters should expect a greater task from them than others, and punish them for not doing it—I say, this single remark is full proof that slaves never did, nor ever will, perform their work either so cheap or so well as those freemen who work by the piece, or the great, and are spurred on every moment by the example of others, by self-interest, and by the glory of excelling." [1]

C. DIVISION OF LABOR

In the preliminary pages opening his *Elements*, Tucker introduces the division of labor as characteristic of man as distinguished from the lower animals:

"Nor do birds, beasts, or fishes discover any disposition to divide the labor of the community into different branches or assign distinct parts to the respective individuals. This, I

[1] *Instruct. for Trav.*, pp. 19 and 20.

think, is the case in general with respect to the brute creation. But if there are any traces of superior abilities, they are so few and inconsiderable as not to deserve a particular inquiry. Nay, whenever any tribe of animals distribute the labor of the community into different parts, as is reported to be the case among the beavers, ants and bees, it hath always been observed that they make some advances superior to the condition of mere animal life." [1]

The social instincts are "for the most part the prerogative of man" [2] and men therefore "naturally seek society to gratify these social instincts." [2] Where they are once together in society a vast number of advantages appear owing to mutual assistance.

"The common labor of the society is branched out into separate and distinct parts. Then it is that each individual chooses a particular course of life, according as his circumstances of genius shall determine his pursuits. I mention genius the more emphatically because some men are formed by nature to peculiar employments, being born with talents (which are a kind of instinctive knowledge) for one pursuit preferably to another. . . . Therefore, among the human species some are employed in the several articles of clothing, others in raising provisions, and third set in preparing materials and building habitations. Thus are the first wants of mankind, viz., food, raiment and dwelling, much better supplied by dividing the general labor into different branches, than if each individual depended on himself alone. . . . And these different parts of the common labor are nothing else, in other words, but distinct trades and manufactures, and may be considered as the first draft or rudiments of commerce." [3]

[1] *Elements*, p. 4.

[2] *Ibid.*, p. 5.

[3] *Ibid.*, pp. 5 and 6.

Tucker's reasons for introducing the discussion of division of labor in his preliminary discourse are obvious. In analyzing human nature he found social instincts; in the societies formed to satisfy these instincts he saw that men by mutual aid make great gains over animals; one of the earliest and greatest of these gains comes from a division of labor. The division to which he refers here is the division into various occupations but even in this he saw one of the advantages true throughout all the more minute divisions viz., that men can labor where their talents will return the most to society. In later discussion he stated a number of the further advantages which labor division brings. Among these as he noted them are (1) the expertness and speed acquired by one who continuously performs a single operation or manufactures a single commodity; (2) the saving of time and of expense; (3) the possibility of utilizing child and woman labor to greater advantage. These thoughts and two others bearing upon division of labor viz., (1) the especial opportunity to secure more minute division of labor in the machine industries and (2) the effect of a narrow market in preventing the gainful division of labor are suggested in one of his instructions to his young traveler. After having advised that the traveler observe what use is made of machinery in a given country, he suggested as his next query:

"Is that labor which is still being performed by the human kind so judiciously divided that men, women and children have their respective shares in proportion to their strength, sex and abilities? And is every branch so contrived that there is no waste of time or unnecessary expense of strength and labor?" [1]

[1] *Instruct. for Trav.*, p. 22.

That he might make his meaning clear he cited an illustration from Birmingham:

"When a man stamps a metal button by means of an engine, a child stands by him to place the button in readiness to receive the stamp and to remove it when received, and then to place another. By these means the operator can stamp at least double the number which he could otherwise have done had he been obliged to have stopped each time to have shifted the buttons; and as his gettings may be from 14d. to 18d. and the child's from a penny to 2d. per day for doing the same quantity of work, which must have required double the sum had the man alone been employed, this single circumstance saves above 80, or nearly 100 per cent., at the same time that it trains up children to a habit of industry almost as soon as they can speak. And hence it is that the *bijoux d'Angleterre,* or Birmingham toys, are rendered so exceedingly cheap as to astonish all Europe." [1]

The influence of a wide market in making possible a very great differentiation of employment he states thus in his discussion of the relative trading strength of poor and rich nations:

"In the richer country, where demands are great and constant, every manufacture that requires various processes and is composed of different parts, is accordingly divided and subdivided into separate and distinct branches, whereby each person becomes more expert, and also more expeditious, in the particular part assigned him. Whereas, in a poor country the same person is obliged, by necessity and for the sake of getting a bare subsistence, to undertake such different branches as prevent him from excelling or being expeditious in any." [2]

[1] *Instruct. for Trav.*, p. 23.

[2] *Four Tracts*, pp. 33-34.

It is, moreover, observable that in country places where there is scarcity of inhabitants, one trade will not be sufficient for a man's subsistence, but several distinct occupations must be joined together in order to obtain a bare and wretched support. By which means it comes to pass that there cannot be the *quantity* of work performed as where every one exercises and improves himself in one particular calling, and as to *quality* or workmanship itself, that must necessarily be clumsy, rude and imperfect." [1]

d. DOMESTIC VS. FACTORY SYSTEM

Tucker favors the domestic system rather than the factory system. He describes the two systems as then in operation and contrasts their effects upon the laborers and upon the product. Raising the question of the relative number of independent manufacturers and of journeymen and the effects upon morals, quality of the product, etc., he tells his traveler the conditions in England:

"This matter is better illustrated by comparing the same manufacture, and the consequences attending it, under the different circumstances here referred to. In many parts of Yorkshire the woollen manufacture is carried on by small farmers and freeholders. These people buy some wool and grow some. Their wives, daughters, and servants spin it in the long winter nights, and at such times when not employed in their farms and dairies. The master of the family either sells this produce in the yarn market or hath it wove up himself. It is then milled, cleansed, and brought to market, generally to the town of Leeds; but when sold there, he can be paid for no greater number of yards than the cloth will measure after having been well soaked in water, by which means all frauds in stretching, tentering, &c., are effectually prevented. The persons who buy this cloth generally act upon commission at

[1] *Elements*, p. 12.

a very low rate, and afterwards cause the cloth to be dyed (if it was not dyed in the wool), and to be properly dressed and finished. Thus the whole passes through various hands independently of each other. And though in fact the spinner, weaver, millman, dyer, dresser, &c., &c., are all of them the journeymen of the agent or commissioner, who stands in the stead of him who is the clothier in other places, yet by acting thus upon a distinct footing they conceive themselves as far independent of him, and of each other, as any buyer or seller whatever. And being thus independent, they are all rivals, all animated with the same desire of bringing their goods to market upon the cheapest terms and of excelling one another. Their journeymen, likewise, if they have any, being so little removed from the degree and condition of their masters, and so likely to set up themselves, by the industry and frugality of a few years, have no conception that they are embarked in an interest opposite to that of their masters, or that they are called upon to enter into clubs and combinations against them. Thus it is that the working people are generally moral, sober and industrious, and that a riot or a mob is a thing hardly known among them. Whereas in Glocestershire, Wiltshire, and Somersetshire the manufacture is carried on by a quite different process, and the effects are accordingly, viz.: One person, with a great stock and a large credit, buys the wool, pays for the spinning, weaving, milling, dyeing, shearing, dressing, &c., &c. That is, he is the master of the whole manufacture, from first to last, and perhaps employs a thousand persons under him. This is the clothier, whom all the rest are to look upon as their paymaster. But will they not also sometimes look upon him as their tyrant? And, as great numbers of them work together in the same shop, will they not have it the more in their power to vitiate and corrupt each other, to cabal and associate against their masters, and to break into mobs and riots upon every little occasion? The event hath fully showed, and is now showing, that these conjectures are too frequently supported by facts. Besides, as the master is placed so high above the condition of the journeyman, both their conditions approach very much nearer to that of a planter and slave in our American colonies than might be expected in such a country as England; and the vices and tempers belonging to each condition are of the same kind, only in an inferior degree. The master, for example, however well disposed in himself, is naturally tempted by his situation to be proud and overbearing, to consider his people as the scum of the earth, whom he has a right to squeeze whenever he can, because they ought to be kept low and not to rise up in competition with their superiors. The journeymen, on the contrary, are equally tempted by their situation to envy the high station and superior fortunes of their masters, and to envy them the more in proportion as they find themselves deprived of the hopes of advancing themselves to the same degree by any stretch of industry or superior skill. Hence, their self-love takes a wrong turn, destructive to themselves and others. They think it no crime to get as much wages and to do as little for it as they possibly can, to lie and cheat, and do any other bad thing, provided it is only against their master, whom they look upon as their common enemy, with whom no faith is to be kept. The motives to industry, frugality, and sobriety are all subverted by this one consideration, viz., that they shall always be chained to the same oar and never be but journeymen. Therefore their only happiness is to get drunk and to make life pass away with as little thought as possible. This being the case, is it to be wondered at that the trade in Yorkshire should flourish, and the trade in Somersetshire, Wiltshire, and Gloucestershire be found declining every day?"[1]

Tucker's distrust of the common people reinforced his opposition to all monopolies in leading him emphatically to condemn any combinations of the laborers in these factories that were developing. This is suggested in the passage above quoted and is directly expressed in the *Essay on Trade* where the prevention of "combinations of journeymen

[1] *Instruct. for Trav.*, pp. 24-25.

against their masters" is characterized as "greatly for the public good."[1]

e. HIGH WAGES AND HOLIDAYS

Instead of upholding the economy of high wages, as a present day writer might do, Tucker, wherever he touches on the rate of wages, argues for a low rate. His eye is on enlarged markets in other lands and he laments that the English workmen do not labor more cheaply. For example, speaking directly to British laborers in explanation of the recurrent stagnations of trade, he tells them that the cause

"is really this, that you do not labor as cheap, and are not content to live and fare as hard as the manufacturers in other countries, and consequently their merchants can afford to sell their goods at the market cheaper than ours. . . . For alas! and this is the ruin of all our trade, too many there are who will not accept of work one part of the week, but on such terms only as may enable them to live in vice and idleness the rest. . . . . In this you are worse, much worse, than the common people of any other nation."[2]

Again, he says that if "the price of labor is continually beat down it is greatly for the public good."[3] At another place he charges that the English common workmen become more vicious, more indigent and idle in proportion to the advance of wages."[4]

In close connection with this arraignment of the English workingmen as too grasping in wage and too inclined to idleness comes his testimony against them because they "lose probably more time in cockfighting, bullbaiting, mob-

[1] *Essay on Trade*, p. 46.
[2] *Six Sermons*, p. 89.
[3] *Essay on Trade*, p. 46.
[4] *Essay on Trade*, p. 41.

bings and electioneering"[1] than the French do "in their too many holidays and great processions."[1]

f. THE UNPRODUCTIVE CLASSES

Tucker considered professional men to be nonproducers. He ranks the professional classes among the "trades which injure the community by flourishing" and says of them.

> "As these scholars and literary gentlemen, lawyers, doctors, divines, live by the labor of others, the increase of their numbers would be so far from adding to the public stock of wealth that it would greatly diminish it in every view. . . . A few, indeed, are necessary in every state, but many are a nuisance, both to themselves and to the public."[2]

He lists[3] as one of the disadvantages in trade of France as compared with Great Britain

> "the number of religious, of both sexes, . . . at lowest computation 300,000, . . . who might be useful in trades; . . . but not only this, they are a heavy burden."

The large number of French nobles, scorning productive labor, is also listed with the disadvantages of France.

g. FIXED WAGES

Consistently with his freedom of trade thesis and with his application of this in opposing government attempts to regulate goods according to some standard, Tucker unreservedly condemns laws for fixing wages. He argues:

[1] *Ibid.*, p. 35. *An Earnest and Affectionate Address to the Common People, etc.* (1787), is a plea against cockfighting, etc.

[2] *Elements*, p. 92.

[3] *Essay on Trade*, pp. 28–30.

"The statutes regulating wages and the price of labor are another absurdity, and a very great hurt to trade. Absurd and preposterous it must surely appear for a third person to attempt to fix the price between buyer and seller, without their own consents. For, if either the journeyman will not sell his labor at the fixed or statutable price, or the master will not give it, of what use are a thousand regulating laws? Nay, how, indeed, can any stated regulations be so contrived as to make due and reasonable allowance for plenty or scarcity of work, cheapness or dearness of provisions, difference of living in town or country, firing, house-rent, &c., &.; also for the goodness or badness of the workmanship, the different degrees of skill or despatch of the workman, the unequal goodness of material to work upon, state of the manufacture, and the demand, or stagnation, at home or abroad? I say, how is it possible to make allowance for all these various and contingent circumstances? And yet were even this possible, a great difficulty still recurs, viz.: Who shall, or how can you, force the journeyman to work, or the master to give him work, unless they themselves shall mutually agree about it? And if they agree, why should you, or I, or anyone else interfere? And what need of any regulations at all? In short, such laws as these can do no good, because they can never be carried into a regular, useful practice. But, on the contrary, they may cause a great deal of mischief, riots, and disturbances, and will infallibly, sooner or later, drive the trade from that country where men are absurd enough to attempt to put them in execution." [1]

Incidentally this passage contains a suggestive analysis of the conditions determining contract wages.

h. APPRENTICESHIP AND SETTLEMENT

In further application of his freedom of trade principle Tucker is everywhere and always the consistent opponent

[1] *Instruct. for Trav.*, pp. 34 and 35.

of the statute of apprentices and of pauper settlements. He deals with these topics at length in both the *Elements* and the *Instructions for Travellers.* Under the head of exclusive privileges he classifies

"that absurd statute of the fifth of Queen Elizabeth, which restrains persons from exercising those very trades they may have the happiest genius for, and in which they may have made great improvements and excelled all that went before them. Yet strong and unanswerable as these reasons are, they are totally overruled by this single law, and the unfortunate ingenious person must be debarred from exercising that trade which nature herself designed him for, and perhaps in which only he could be of use to his country, because, forsooth, he had not served a regular apprenticeship!" [1]

Tucker criticises the pauper and parish settlement acts many times in his works. He opposes these laws because the parishes in particular are injured and because the trading and manufacturing nation, as a whole suffers through an ill distributed labor force. He says:

"The present set of pauper and parish settlement laws are absurd and unjust, nor have they one good consequence. . . . The parishes are injured, . . . put at war against the rest of the kingdom. . . . Law suits cost more than charity would. . . . The public at large suffers. In a commercial state, all able and willing should be provided with work; . . . cannot do this unless . . . can provide work for all at home at all seasons (an extravagant supposition), or let them seek it wherever they choose. . . . The poor suffer greatly by these unjust laws. . . . Sent to the parish to be a pauper when he could have a flourishing business elsewhere." [2]

[1] *Instruct. for Trav.*, p. 34. For a general scoring of all trade restraints due to exclusions and including the statute of the 5th of Elizabeth see *Elements*, pp. 79–92.

[2] *Elements*, pp. 20 and 21.

Again:

"The statutes relating to pauper settlements are another great confinement and disadvantage to trade, without being of real benefit to any set of men whatever, the lawyers excepted."[1] "The restraints that villains should not stir from manors probably suggested the later law that the poor be confined to their parish (originally coextensive with the manor). This indicates a failure to distinguish the difference of times and the variation of circumstances. For, in a commercial country, the people must follow their work, be it near or far, and as trade and manufactures are always shifting places, . . . it seems unavoidable that people should be permitted to remove as their work removes," &c.[2]

i. SLAVE LABOR

Tucker opposes slavery both upon ethical and economic grounds. He couples these two classes of objections when he says

"We make slaves of these poor wretches (the African blacks) contrary to every principle, not only of humanity and justice, but also of national profit and advantage, as I have often proved in several of my writings, both commercial and theological. We, I say, the boasted patrons of liberty and the professed advocates of the natural rights of mankind, engage deeper in this murderous traffic than any nation whatever."[3]

Under the discussion of piece work above and in the earlier chapter on *Fundamental Notions,* passages were cited giving one of Tucker's arguments against the economy of slave labor. The gist of all these arguments is

[1] *Instruct. for Trav.*, p. 34.

[2] *2nd Lett. on Naturalization*, p. 6, Note. Similar statements are made in *Manifold Causes Increase of Poor*, p. 8, and *Thoughts on Public Affairs, Gent's Mag.*, vol. 1, pp. 132–133.

[3] *Series of Answers*, p. 21.

"Little industry can be expected from any poor wretches who know beforehand that a greater exertion of industry on their parts would only be an increase of labor painful to themselves and solely beneficial to their masters."[1]

III. Capital and Interest

The third important topic under the general head, *Manufactures,* is Capital and Interest.

a. CAPITAL

Tucker has but little to say about capital. He theorizes neither about its origin nor about its share in distribution. The one thought concerning it which he expands at all is the importance to the merchant, to the manufacturer, and to the nation, of having capital in large amounts. By means of their large capitals he notes that British manufacturers and traders can "give longer credits . . . and receive none;"[2] "always command the market in buying raw materials at the best hand;"[3] can make . . . costly experiments or embark in . . . expensive and longwinded undertakings;"[4] and can vend "all goods on the cheapest terms."[5]

It is because of their large capitals bringing to them these advantages that British merchants are the leading traders of the globe. He states that the combined capitals of British citizens give Great Britain, as a nation, a capital greater than that of any other nation, so great indeed, that "the trade of

[1] *Series of Answers*, p. 39. Tucker's most extended argument against the economy of slave labor occurs in *Reflect. Present Matters in Dispute, etc.*, pp. 11–17.

[2] *Series of Answers*, p. 30.

[3] *Four Tracts*, p. 34.

[4] *Ibid.*, p. 32.

the world is carried on in a great measure with British capital." [1]

In particular he argues that Great Britain has a great advantage over France in that "its capitals in trade are much larger . . . . no uncommon thing for an English manufacturer to have 20,000£ in trade" whereas in France "as soon as they get 10,000 £ is it not a common practice with them to buy some charge in order to ennoble their families and so wipe off the disgrace of having been once useful to their country?" [2]

b. INTEREST

Tucker deals with but one phase of the subject of interest, at any length. With this one exception, all of his remarks concerning it are incidental. All that he says may be presented under the heads (1) the rate of loan interest (2) discrimination between loan interest and profits and (3) the ethics of loan interest.

(1) Concerning the rate of loan interest he states that an increase of the money supply causes a lowered rate of interest;[3] that "the low interest of money will insure, the vending of all goods on the cheapest terms,"[4] i. e. that prices vary as the rate of loan interest; and lastly, that rents vary inversely as the rate of loan interest. This last point he argues in his longest passage treating of interest, in which he says:

"Enquire the relative price both of land and of money;

[1] *Series of Answers*, p. 31.

[2] *Reflect. on Turkey Trade, Append.*, pp. 28–29.

[3] *2nd Lett. on Naturalization*, p. 39.

[4] *Four Tracts*, p. 34. In *Essay on Trade*, p. 39, he states that higher interest makes higher prices.

criteria like the alternate buckets of a well, where the ascent of one necessarily supposes the descent of the other. . . . Where interest of money is high the price of lands must be low, because the height of interest is a proof that there are many to borrow yet few to lend. And if so, then it follows that wherever there are but few lenders of money there cannot be many purchasers of land. On the contrary, were the interest to be exceeding low, the price of lands must rise in proportion, because the lowness of interest is an infallible proof that there are many persons in that state capable of making purchases, and yet but few who want to sell or mortgage their estates. But the effects of high or low interest are yet to be extended a great deal further, inasmuch as the employment or non-employment of a people, and consequently their riches or poverty, will be found to depend, in a considerable degree, on one or the other of these things." [1]

(2) He distinguishes between loan interest and profits. In contrasting England and France he says that interest is lower in England and that "therefore a master manufacturer is content with less profits . . . for no man would run risks and take fatigue of trade if he could get as much, or nearly as much, by living upon the interest of his money." [2] It may be noted here that this remark contains the substance of all that Tucker has to say about profits.

(3) Tucker condemns laws against interest taking. Speaking of historic days where English princes were using the Jews "as sponges to suck up the treasure of the nation" [3] he says:

"It must be observed that both church and state had in those

[1] *Instruct for Trav.*, p. 59.

[2] *Reflect. on Turkey Trade, Appendix*, p. 28. A similar remark occurs in *Instruct. for Trav.*, p. 59.

times enacted several foolish, absurd laws, that no Christian should lend money upon interest." [1]

Remembering that Tucker was a churchman, it is interesting to note that he continues by commenting that both church and state erred in "grossly mistaking the meaning of the Scripture" on that head. In a note he refers to the Mosaic precept against interest saying:

"Moses, in settling the property of the land of Canaan, seems to have kept the happy medium between an absolute agrarian law and an unlimited monopoly of land. And, therefore, he allowed the rich and the industrious to purchase from the poor or the idle for the space of 49 years, and no longer. The consequence of which was that personal industry received a sufficient encouragement, at the same time that an effectual guard was placed against the laziness and luxury of an overgrown fortune. But this excellent scheme would still have been eluded had the Israelites been permitted to lend money to each other upon interest, because it would have proved the same thing in fact, whether the paternal estate was bought forever or mortgaged forever. He, therefore, ordained that they should not take usury or interest of one another. This is the true reason for that remarkable prohibition, but the clergy and laity of the times we are now speaking of little understood it." [2]

IV. Machinery

The last topic worthy particular treatment under the general head of *Manufactures* is machinery.

Tucker's theory of the effects of machinery, formulated in 1757, at the very beginning of the industrial revolution

[1] *2nd Lett. on Naturalization*, pp. 36 and 37. For other condemnations of usury laws see *Ibid.*, pp. 26 and 39.

[2] *2nd Lett. on Naturalization*, p. 37, *Note*.

in England is one that may be approved even to-day, when the economist has a century and a half of world-experience with machinery, upon which to reflect. In his *Instructions for Travellers* he advises his traveler to find out what machines are being used in each country that he visits and what effect these machines have upon the price of goods, and upon the number of persons employed. To illustrate his meaning he thus states [1] his own ideas concerning the use of machinery in England:

"Few countries are equal, perhaps none excel, the English in the numbers and contrivance of their machines to abridge labor. Indeed, the Dutch are superior to them in the use and application of windmills for saving timber, expressing oil, making paper and the like. But in regard to mines and metals of all sorts, the English are uncommonly dexterous in their contrivance of the mechanic powers; some being calculated for landing the ores out of the pits, such as cranes and horse-engines; others for draining off superfluous water, such as water-wheels and steam engines; others, again, for easing the expense of carriage, such as machines to run on inclined planes or roads down hill, with wooden frames, in order to carry many tons of materials at a time. And to these must be added the various sorts of levers used in different processes; also the brass battery works, the slitting mill, plate and flattening mills, and those for making wire of different fineness. Yet all these, curious as they may seem, are little more than preparations or introductions for further operations. Therefore, when we still consider that at Birmingham, Wolverhampton, Sheffield, and other manufacturing places, almost every master-manufacturer hath a new invention of his own, and is daily im-

[1] The passage has been reprinted here in full not only because it gives Tucker's thought upon machinery, but because (1) the first part of it is an outline account by an eye-witness of manufacturing England in 1757, and (2) it well illustrates Tucker's substance and style both as recorder of observations and as theorist.

proving on those of others, we may aver, with some confidence, that those parts of England in which these things are to be seen exhibit a specimen of practical mechanics scarce to be paralleled in any part of the world. As to machines in the woollen and stuff way, nothing very considerable hath been of late attempted, owing, in a great measure, to the mistaken notions of the infatuated populace, who, not being able to see farther than the first link of the chain, consider all such inventions as taking the bread out of their mouths, and therefore never fail to break out into riots and insurrections whenever such things are proposed. In regard to the silk manufacture, the throwing mills, especially the grand one at Derby, are eminent proofs of the abridgment of that species of labor. And some attempts have been lately made towards the cotton and linen manufactures by means of certain engines.

" In regard to the other part of the query, viz.—What is the consequence of this abridgment of labor, both regarding the price of goods and the number of persons employed?—the answer is very short and full, viz.: That the price of goods is thereby prodigiously lowered from what it otherwise must have been, and that a much greater number of hands are employed. The first of these is a position universally assented to; but the other, though nothing more than a corollary of the former, is looked upon by the majority of mankind, and even by some persons of great name and character, as a monstrous paradox. We must, therefore, endeavor to clear away these prejudices step by step. And the first step is that cheapness, *ceteris paribus,* is an inducement to buy, and that many buyers cause a great demand, and that a great demand brings on a great consumption, which great consumption must necessarily employ a vast variety of hands, whether the original material is considered, or the number and repair of machines, or the materials out of which those machines are made, or the persons necessarily employed in tending upon and conducting them, not to mention those branches of the manufacture, package, porterage, stationery articles and bookkeeping, &c., &c., which must inevitably be performed by human labor. But to come to some determinate and striking instance, let us take the plow, the harrow, the cart, the instruments for threshing and winnowing, and the mills for grinding and bolting, as so many machines for abridging labor in the process of making bread. I ask, do these machines prevent or create employment for the people? And would there have been as many persons occupied in raising of corn and making of bread if no such engines had been discovered? The obvious reply to this query is that probably the wheaten loaf had been confined to one or two families in a state, who, on account of their superior rank and vast revenues, could have afforded to give an extravagant price for this delicious morsel. But it is impossible that under such circumstances it ever could have become the common food of the kingdom. And the same remark would hold good were it to be applied to the art of printing, and to the numbers of people from first to last therein employed. For printing is nothing more than a machine to abridge labor and reduce the price of writing. But examples are endless, and surely enough has been said to convince any reasonable man—though even the great author of *L'Esprit de Loix* should once be of a different mind—that the system of machines, which so greatly reduces the price of labor as to enable the generality of a people to become purchasers of the goods, will in the end, though not immediately, employ more hands in the manufacture than could possibly have found employment had no such machines been invented. And every manufacturing place, when duly considered, is an evidence in this point." [1]

[1] *Instruct. for Trav.*, pp. 20 to 22.

CHAPTER V

COMMERCE

THE next chapter of the great work continues the analysis of the broadly defined subject of manufactures. Intra-national trade having been treated, international trade is next considered. To it the freedom of trade thesis is applied. The dean-philosopher appears and calling up his fundamental principle that religion, government and commerce are in essential harmony, he argues that a truth of religion is therefore applicable to commerce. He proceeds to apply the golden rule to commerce

"And then monopolies would immediately be at an end; a general encouragement would be given to the diligent and industrious of all professions; a general emulation would excite their genius and improve their abilities; and every man would find his own account in doing to his neighbor as he wishes to be done to himself." [1]

Like many other passages in Tucker's works, this one may be interpreted to indicate that he championed free trade in the full present day signification of the phrase. But freedom of trade, when applied to commerce between nations, means to him just what it means to him when applied to inland commerce, i. e. that individuals or corporations shall not be given exclusive charters—this and no more. The injunction

[1] *Seventeen Sermons*, pp. 140–141.

"give universal freedom to trade, and do not confine it by gilds, or companies, or corporations, or fetters of any kind," [1]

is fairly typical of his thought. In harmony with his whole writing, with his evident intent as judged by contexts, it must be interpreted to mean simply that the conditions of the trade, so far as the government is concerned, are the same for all who desire to engage in it. In other words, Tucker does not advocate complete trade freedom. He is a believer in bounties and in duties as will be clearly shown later. It seems difficult to understand how one who is so truly cosmopolitan in the spirit of much of his writing, who states so forcefully the many advantages of exchange between nations, who condemns trade jealousy and war for trade's sake in unsparing terms, who claims to be a foe to all monopoly, who makes out so overwhelming a case against the British exclusive companies for foreign trade, who eulogizes the duty-destroying career of minister Walpole, who proclaims the advantages of trade, untrammelled by customs or duties of any kind, between England and Ireland, and who several times asserts the perfect parallel of intra-national and international trade—it is difficult to understand how such a man failed to follow his thought to the conclusion that should make him an advocate of complete freedom of trade between nations. But he does fail. There are more than glimpses of this full trade freedom in his writings, sometimes a phrase or a sentence seems to state it, but the context invariably shows that the writer pleads only for an abolition of special, chartered, privileges to individuals or to companies. *General* interference, by the government offering bounties to all who care to enter a given industry or levying duties upon all imported goods, whoever may be the importer, finds a staunch supporter in

[1] *Gent's Mag.*, vol. 1, pp. 132–133.

Tucker. In short, as will be shown farther on in this chapter, he lacks little of being a full-blooded mercantilist.

It is in place to call attention to the type of statement in Tucker's writings which seems to declare complete freedom of trade but which, interpreted by the spirit of the whole passage in which it occurs, clearly means no more than opposition to exclusive privileges:

"All merchandise should be free and open; . . . no impediments should lie in the way of commerce, but everything be calculated to promote and extend it."[1] "All trade ought to be laid free and open, in order to induce the exporters to rival each other, that the public may obtain the general good of their competitorship."[2] He hopes that "the time will come when English trade is entirely free from shackles of all kinds."[3]

In each of these cases the context unmistakably points opposition to special privileges in trade, and to this only.

Some passages showing that Tucker was far on the way of arriving at the full freedom of trade thought are:

(1) He pays a glowing tribute to Sir Robert Walpole declaring that

"his plan of commerce was manly and rational; that his endeavors to prevent an infatuated people from quarrelling with their best customers were truly patriotical. . . . He did more for general trade promotion than any other minister of the world, not forgetting the Sullys, Colberts, and Fleurys of France."[4]

(2) He condemns the Navigation Act, as has been shown

[1] *Lett. on Naturalization*, Mss. p. 8.

[2] *Essay on Trade, 3rd ed.*, p. 82.

[3] *Appendix to Turkey Trade*, p. 26.

[4] *Four Tracts*, p. 79.

in presenting his thought upon monopolies, and argues that

"it is highly absurd to prefer the interest of the single waggoner [1] to that of the whole community. . . . Confining the freight of goods to one set of waggoners is evidently a monopoly," [2] and therefore objectionable. Great Britain should rather trust competition between seamen, and there will be an adequate and acceptable supply of vessels.

(3) Most striking of all of Tucker's passages, which seem to lead directly to full free trade, are those with reference to the trade relations between England and Ireland:

"It is since the year 1759 that we have repealed that very injudicious tax, which discouraged, and in a manner prohibited, the importation of butter, tallow, lard, and other articles of like sort, from Ireland into Great Britain. . . . Since a permanent repeal, . . . the mutual intercourse of England and Ireland hath prodigiously increased; and, of course, our shipping and navigation have greatly increased likewise." [3]

"The present clamors for protective duties and prohibitory laws would cease (another good circumstance)—clamors which betray a total ignorance of the true interest of that country, because Ireland ought always to excite an emulation, among her mechanics and manufacturers, to excel her rivals, instead of checking and preventing it by monopolies, pains and penalties. . . . Each county and each part of the island must enjoy their own peculiar advantages, natural or artificial, without let or molestation. At this instant, Yorkshire is getting the clothing trade from the west of England by means of its superior frugality, economy, mechanic skill and industry. . . . The west must adopt the like measures, and police with the

[1] Tucker illustrated with land carriage by wagons and applied the conclusion to vessels as "sea-waggons."

[2] *Present Posture—Further Thoughts.*

[3] *State of the Nation.*

north, or deservedly suffer for their folly. . . . And above all, Ireland should never use such a conduct towards other nations, especially towards the English . . . as would provoke them to retaliate the injury upon herself with redoubled vengeance."[1]

It is something of a mystery how a keen and logical mind, prone to bold generalizations, could write these lines and yet embrace mercantilism. Perhaps being a citizen of out-port Bristol, Tucker through his patriotic efforts to break down the exclusive chartered privileges of London companies was led unconsciously to expend all of his energy in emphasizing but half of the truth. Or, it is barely possible that the above statement represented his changed view, late in his life. *Union and Separation,* in which this passage occurs, was written in 1785. It is conceivable that Tucker may have read the *Wealth of Nations* and may have been converted to a belief in full freedom of trade. But the facts (1) that he was at this time seventy-two years of age, an age at which few men change creeds, and (2) that he had worked out the mercantilist thoughts satisfactorily to himself and had championed it for more than thirty years, make this hypothesis very improbable, as well as the farther fact that he has nowhere, in publication or in letters, indicated that he had read, or had even heard of, the *Wealth of Nations.*

But if Tucker did not go the full length that his thought seemed to lead him, he was forceful and aggressive in presenting and applying the truth which he did see. His endeavor in the *Elements* chapter on *Foreign Trade* is expended in demonstrating the

"right notion of national industry and riches, and in confut-

[1] *Union or Separation*, pp. 18 and 19.

ing the popular errors concerning the balance of trade and the nature of money." [1]

He concentrates his attacks upon the chartered companies and is a powerful and persistent pleader against their special privileges. His plea is given especial force by the fact that his judgment is not a sweeping *a priori* one but is delivered against the existent companies and for particular reasons. He takes up the argument he had begun against these companies in his *Essay on Trade*. In that *Essay*, with an impartiality and breadth of view, well illustrative of his historical sense, he does not for all time and all places condemn exclusive trade companies but he allows

" that in certain cases, and at certain junctures, exclusive companies might have been a prudent institution, calculated for the public good, as: (1) To intruduce arts, sciences and manufactures among a barbarous people, *e. g.*, the Czar of Muscovy . . . gives such extraordinary privileges . . . to overbalance the temptation of self-interest for residing elsewhere. (2) To induce skillful artisans to come and instruct an ignorant people, *e. g.*, England granted so many privileges and exemptions to Flemish and other foreign manufacturers 200 years ago. (3) To conquer deep-rooted laziness of people, ... bringing an example of industry before them, *e. g.*, the Spanish court is now desirous to bring foreign manufacturers to Spain. (4) In order to have large capital to embark a hazardous undertaking calling for great sums. (5) When the government credit is not good—may incorporate a body from which to borrow money." [2]

But while he thus recognizes the possible good reasons for exclusive companies he cautions that

[1] *Elements*, p. 93.

[2] *Essay on Trade, 3rd edition*, pp. 66–68.

"In the course of time the reasons for continuing them cease, and the trade should be laid open."[1] "The establishment of exclusive companies, . . . be the motive what it will, . . . may be compared to the hedgehog in the fable, . . . a most humble petitioner for a night's lodging, but once in possession, sets up bristles, and too strong to be removed."[2]

He notes that these companies always have special "pretenses" to offer in justification of a retention of their privileges. These pretenses he considers *seriatim.* (1) To the pleas that these companies maintain forts necessary for trading in foreign lands he replies, that either forts are unnecessary altogether, or that wherever really necessary, since the consumers of company goods pay for them anyway, the nation had better erect and man the forts, guaranteeing protection to any of her citizens, desirous of trading with the foreign people.[3] (2) He freely condemns the companies when they plead that they are enabled to sell British goods dearly and to buy foreign wares cheaply. His reply is that more British goods would find market if sold more cheaply, and that the fact that companies purchased foreign goods cheaply was no guarantee that they would sell them cheaply in Great Britain. (3) He points out the error of the argument for prevention of bullion export. (4) He regards the maintenance of state and of strength unnecessary, citing successful trade with China, etc., without this. (5) To the claim that exclusive companies must be right because all nations have them, and what is universal is reasonable, he replies, that according to this there could be no progress

[1] *Essay on Trade, 3rd ed.*, pp. 66-68.

[2] *Elements*, p. 110.

[3] The full argument here briefly summarized is in *Elements*, pp. 94-113.

and that a study of the origins of the companies will amply disprove this claim.

He then enters upon a consideration of the British exclusive companies actually engaged in trade at that time. These companies appear to him to be relics of Gothic despotism in government:

> "We still want that glorious revolution in the commercial system which we have happily obtained in the political. Then, indeed, and not till then, may we be said to have abolished all the remains of ancient despotic power and Gothic barbarity. For as long as these charters and exclusive companies remain, we bear about us the marks of our former slavery." [1]

The companies he particularly opposes are the Turkey Trade Company,[2] the Hudson's Bay Company,[3] and the East India Company.[4] The arguments against these three companies are extensive and exhaustive, and no brief summary can do them any justice. The trend and flavor of the extended treatment may, however, be suggested by citing some characteristic passages.

He begins the attack upon these companies in his *Essay on Trade*. A single paragraph of this early and bold assault upon huge, established monopolies conveys its spirit and illustrates its power and its comprehensiveness:

> "Our monopolies, public companies, and corporate charters are the bane and destruction of free trade. By the charter of the East India Company, at least 9,999 British subjects out of 10,000, without having committed any fault to deserve such a

[1] *Elements*, pp. 88-89.

[2] *Ibid.*, pp. 113-119, for extended argument.

[3] *Ibid.*, pp. 120-132.

[4] *Ibid.*, pp. 132-133. He calls the East India Company "the most unwieldly monster of them all."

punishment, are excluded from trading anywhere beyond the Cape of Good Hope. By the charter of the Turkey Company, a like or greater number are excluded from having any commerce with the whole Turkish empire. The Hudson Bay Company engrosses all the fur trade with the Indians in an extent of country almost as large as half of Europe. Thus the interest of 9,999 fellow-subjects is sacrificed in so many respects for the sake of a single one. The whole nation suffers in its commerce, and is debarred from trading to more than three-fourths of the globe, to enrich a few rapacious directors. . . . . And as to corporate charters and companies of trade, they are likewise so many monopolies in the places to which they belong, to the great detriment of national commerce." [1]

This paragraph simply outlines his field of operations against the chartered companies. He deals with them in great detail. Nearly a hundred pages of this same *Essay* [2] are devoted to an argument against the Hudson's Bay Company, in which every plea of that company is analyzed and refuted and a long list of well sustained charges is brought against it. Two editions of the tract [3] on the trade to Turkey denounce the privileges granted to the Turkey company. In the *Elements* he returns to the attack upon both of these companies and adds a stinging paragraph against the East India Company. In opening this argument he thus characterizes the oppressive practices of these companies:

" Introduced in the ages of ignorance, tyranny and barbarity, and settled by long custom, covered with the sacred dust

[1] *Essay on Trade*, p. 45.

[2] *3rd edition*, 1753.

[3] Postlethwayt in his *Universal Dictionary of Trade and Commerce*, 2nd Ed. (1757), selected this tract of Tucker's as the best representative of what had been argumentatively urged for opening the Turkey trade and abstracted it. See vol. ii, pp. 384-86.

of time, a multitude of arguments have been coined to gloss over these practices." [1]

Tucker rounds off the argument refuting the company pretenses of right and reasons, by tracing the history of monopoly in England from the days of Elizabeth. He quotes [2] Townshend's *Historical Collections* to show the prevalence and despotism of monopolies under the good Queen Bess and cities at length [3] the report made in the 3d of James I by Sir Edward Sandys against the vicious monopolies of the day. The conclusion he draws from this historical review is that

"Every plea, pretense, or apology urged at this day in defense of these things, is nothing else but a nauseous repetition of the same idle, canting story which hath been confuted a thousand times over." [4]

His appeals against these intrenched companies are often artfully made. The following, for example, is a skillful description of the immortal tactics of legislatively privileged classes:

"Whenever an attempt hath been made to free the nation from this destructive and impolitic restraint, great is the cry of Demetrius and his craftsmen: 'Sirs, this is the artifice by which we have our wealth; by which we are freed from disagreeable rivals and competitors, and can secure the trade of the kingdom to ourselves, and put what price we please on our commodities. But, as this is not proper to be publicly avowed, therefore let us apply to the passions and foibles of our coun-

[1] *Elements*, p. 82.

[2] *Ibid.*, pp. 137 sqq.

[3] *Ibid.*, pp. 154 sqq.

[4] *Ibid.*, p. 167.

trymen, and harangue upon such popular topics as may keep them still in the dark. For, if they were to know the true state of the case, how soon would all our schemes be rendered abortive? And how quickly would the popular odium fall upon ourselves?" [1]

Tucker has full hope that a new era will come when special trading privileges will be abolished and this hope he voices thus:

"Mankind begin to see more and more into the base and slavish original and present iniquitous chicane of all exclusive charters; nor will they be led blindfolded much longer by those whose interest it is to deceive them." [2]

A leading thought running through this entire discussion is that trade supremacy comes to that nation which can sell the best goods for the least money. This is an idea which he emphasizes many times in his works. The whole of *Tract II* is devoted to an argument to prove, contrary to a popular notion, championed even by historian Hume,[3] that a rich nation can undersell a poor one. A strong statement for the need of good, cheap goods to the nation that would win world-trade appears in his letters addressed to M. Necker. He says that there is only one of three things which can be done in competition with France:

"(1) Knock all Frenchmen on the head wherever met with, because of their unpardonable crime of making goods cheaper than the English. (2) Knock all customers on the head,

[1] *Letter upon Naturalization*, Mss. p. 7.

[2] *Appendix to Turkey Trade*, p. 32.

[3] This tract was the result of a correspondence with Hume in 1758. Tucker claimed Hume as a convert to his view on this subject. See *Preface* to *Four Tracts*.

native or foreign, who dare to buy such goods instead of purchasing at the English shops. (3) Make goods better and sell them cheaper, as a means of attracting the general course of trade to ourselves, without doing violence to our neighbors." [1]

He suggests that the first two are immoral and dangerous and that the third only is left as the rational choice for the "shopkeeping nation" Great Britain.

The topics, suggested by the outline above given and broadly enough treated in Tucker's works to deserve especial presentation in connection with foreign trade are: I. The philosophy of exchange; II. Trade jealousy between nations; III. Mercantilism; IV. Bounties; V. Colonies and VI. Statistics.

I. Philosophy of Exchange

Tucker develops a complete philosophy of exchange. He observes that different peoples have aptitudes for different kinds of production and that they are environed by differing resources, the two factors which make for specialization in production. He observes also the factor which makes for universality in consumption, viz., the wide range of human wants. These three facts indicate to him that the world-plan demands an exchange of products. He thus sees accurately that exchange alone solves the contradiction between universal wants and endowments for specialized production. The passage which most clearly and fully presents these thoughts is in the second of the *Four Tracts*. In part it reads:

"In the natural world our bountiful Creator hath formed different soils and appointed different climates, whereby the inhabitants of different countries may supply each other with

[1] *Cui Bono*, p. 35.

their respective fruits and products, so that by exciting a reciprocal industry they may carry on an intercourse mutually beneficial and universally benevolent. Nay more, even where there is no remarkable difference of soil or of climate, we find a great difference of talents, and, if I may be allowed the expression, a wonderful variety of strata in the human mind. . . . Moreover, the instinct of curiosity and the thirst for novelty, which are so universally implanted in human nature, whereby the various nations and different peoples so ardently wish to be customers to each other, is another proof that the curious manufactures of one nation will never want a vent among the richer inhabitants of another, provided they are reasonably cheap and good." [1]

II. Jealousy of Trade

The second of these special topics is jealousy of trade between nations.

Tucker was a citizen of the world as he consciously strove[2] to be. He was truly cosmopolitan in his views upon commerce. His religious thought was, in part, responsible for this, or at least, it supported him in this attitude. Witness his words:

" But surely the benign Saviour of all mankind hath nowhere enjoined that any person, because he happened to be born on one side of a river, a mountain, or an arm of the sea, should not freely negotiate business or purchase a piece of land on the other. . . . Have we not all one Father?" &c.[3]

[1] *Four Tracts*, pp. 75 to 78. Similar passages in *Ibid.*, pp. 50–51, and in *Essay on Trade*, p. v and vi.

[2] See quotation from *Cui Bono*, in chapter on *Life*, etc.

[3] This is from a note, in Tucker's handwriting, upon the margin of the Mss. of the *Letter on Naturalization* (p. 11) in the British Museum Library. See *Mss.* number 4207, 2.

His application of religious thought to politics and to commerce, his cosmopolitanism and his hatred of war are all in evidence in a striking passage condemning that spirit of bellicose patriotism so characteristic of the nation-building era and not altogether extinct to-day:

"The love of country hath no place in the catalogue of Christian virtues. The love of country is, in fact, a local affection and a partial attachment; but the Christian covenant is general, comprehending all mankind within its embraces. Judge, therefore, with what propriety such a narrow, contracted passion can have any place in the diffusive, benevolent scheme of Christianity—a passion, however glittering and glorious in appearance, which hath been productive of more injustice, barbarity and bloodshed in the world than any other disgrace of human nature—a passion, in short, fit only for the enthusiastic rage of an old Roman robber, when cruelly exulting over the unhappy victims of his lust of power and dominion—but altogether unworthy of the breast of a Christian, who is commanded to regard all mankind not only as his countrymen, but as his brethren, doing to others as he would be done by, and helping and assisting even his enemies in distress. Indeed, so far as the love of country means no more than a principle of self-defense against invaders, so far it is justifiable, and so far hath Christianity provided for due exertion of it, by inculcating obedience to the respective powers set over us. But as to the ideas of honor, and glory, and conquest, and dominion, and the other fine things usually implied in the love of country, they are so foreign to the Christian plan that in this sense the love of country neither is, nor ought to be, a part of the Christian scheme of universal love and benevolence. And let the infidels make what uses they please of the concession." [1]

Tucker's cosmopolitan spirit is clearly shown by his op-

[1] *Seventeen Sermons*, pp. 285-286.

position to the current jealousy of trade, especially, that jealousy existing between Great Britain and France. He condemns absolutely " going to war for the sake of trade." [1] His position with reference to trade-jealousy and to the effects of war upon commerce is thus stated:

> " But is this spell, this witchcraft of the jealousy of trade, never to be dissolved? And are there no hopes that mankind will recover their senses as to these things? For of all absurdities, that of going to war for the sake of getting trade is the most absurd, . . . so extravagantly foolish." [2]

He holds that " no trading nation can ever be ruined but by itself, by decline of industry." [3]

The thought that had so long been a foundation of a widely prevailing system of trade philosophy he distinctly repudiates. " That one nation can thrive only by the downfall of another, cannot grow rich but by impoverishing another " [4] he classes with illusions. On the contrary, he believes that since nations are mutual customers, they must share in each other's prosperity or decline:

> " But to excite that man, whom perhaps they have long called their enemy, to greater industry and sobriety, to consider him a customer to them, and themselves as customers to him, so that the richer both are, the better it may be for each other; and, in short, to promote a mutual trade to mutual benefit; this is a kind of reasoning as unintelligible to their comprehensions as the antipodes themselves." [5]

[1] This is the title and opposition to it, the theme, of *Tract II* of the *Four Tracts*.

[2] *Four Tracts*, p. 82.

[3] *Ibid.*, p. 42.

[4] *Ibid.*, p. 61.

[5] *Ibid.*, p. 97.

Again:

"A private shopkeeper would certainly wish that his customers did improve in their circumstances rather than go behind hand, because every such improvement would probably redound to his advantage. Where, then, can be the wisdom of the public shopkeeper, a trading people, to endeavor to make the neighboring states and nations that are his customers so very poor as not to be able to trade with him? . . . The only possible means of preventing a rival nation from running away with your trade, is to prevent your own people from being more idle and vicious than they are; and by inspiring them with the opposite good qualities." [1]

The gains to come from open international trade appear to him as natural and as certain as those coming from intranational trade. This argument for the promotion of peaceful commerce between the nations he several times enforces. For example:

"If mankind would but open their eyes, they would plainly see that there is no one argument for inducing different nations to fight for the sake of trade but which would equally oblige every county, town and village—nay, and every shop, among ourselves—to be engaged in civil and intestine wars for the same end. Nor, on the contrary, is there any motive of interest or advantage that can be urged for restraining the parts of the same government from these uncertain and foolish contests but which would conclude equally strong against separate and independent nations making war with each other on like pretexts." [2]

Especially does he oppose the traditional trade jealousy between Great Britain and France. He argues that it is the true interest of Great Britain

[1] *Four Tracts*, p. 97.

[2] *Ibid.*, p. 77. A similar passage, *Ibid.*, p. 62.

"to promote the prosperity of France by all just and honorable means. . . . If France should grow poorer, she must be so much the worse customer of England. If richer, probably so much the better. This is so plain a case that one would think national prejudice itself could not be able to prevent such an evident truth from being universally acknowledged." [1]

Tucker was particularly opposed to war as an alleged means of enlarging trade. His opposition was accentuated by the losses to trade and the resulting general business depression in Bristol [2] during the seven years' war. This was another object lesson from his Bristol environment. Idle ships and standstill trade taught him very effectively that war causes economic loss.

He recognized Great Britain as a trading nation and lamented throughout the whole of his author life, the persistently belligerent attitude of her people. Speaking in this vein he says to the British:

"It is our misfortune to aim at things which are incompatible. Unhappily for us, we are continually wishing to be a nation of heroes and a nation of traders and mechanics at the same time. We expect to give laws to all the world, especially at sea, and yet to be considered by this world as a quiet, harmless, unoffending people. . . . . The honors of war and the sweets of peace, the glories of conquests and the rewards of industry, the dissipation of a vast, scattered and unwieldy empire and the economy of a moderate compact state, cannot

[1] *Cui Bono*, p. 46.

[2] Writing to Dr. Forster, May 19, 1756, he says, "Our ships are still tied up in the key, which at this season of the year used to be prosecuting their voyage, and almost every branch of trade is at a stand." See *Forster Mss.* Brit. Museum. Similar thoughts are expressed in letters to Dr. Birch written Nov. 30, 1756, and Nov. 2, 1761. See *Birch Mss.* Brit. Mus.

be made to unite together."[1] There is "something ridiculous in the farce that a shopkeeper should bully his customers to compel them to deal with him against their interests."[2]

When Rome was lauded as a world-conquerer, worthy of Britain's imitation, Tucker's reply was:

". . . Romans were not so mad as to fight for trade. They fought only for conquest and dominion, which may be acquired by fighting. But to fight for the sake of procuring trade is a species of madness reserved only for Britons."[3]

And the result of Rome's centuries of conquest was that her soldier-citizens came to look upon honest industry and trade as degrading and with the exception of a "haughty rich few"[4] they became "illustrious brother beggars."[4] The lesson of history, as Tucker interprets its message, relative to war for trade's sake is, that "victors in vanquishing others only prepare a more magnificent tomb for their own interment."[5] "There is nothing to be gained by war that could not better be accomplished by peace."[6]

Tucker thinks that the very classes of men who favor war are a standing warning against entering upon it for the sake of commerce. He cites as war advocates[7] (1) Mock patriots, desirous of plunging the ruling ministry, which they oppose, into a costly war (2) The "hungry pamphleteer who

[1] *Proposals for General Pacification*, *Gent's Mag.*, vol. 1, p. 222.

[2] *Treatise on Gov't*, p. 233.

[3] *Four Tracts*, pp. 70–71. *Cf.* "Rome's trade was to wage war with the world." See *Invasions and Subsidies*, p. 21.

[4] *Ibid.*, pp. 72–73.

[5] *Ibid.*, p. 75.

[6] *Ibid.*, p. 83.

[7] *Ibid.*, pp. 83–95, give these classes and comment upon them.

writes for bread—a jackall to the patriot-lion" (3) the gambler of change-alley. (4) Newswriters—"a fourth species of fire brands . . . . This country is news-mad and news-ridden now." (5) Jobbers, contractors, paymasters etc., in army employ; (6) Some traders who reap individual advantage from public calamity (7) Land and sea officers. War "is their business and their promotions come so."

Tract II closes with expressed fear in his day of "the mob, the bloodthirsty mob, no arguments and no demonstrations whatever can persuade them to withdraw their veneration from their grim idol, the god of slaughter;" but there is hope in posterity:

"A few may yield to these arguments, their numbers may increase, and possibly at last the tide may turn so that our posterity may regard the present madness of going to war for the sake of trade, riches and dominion with the same eye of astonishment and pity that we do the madness of our forefathers in fighting under the banner of the peaceful cross to recover the Holy Land." [1]

III. Mercantilism

The third topic worthy of particular consideration under foreign trade is mercantilism.

Tucker is a neo-mercantilist. He agrees, in very large measure, with the mercantile thought. In four points he is at variance with the simon-pure early tenents of this system of thought: (1) He is quite clear upon the difference between heaps of gold and national riches. (2) As a corollary to the proposition that bullion is not riches, he condemns prohibitions of precious-metal exports. (3) He distinguishes between a trade balance which is acceptable to an

[1] *Four Tracts*, p. 97.

individual merchant and one which is acceptable to a nation. (4) He takes issue with an underlying principle of old-line mercantilism, viz., that in exchange what one party gains another must lose. In all other points he accepts the tradition of the mercantile fathers. He insists that encouragement should be given by a nation to the export of its manufactured goods and to imports of raw materials and food supplies. He favors duties upon the import of foreign manufactures and upon the export of raw materials. He emphasizes the importance of manufactures, and advises discouragement of any export until the commodity is in its ripest condition, fully prepared for the final consumer. And although he ridicules the idea that gold is, in itself, riches, he still affirms that the ultimate goal of national trade is to secure a balance in gold and silver.

Evidence to show that Tucker was a mercantilist will first be presented, and then the evidence that he took issue with mercantilism in some points will be given.

a. TUCKER A MERCANTILIST

To present first his credentials as one of the mercantilist persuasion—a single selection eptomizes the ideas to be found in many of his writings. He gives a criterion for testing whether taxes are properly applied to goods entering or departing from the kingdom in this passage:

"Let him suppose the state to be a living personage, standing on the key of some great seaport and examining goods as loading or unloading. In the former case, if the goods to be exported are completely manufactured, having undergone the full industry and labor of his own people, he ought to lay no embargo whatever upon them, but to show exporters all the favor he can and to protect them in that good work. Whereas, if the goods are only manufactured in part, or, what is worse still, if they are absolutely raw materials, he should lay such taxes upon them to check and discourage their going out of the kingdom in that condition as may be proportionate to their unmanufactured or raw-material state. That is, if they are absolutely raw materials, they ought to have the highest tax laid upon them, and, in some cases, even such as may amount to a prohibition. But if they are partly manufactured and partly otherwise, the tax should be lessened in proportion as they recede from the state of raw materials and approach to complete manufactures. In regard to goods imported, his conduct ought to be just the very reverse of the former; that is, he ought to lay the highest and most discouraging taxes upon foreign complete manufactures, in order to prevent their being worn or used in his kingdom, a less discouraging upon others that are incomplete, and still less upon those that are but little removed from the raw-material state. As to raw materials themselves, they ought to be admitted into every port of the kingdom duty-free, unless there are some very peculiar circumstances to create an exception to this general rule. Now, the grounds or foundation of all this reasoning is national industry and labor, because these are the only riches of a kingdom." [1]

The mercantilist plan for customs-duties could scarcely be more plainly stated than it is here stated. It is of interest to find that, applying the above tests to the British custom-laws of that year of grace 1757, Tucker found but five taxes which he pronounced " strictly bad," viz., the duties upon imported salt, coals, soap and candles, leather and coarse olive oil. And he comments:

[1] *Instructions for Trav.*, pp. 38-39. In *2nd Lett. on Naturalization*, p. 13, Tucker condemns the policy of the kings before the Revolution because they (1) chartered privileged companies; (2) taxed home manufactures; (3) admitted foreign manufactures freely or at low duties; (4) taxed imported raw materials; (5) had no special care for manufactures; (6) granted no drawbacks on re-exported goods.

"And having thus finished the present examination, it may not be improper to add, for the credit of our country and praise of the legislature, that, upon the most impartial survey, there seem to be only these five taxes of any consequence which can strictly be denominated bad."[1]

That Tucker includes articles of food under his list of free imports is shown by this sentence:

"Rice is free now and should be, for it is a raw material and an article of food, and it ought never to have been taxed."[2]

Once only, and that in his earliest economic work, Tucker states, as his ultimate thought, the ultra-mercantilist balance of trade view:

"The science of gainful commerce consists ultimately[3] . . . in procuring a balance of gold and silver to ourselves from other nations."[4]

He does not repeat this proposition, but, on the other hand, he nowhere later either retracts or refutes it, and it therefore commits him to the mercantilist doctrine as to balance of trade.

This completes the mercantilist creed. The more extended statement given above is from the last important work written during Tucker's economic decade. It, therefore fairly represents his matured view, and should overrule any incidental remarks he may have elsewhere offered.

[1] *Instructions for Trav.*, p. 41.

[2] *Humble Address, etc.*, p. 58.

[3] Tucker makes it clear here that he means that all the trade with all the nations must be accounted, *e. g.*, India and the Baltic nations have a trade balance always against England, but England re-exports their goods.

[4] *Essay on Trade*, p. vi.

Some passages, as has been mentioned in treating of freedom of trade, are susceptible of interpretation as advocating full freedom of trade, but in the presence of the above given clear confession of faith, there seems to be no doubt that Tucker is to be classified as a mercantilist.

b. TUCKER A NEO-MERCANTILIST

Tucker is a neo-mercantilist in the sense that he takes issue with old-line mercantilism in some points: (1) He does not deify the precious metals; (2) he favors the seed-time-and-harvest export of gold and silver bullion; (3) he does not identify the nation's and the merchant's ledger balance; (4) he does not advocate annihilation of commercial rivals.

(1) In regard to gold and silver, he says:

"Heaps of gold and silver are not the riches of a nation. Gold and silver got in the ways of idleness will prove to be destructive likewise; it is wealth in appearance, but poverty in reality. Gold and silver got by industry and spent in idleness will prove to be destructive likewise. But gold and silver acquired by general industry, and used with sobriety and according to good morals, will promote still greater industry. . . . An augmentation of money by such means as decrease industry is a national curse, not a national blessing. . . ."[1] Again: "The capital mistake that money is riches, is the basis of all."[2] . . . "Industry and labor are the only real riches, money being merely the ticket or sign belonging to them. . . . If Great Britain hath industry and another country money, the industry of the one will soon extract the money of the other, in spite of every law, penalty and prohibition that can be

[1] *Four Tracts*, pp. 43-44. This will be recognized as an application of one of his theory-of-prosperity principles.

[2] *Elements*, p. 162.

framed. . . . Suppose a country, separated from all the world, and yet abounding in . . . gold and silver, and the inhabitants of it (may be) much poorer than the poorest beggar in our streets. . . . Suppose that the inhabitants are . . . industrious: . . . let us suppose that all the gold and silver was annihilated in one night, and what would be the consequences but plainly this, that the inhabitants would then devise some ticket or counter for the exchange of mutual industry." [1]

(2) Tucker's opposition to prohibition of precious metal exports is thus stated:

"The continuance of the prohibition against the exporting coin or bullion is another absurdity and tyrannical imposition. It is an absurdity because the chief call for money in Turkey, according to the Company's own account, is to purchase raw silk and mohair yarn. Judge, therefore, which deserves the preference among a manufacturing nation, a lump of gold or silver, or a bale of merchandise. . . ." [2] "If the bullion is carried out to purchase raw materials for the employment of our people, the trade is good and beneficial to the state." [3]

These pleas for freedom of bullion export are strongly mercantilistic, since they are made on the ground that the bullion brings back the raw material, and thus affords the glorious opportunity for the British, by hard labor, to work this raw material up into a finished product and export it for more raw material and a further opportunity to labor, and so on. The "ultimate" balance of trade looms up back of all this.

[1] *Elements*, pp. 99 and 100. Similar statements are in *Elements*, p. 103, *Invasions, Subsidies, etc.*, pp. 38–46, *Union and Separation*, pp. 20 and 21. Spain is cited here as a decadent nation whose decadence is due to heaps of gold and silver which begot idleness.

[2] *Elements*, pp. 118–119.

[3] *Ibid.*, p. 99.

(3) Tucker's leading caution, with reference to the balance of trade, is that the national balance of trade and the merchant's balance of trade are not the same:

"The business of the merchant is to get as large (profits) as he can upon small exports, . . . but the interest of the nation is to promote general industry and labor at home; which consists in exporting the greatest quantities at the smallest profits. . . . The views of the merchants are merely and solely for money. If he can get this by employing the fewest hands, he thinks it so much the better; whereas the views of the nation should be wholly and solely to promote industry, and then national industry will always command as much cash and credit as are wanted." [1]

(4) Tucker is positive upon the proposition that rival nations may both gain by their exchanges. He says:

"We may lay it down as a universal rule, subject to very few exceptions, that an industrious nation can never be hurt by the increasing industry of its neighbors. . . . All people . . . have a strong bias towards the produce and manufactures of others, so it follows that . . . the respective industry of nation and nation enables them to be so much the better customers, to improve in friendly intercourse, and to be a mutual benefit to each other. . . . Where can be the wisdom in the public shopkeeper, a trading people, to endeavor to make the neighboring states and nations that are his customers so very poor as not to be able to trade with him?" [2]

[1] *Elements*, p. 162. A similar distinction is made in *Four Tracts*, p. 44.

[2] *Four Tracts*, p. 43. In *Ibid.*, pp. 61 and 62, Tucker develops the thought that as neighboring towns or districts wish each other to thrive so should neighboring states. In *Cui Bono*, pp. 58 to 62, he applies this thought particularly to England and France.

IV. Bounties

The fourth important topic relating to foreign trade is bounties.

Tucked considers Great Britain the habitat of the bounty; "more [1] (bounties, premiums and drawbacks) being introduced into our commercial system, within these sixty years, than are to be met with in all Europe beside." He classifies these as of two sorts, the first used to promote the export of manufactures, and the second to promote the import of raw materials. He defines and distinguishes between the bounty and the drawback:

"The one being a sum actually given or paid by the people in general to particular exporters; the other being no more than a return of that tax or duty upon exportation, which was, or would have been levied upon the goods if used for home consumption." [2]

The nature and use of the bounty is well developed by him. He recognizes

"Four ways of turning trade into new channels and stopping up the old one: (1) Laying additional duties on the commerce of one country and not of the other . . . to be used with wari-

[1] Tucker catalogues these thus: "Commodities entitled to bounty now are corn, spirits distilled from corn, fish and flesh, gunpowder, coarse linens, sail cloth and some sorts of silk manufacture and a peculiar case of bounty on tonnage of ships in the Royal British and Greenland fisheries. Commodities entitled to drawbacks are refined sugars, soap, candles, starch, leather, leather manufactures, paper, ale, mum, cider, perry, spiritous liquors, wrought plate, gold and silver lace, glass, foreign silks, calicoes, linens and stuffs, if printed, painted, stained or dyed in Great Britain. Bounty on raw materials from Colonies are pitch, tar, turpentine, naval stores and indigo." *Instruct. for Trav.*, p. 33.

[2] *Instruct. for Trav.*, p. 33.

ness . . . every such additional duty put upon the commodities of a foreign country will be looked upon by that country as an act of hostility committed upon its trade . . . which it will be sure to revenge . . . incline the scale gradually . . . violently high duties and the favored country . . . not ready for a time to supply the increase wanted. (2) More commodious and less exceptionable way . . . to grant certain privileges and exemptions . . . which shall continue until . . . the merchant can find it worth his while to engage in it without being paid at the public expense. (3) Bounty upon importation. (4) Personal premium to the merchants importing most and best." [1]

The changed trade-channel referred to here is evidently in an import class of goods. It is to be noted that Tucker here expressly prefers "special privileges and exceptions" to duties as a means of obtaining the desired end. Elsewhere he as expressly prefers bounties to chartered privileges. In connection with his statement of this last mentioned preference he completes his analysis of the bounty by recognizing that it is a burden upon society, endured for the sake of expected future gain from the stimulated industry. In this passage he argues that if private persons will not voluntarily embark in an enterprise

"the better way would be to give a bounty or premium to encourage all adventurers, rather than to grant exclusive privileges to a few. For both the one and the other are a charge upon the public; but the monopoly is by much the worse, the dearest and the most difficult to be broken through." [2]

He is careful to warn frequently against the danger of continuing too long the aid to any given kind of industry.

[1] *Essay on Trade, 3rd ed.*, pp. 100–102.

[2] *Ibid., 3rd ed.*, p. 67, *note*.

Thus he is of opinion that the bounty upon the exportation of corn, which had opened up markets in foreign lands and "which in the infancy of agriculture was so essentially necessary, ought to receive at present, very considerable amendments and reductions." [1] But the best illustration of his caution against undue use of national bounties occurs in connection with a remarkably clear presentation of the infant-industry argument. As has been noted above, Tucker, seems to favor the bounty rather than either chartered privileges or customs-duties, as a means for encouraging industry. This accounts for his presentation of the infant-industry argument in connection with bounties. He several times states the complete infant-industry argument. The passage here given in full, is his best statement of it and is so modern in cast that it reads as though it might have been taken from an economic treatise of the last decade:

"Such infant manufactures or raw materials as promise to become hereafter of general use and importance, ought to be reared and nursed, during the weakness and difficulties of their infant state, by public encouragement and national premiums. But it doth, by no means, so clearly appear that this nursing and supporting should be continued forever. On the contrary, it seems more natural to conclude that, after a reasonable course of years, attempts ought to be made to wean this commercial child by gentle degrees, and not to suffer it to contract a lazy habit of leaning continually on the leading strings. In short, all bounties to particular persons are just so many taxes upon the community; and that particular trade is not worth having which never can be brought to support itself. Were all manufactures to receive a bounty (and all have equal right to expect it), this reasoning would appear unanswerable." [2]

[1] *Instruct. for Trav.*, p. 18.

[2] *Ibid.*, p. 33. Similar infant-industry arguments are given in *Elements*, pp. 85-86, and in *Reflect. on Wools*, pp. 24-27.

It thus appears that Tucker believed that the bounty system of Great Britain had worked successfully. He several times proposes new bounties to encourage enterprises he favors,[1] and especially he favors a duty or bounty "to encourage trade in naval stores, . . . not to be too dependent on Sweden, Russia and Denmark in war." [2]

V. Colonies

The fifth leading topic dealt with rather fully by Tucker, in his consideration of foreign trade, is that of colonies. There is development in his treatment of this subject. In his earlier writings he gives rules for maintaining satisfactory relations with colonies. The reasonable implication is that he accounts them beneficial, or, at least, that he is not opposed to them. But when the American controversy arises, he appears as the consistent opponent of distant colonies. The years had increased his aversion to war, and had led him to a belief that trade relations, fully as lucrative to the mother country, will exist with a given district, whether it is a colony or not; that costly wars must be fought for the infant colonies' sake; that emigrants leave the mother country and add to the population of the colony; and, finally, that the colony, in the natural evolution of its new life, inevitably seeks and obtains independence. This development in Tucker's thought concerning colonies, is normal, and may be easily explained.

During his economic decade there had appeared only the suggestions of a coming severance of the American colonies from Great Britain. That Tucker perceived this shadow

[1] *E. g.*, he proposed an export bounty of 3/2d per yard on coarse woollens sent to the Baltic countries, see *Reflect. on Wools*, pp. 17 *sqq;* he favored "a double premium on fisheries on the north coast of Scotland," see *Essay on Trade, 3rd ed., Appendix*, pp. 18 and 19.

[2] *Essay on Trade, 3rd ed.*, p. 93.

cast before, seems probable from the fact that he emphasized the need of considerate treatment if the colonies were to be kept subservient. Indeed, he expressly stated in his very first economic treatise, in 1749, that the colonies would seek independence if they saw that they did not need Great Britain's assistance. The statement occurs in the passage where he outlines the policy for treatment of colonies:

"If we fear they may revolt, let us not drive them into independence. . . . This they will seek if they see that they do not need our assistance. If we keep them dependent and subservient to the welfare of the mother country, we must make it to their interest to be. . . . . (1) They must not interfere with the mother country in their products. (2) They should be encouraged to send raw materials to England . . . (3) We must permit them to furnish us, under reasonable and easy duty, such luxuries as we are wedded to and must buy elsewhere . . . . (4) Even the farthest colonists must be considered . . . and encouraged to do what they can lest they be employed in planning against the mother country." [1]

This is evidently the outline of the accepted eighteenth century policy, based upon the belief that colonies exist for the benefit of the mother country. The counsel is temperate only because a practical man is aiming to point the way to largest results with least friction. There is no hint in the passage that its author believes that it is inexpedient or economically unwise for a country to have colonies; on the contrary, the clause, "if we would keep them dependent and subservient to the welfare of the mother country," evidences that he believed real gain could come from the possession

[1] *Essay on Trade, 3rd ed.*, pp. 96–98. Other early references to colonies are *Reflect. Nat. For. Prot.* Part II, pp. 36 sqq., where he advises that emigration to the colonies be allowed, and *Elements*, pp. 108–110, where he states that conquest without colonization is an absurdity.

of colonies. He goes still further in the *Elements,* and expressly advocates the founding of a colony in the Hudson Bay country, and declares that "such a colony would be most profitably connected with Great Britain." [1]

But the seven years' war had been fought to a victorious ending, and the American colonies were freed from all danger of French domination. Almost immediately the colonies grew openly and menacingly restive. British thought centred upon them more fully, both because of their growing strength and increasing readiness to resent dictation, and because, foreign relations being peaceful, there were no international complications to distract the British attention from intra-imperial conditions. Tucker was one of the earliest to open a pamphleteer consideration of the American colony relations. His attention for the first time was now centred upon the colonies. Before, what he had written concerning them had been incidental to his treatment of trade relations with France, in particular, or with the world in general. He now reviewed the history of the colonies. He realized that the whole heavy expense of the Seven Years' War had come because of them. He foresaw a coming costly, prolonged and hopeless struggle to retain them. He noted that good-class British citizens were going to the colonies to live, thus further decimating the British population, which his studies had led him to regard as already far too small. He applied his self-interest canon to determine trade tendencies, and concluded that any truly profitable commerce would continue even if the new world were independent. He traced the life record of important colonies in history, and concluded that the American colonies were but repeating that history. These thoughts led him to his later and final view, that distant colonies are expensive appendages to any

[1] *Elements*, p. 125.

state, and that Great Britain would be wise if she yielded to the colonies the independence they were beginning to seek, and turned to people and to develop the waste lands within her island borders with the emigrants and soldiers whom the colonial wildernesses were swallowing, and with the wealth she would squander in protecting, coddling, and endeavoring to compel the colonies. This final position is well stated in his *Treatise on Government:*

"Colonies of every sort and kind are and ever were a drain to and an incumbrance on the mother country, requiring perpetual and expensive nursing in their infancy and becoming headstrong and ungovernable in proportion as they grow up and never failing to revolt as soon as they shall find that they do not want our assistance. And that even at the best, those commercial advantages, which are vulgarly supposed to arise from them, are more imaginary than real because it is impossible to compel distant settlements to trade with a parent state to any great degree beyond what their own interest would prompt them." [1]

Tucker condemns the two parties in the kingdom because they agree in nothing

"but in maintaining and propagating one grand capital mistake relative to the welfare of this nation, viz.: That colonies are necessary for the support, preservation and extension of commerce, a fatal error which has ruined every country in proportion as it has been adopted." [2]

A detailed argument against the alleged false position of the parties follows the above statement. It maintains: (1)

[1] *Treatise on Government*, p. 253.

[2] *Further Thoughts, etc.* The outline given is of the argument in this tract.

That British trade with other countries is as lucrative as that with colonies. (2) That "keys," such as Gibraltar and Port Mahon

"have never opened one passage to the English, which was not open before nor have they once shut the door against our enemies and our rivals in peace or in war, nothwithstanding the immense sums they have cost and the great number of troops stationed there." [1]

(3) That if colonies enable a country to buy more cheaply, Britain should plant colonies in every clime whose products she desired. (4) That if an increase in the shipping is desired, as is the aim of the Navigation Act, the sure way to get it, and the only way to get it, is to increase the goods for export, and thus make a demand for "sea waggons." (5) "States may be too great as well as too small; . . . . added colonies in far parts of the world are exposed to constant attack; . . . . the centre is weakened to protect the colonies." (6) It would be better to reclaim England's wastes than to develop colonies.

"Would not a judicious application of one thousandth part of the sums of money which have been lavished in fighting for America, and one hundredth part of the lives sacrificed in the same cause . . . have rendered these English wastes and deserts, some of the best cultivated, the most fruitful and populous parts of the whole kingdom?" [1]

(7) These same wastes, when peopled, will aid in national defence: but America, even had she remained loyal, is too far away to render timely assistance.

In his *Letter to Burke,* he cites Spain's history as proof that colonies enfeeble a land. He argues that

[1] *Further Thoughts, etc.*

"Spain . . . before it was seized with an epidemic madness of settling colonies in America was one of the richest, the best peopled, the best cultivated and the most flourishing countries in Europe . . . But alas, how fallen! What is Spain! Where are its manufactures! Where its inhabitants! . . . Is Spain, with its diminished population and with vast colonies in South America, richer than formerly?" [1]

Tucker's belief in the inevitableness of colonial independence is best formulated in the following passage:

"There is nothing in our present situation with respect to the American colonies, to amaze the philosopher or politician. Where is the wonder that Americans should forget their obligations to the mother country, and revolt against her authority, when they need no further protection? Or that we should be too weak to bring them back to submission and dependence? If a spirit of national pride and vanity could permit us to reason calmly on these subjects, if it would suffer us farther dispassionately to turn over a few pages of authentic history either ancient or modern we should see that colonies while in their infant state are always humble and modest; and while their very existence results from, and every hope is cherished by, the fostering care of a mother country, make suitable returns of gratitude, duty and affection. But as they rise in strength and approach maturity, they become proud and insolent; impatient even of the most equitable restraints and incessantly aiming at emancipation. And this is but a picture of what every day passes in natural life where the connection is much stronger and more endearing. The child, advanced to man's estate and in possession of the means of subsistence withdraws from the authority of his parent . . . the stamp act therefore only hastened that struggle which might otherwise have been deferred a short time longer; but must assuredly have taken place before the expiration of many years." [2]

[1] *Lett. to Burke*, p. 40.

[2] *Dispassionate Tho'ts on Am. War*, pp. 24-26.

One may approve this theory as a just deduction from history, bearing in mind that it is formulated on the hypothesis that the mother country is to seek to develop, in eighteenth century style, a colony which shall be both profitable and subservient to her.

Tucker's final judgment upon the relations of Great Britain to the American colonies is expressed in a letter to Lord Kames, in 1782:

"In short to sum up all at once I look upon it to have been a very imprudent act to have settled any distant colonies at all whilst there remained an inch of land in great Britain capable of further cultivation; afterwards to have been very foolish and absurd to have engaged in their disputes either with the French or Spaniards and to have espoused their quarrels; and lastly, to have been the height of absurdity to have endeavored to conquer them after they had broken out in open rebellion. They were always from first to last a heavy weight upon us; a weight which we ourselves ought to have thrown off if they had not done it for us." [1]

VI. Statistics

The fifth special topic to be presented is statistics. The topic relates to commerce, as well as to any other of the subdivisions under which Tucker's work is being presented. It really relates to them all.

Upon the subjects with which Tucker dealt, he could secure but little statistical material, and there are very few and minor statistical references [1] made by him. One tract,[2] however, gives an interesting forecast of the modern national census. It was written in 1778. It suggests an outline for an investigation, which Tucker advises the malcontents of

[1] *Memoirs of Kames*, vol. iii, pp. 180–181.

[2] *State of the Nation*.

the day to make. He prophesies that if a comparison be made between the year 1777 and "the famous era of 1759, that period of glory and conquest, when everything was supposed to go right," it would be discovered that Great Britain had made progress. He suggests a "nine-fold inquiry," and says that "each of these is a proper subject for a Parliamentary inquiry, and all of them, taken together, form the complex idea called 'the State of the Nation.'"

The nine subjects for investigation which he presents are, in his order: (1) population, (2) agriculture, (3) manufacture, (4) land and fresh-water carriage of goods, (5) salt-water carriage of goods, (6) state of our fisheries at home and abroad, (7) tendency of our taxes, (8) the clear annual amount of the revenue, (9) the national debt. Under each of these subdivisions he offers a number of questions. An idea of the whole may be obtained from the questions asked under one topic. The paragraph treating of agriculture reads:

> "Here let the inquiry proceed in the following manner: What was the state of agriculture last year, 1777, compared with the year 1759? Has it advanced or declined since then? Are our old farm houses, barns, outbuildings, now tumbling down? Are there no new erections of the like sort? Are our inclosures, hedges, fences, drains, etc., etc., running fast to decay? And are there no new ones making? Is there less land under tillage or used for meadow and pasture at present than in 1759? Is this land less drained or watered, less manured, cultivated or improved? Are our farmers grown poorer than heretofore? Can we get no substantial tenants now to occupy farms? And are there no instances of late years of farmers buying estates for themselves? I will add no more, but any gentleman who trembles with apprehensions that we are now on the brink of ruin, would do well to produce his list of grievances respecting agriculture for the year 1777, compared with the happy days of 1759."

Similar series of questions occur under each topic, and it is evident, from the detailed nature of the questions, that had they been answered in a series of volumes in the year 1778, Great Britain would have led the world in comprehensive and complete inventory of her own population, resources, industry, trade and finance.

Tucker appears to have realized the great value that would attach to such a publication. In the very connection in which he suggested its use lies one of its chief values, viz., that a nation may thereby learn whether it is making progress.

In the " skeleton " of his great work, he had planned a section upon " An Annual Survey and Register of Inhabitants." Judging from the *State of the Nation,* this section, had he drafted it, would probably have been a reasonably complete scheme for a national census.

CHAPTER VI

MONEY AND PRICES

THE " skeleton " for Tucker's great work, which he gives at the end of his *Elements,* maps out for Chapter III, of Book II, a treatise on " Coin and credit as the medium of commerce." The eight sections, fully headlined for this chapter, give promise of a quite complete discussion of the functions of money, its kinds and their relative merits, market price and value, the reasons why gold and silver are the money metals, the nature of paper money, the ratio of gold and silver, the theory of exchange, the par of exchange, the nature of banking, the need for more metallic money, and a plan for breaking up the national debt into interest-bearing bonds of small denomination. Unfortunately, none of these sections was ever expanded as a part of the great work, and only by suggestions and fragmentary expositions appearing incidentally in others of Tucker's works, can a further idea be formed of their intended contents. Fortunately, on the other hand, the section headings in the skeleton are sufficiently full to give a fair concept of what the expanded chapter would have been. To these section headings the reader must be referred [1] for all the topics mentioned above, except (I) the functions of money, (II) the standard of value, (III) market price, (IV) the philosophy of exchange, and (V) the scheme for subdividing the public debt. Upon all other money and credit topics the skeleton headings tell all that is told anywhere in

[1] See *Appendix* of this volume for the " Skeleton," Book II, Chap. III.

Tucker's writings. Upon each of those five subjects he has left something in other parts of his works, and what he has left is here topically arranged.

I. Functions of Money

Tucker understands the leading two functions of money. He sees clearly that it is a medium of exchange, and so defines it in the "skeleton."[1] Elsewhere he queries:

> "What is money but a common measure, tally, counter to set forth or denominate the price of labor in the several transfers of it?"[2]

This expressly makes money a measure of the contained labor in commodities, or a measure of value.

II. Standard of Value

In the "skeleton" Tucker promises to explain the "true meaning of the relative terms, market price, and value of commodities, cheapness, dearness, scarcity, plenty, &c., &c."[3] Nowhere in his other writings does there appear any discussion of value. The incidental statements which do occur seem to show that he is a believer in a labor standard of value. In the body of the *Elements* he says:

> "Industry and labor are the only real riches, money being merely the ticket or sign belonging to them and the use of money is to certify that the person possessing that piece of coin hath likewise been in possession of a certain quantity of labor which he hath transferred to other hands and now retains the sign of it. Money therefore being nothing more than a certificate of labor, etc."[4]

[1] See *Appendix* of this volume, book ii, chap. iii, section ii.

[2] *Reflect. Nat. For. Prot.* Part II, p. 19.

[3] See *Appendix*, Skeleton, book ii, chap. iii, sect. iii.

[4] *Elements*, p. 99.

Again:

"Labor is the true riches and money only the sign or tally." [1]

III. Market Price

There is little concerning prices in Tucker's works. He (1) states that supply and demand determine market price, and (2) he opposes any attempt by the state to keep goods, offered in the market, up to any arbitrary standard. These two positions comprehend his whole expressed thought upon prices.

(1) The market-price formula is thus worded by him:

"The prices of all commodities whatever depend on the quantity at market and the demand for the same. It must therefore follow that when the demand decreases and the quantity increases the price must fall and vice versa." [2]

That the quantity of money affects the prices is only hinted at by him. In unfolding his thesis that mere money is not riches, he supposes England to receive suddenly a large sum of money, through a mine discovery or successful privateering, and says that prices of provisions and manufactures would rise to a " most enormous price whilst the flush of money lasted." The reasons he gives for this are, that

"First the people, enriched by so improper means would not know the real value of money and (would) give any price asked. Secondly, the cart, plow, anvil, wheel and loom would certainly be laid aside for these quicker and easier arts

[1] *Reflect. Nat. For. Prot.* Part II, p. 19.

[2] *Reflections on Wool*, p. 14. He applies this principle elsewhere, *e. g.*, *Elements*, pp. 73, 96 and 98.

of getting rich . . . and the quantity (of provisions and manufactures) raised in the kingdom would be less than ever."[1]

Reason number one emphasizes that the extravagance of those easily enriched, rather than the large quantity of money, acts as a cause in raising prices. Reason number two simply applies his supply-and-demand formula.

(2) His opposition to governmental attempts to regulate the manufacture of goods according to set standards is twice stated very emphatically. In *Instructions to Travellers,* he numbers statutes fixing standards among the "bad laws relating to trade and manufactures (which) are now subsisting."[2] Of them he says:

"The statutes for the due ordering and making particular sorts of goods, keeping them up to a standard, regulating their lengths and breadths, appointing of what materials, or at what seasons of the year they shall be made, etc., etc., are also a useless farce and burden, and only serve now and then as an handle for one litigious or lazy rival to vex his industrious or ingenious neighbor. For as to general use they are absolutely impracticable and ever will so remain as long as buyers and sellers vary in their prices, fancies, tastes, etc. In one word if the buyer is not deceived in buying them, that is, if they shall prove throughout such as they appear to be, and are in reality the same he bought them for, it is no sort of consequence, when, or how or where or with what materials they were made or whether the goods are longer or shorter, broader or narrower, coarser or finer, better or worse than those usually made before them."[3]

[1] *Four Tracts*, p. 23.

[2] *Instruct. for Trav.*, p. 33.

[3] *Instruct. for Trav.*, p. 34. For a similar statement see *Elements*, p. 83.

IV. Philosophy of Exchange

This topic was treated in the preceding chapter, as more naturally introductory to a presentation of Tucker's thought upon trade.

V. Circulating Bond Scheme

Twenty-five years after the "skeleton" promise of a polity for changing part of the "dead national debt" into circulating certificates, Tucker outlines the plan which he then probably had in mind. He advises that Parliament should

"pass a law to enable 3% bonds, now £60 each, to be exchanged for equivalent sums in £10 notes, each with a 6d. stamp and bearing 6s. annual interest, payable each six months to the bearer like East India bonds. And when a great quantity of such notes are in circulation it would be right to allot a place or two in each county to pay the interest. The 6d. stamp would meet all the expense of the new officers needed by this . . . banks would be glad to be places of payment. By these means every man in the kingdom from the highest to the lowest who had £10 to spare for ever so short a time would get after the rate of 3% per annum for the money which otherwise must have lain dead. And poor men in particular, journeymen, laborers, man servants and maid servants, would have a safe deposit for their little earnings and a regular interest in order to induce them to save more." [1]

[1] *Thoughts on Public Affairs, Gent's Mag.*, vol. l, p. 133.

CHAPTER VII

TAXATION

TAXES play an important rôle in Tucker's economic system. He recognizes that revenue-raising plans have been responsible for great changes in history.[1] Very many of his "polities" find their sanctions in proposed taxation. An entire "Book" of the great work was to have been devoted to a full development of the subject of taxation. The outline of this book, given in the "skeleton," shows that Tucker had planned to treat this theme as he treats others, viz., first to discuss the theory of taxes in general, and secondly to apply the theoretical principles arrived at to existent British taxes, approving, disapproving, suggesting alterations and additions. Though this outline was nowhere elaborated to completeness by him, it can be measurably filled in by a collect of taxation passages scattered throughout his works. The most serious loss, in the consideration of this subject, is the dissertation upon "the nature, reason, and use of taxes," with which he purposed to open his treatment in the great work. Nowhere does he present this. But a reasonably complete idea of the probably intended content of the remainder of this "Book" on taxation may be ob-

[1] He notes that the Stuart monarchs had a choice: either (1) to command Parliament to levy some tax, and in case they refused, to raise the tax by royal prerogative without asking consent, or (2) to yield to the times in good grace and sue for revenue as a favor. "They chose the former and the result was a civil war which at last begot the expulsion of the family." *Treatise on Government*, p. 66. *Cf. Elements*, pp. 151–153.

tained by a study of all his works. A result of such a study is presented below, under three divisions: I. The tax criterion. II. Application of this criterion to the British tax system. III. Taxation miscellany.

I. Tax Criterion

Tucker's central taxation principle is stated a number of times in his works. He recognizes that

> "Two uses may be made of taxes, a primary and a secondary. The primary use is to support government and to defray the several expenses, military and civil, incurred or to be incurred thereby. . . . . The secondary is to provide for these expenses in such a manner as shall render the subjects in general more industrious and consequently the richer and not the poorer by such a mode of taxation. And I do aver that every judicious tax tends to promote the latter of these uses as well as the former." [1]

It is this secondary use which he constantly emphasizes, so much so that the policing and fructifying function of taxes may be called his financial hobby. It is necessary, in his thought, to raise a given revenue, but also quite essential so to levy the taxes as to encourage industry and morality, and to discourage idleness and vice. Indeed, he sometimes regards this latter regulative function as the more important. Thus, he states that

> "the sum produced into the exchequer ought not to be so much the principal consideration as the nature and tendency of the tax." [1]

From among the many statements of this fundamental

[1] *Treatise on Gov't*, p. 67.

test for the merit of any tax, the following are selected as fairly conveying his thought:

"A good tax is that which tends to prevent idleness, check extravagance and promote industry. A bad tax on the contrary falls the heaviest of all upon the industrious man, excusing or at least not punishing the idle, the spendthrift, or the vain." [1]

"The nature of taxes is such that they may be compared to the pruning of fruit trees, an operation which all will allow not only to be useful but in some sense necessary. Now if this should be judiciously performed the trees will be much healthier and bear abundantly the better—but if ignorantly and unskillfully done the trees will bear nothing or next to nothing and perhaps will sicken and die away." [2]

"If you have a mind to have your people in general honestly and usefully employed lay your chief taxes upon idleness and pleasures. For such taxes will make all people frugal and industrious, and frugality and industry necessarily create wealth. The infallible consequence of wealth is enjoyment and enjoyment is the proper subject for taxation. Thus therefore the circle goes around the more taxes (of this sort) the more riches; the more riches, the more pleasures; the more pleasures the more taxes, etc., or if you prefer to consider the subject in another view then I would say abolish every tax and remove all impediments whatever which might prevent self-love, the grand mover, from operating for the public good. But bar up with high taxes, duties and impositions, all the avenues and byepaths which might make an opening for irregular or corrupt self-love to decline from the great road of private virtue and public happiness. And when you have set this plan once in motion you have all the certainty which is to be expected in human affairs that it will not miscarry.

[1] *Instruct. for Trav.*, p. 36.

[2] *Treatise on Gov't*, p. 79.

For the daily and hourly collection of the revenue is a constant and never ceasing agent in the execution of your system, whereas all other applications to law and justice can proceed, even at the best, only by fits and starts." [1]

II. The Criterion Applied

His criterion being determined, he tests, by it, the prevailing systems of British taxes.

He finds:

(1) "The Land tax is become of late years a most excellent tax for the exciting of industry and all kinds of improvements; inasmuch as the increase of produce and advancements of value pay no higher tax than the grounds would have paid had there been no improvement at all. Therefore this impost doth now operate in the very manner which every tax ought and every good one necessarily will do: that is, it punishes the idle and the sluggards for not improving their estates but exempts the diligent and industrious. . . ." [1]

(2) "In regard to the excise, many branches thereof are very proper taxes, and fit to be continued; those especially which are laid on intoxicating liquors, or on articles of parade, expense, and pleasure. For, the further any article is removed from the unavoidable wants, the fitter it is to contribute towards the support of the state by paying a tax. And as to intoxicating liquors, they are the farthest removed of any whatever, and the most detrimental to the state in their effects and consequences; therefore in every view, they are the properest to have very high and discouraging duties laid on them." [2]

(3) Upon customs duties Tucker takes an unequivocal mercantilist view. His thought upon them has been given in presenting his treatment of mercantilism, which see.

[1] *Elements*, pp. 169–170. Similar statements to those here quoted are in *Essay on Trade, 3d Ed.*, pp. 126–127, *State of the Nation*, and *Manifold Causes Inc. Poor*, pp. 6 and 7.

[2] *Instruct. for Trav.*, p. 38.

(4) "The last article of taxes is the stamp duties; and as some of them are very proper and none of them amiss, we shall here conclude this head of the query with one short reflection, viz., as that tax which promotes labor, and checks idleness, is a very good one, so no others ought to be esteemed absolutely bad, but such only which produce the contrary effect." [1]

In further application of his criterion for determining good taxes, Tucker states what particular British taxes should, in his judgment, be repealed:

(1) "The salt tax can have no shadow of an argument to plead in its behalf. For if salt is a good manure for lands, the taxing of salt, is the taxing of manure. And surely all manures are raw materials of the most important, most extensive nature. . . . . Further salt is an absolute necessity of life, administering to no pride, vanity, or excess whatever and consequently the most improper to be taxed." [2]

(2) "The duty on coals is a very pernicious duty and subject to all the objections of the former; only some of them in a lesser degree." [1]

(3) "The duty on soap and candles is not a good tax and yet not wholly bad. That part which affects the poor or even the middling people, must certainly be bad. But the soap and candles used by the great, in which the chief consumption and extravagance consist ought to pay a duty; and it would be really a pity that beaux and belles should not contribute something to the support of government in proportion as they frequented balls, assemblies, operas, plays, masquerades, routs, drums, etc., etc." [3]

(4) "The duty on leather is subject to some objections as it

[1] *Instruct. for Trav.*, p. 39.

[2] *Ibid.*, pp. 39 and 40.

[3] *Ibid.*, p. 40.

affects the poor almost equally with the rich. And yet of bad taxes it is far from the worst."

(5) " The extravagant duty upon the importation of coarse olive oil, a raw material incapable either of excess, vanity, or waste of time, and a most necessary article for our woollen manufactures and in making Castile soap, is one that calls the loudest for redress." [1]

And he adds:

" having thus finished the present examination, it may not be improper to add, for the credit of our country and the praise of the legislature, that upon the most impartial survey, there seems to be only these five taxes of any consequence, which can strictly be denominated bad." [1]

Additions to the tax system are next considered. As an improvement to the customs system, he advocates the institution of warehouses:

" To permit, though not to oblige, the merchants to land their goods without prompt payment of duties at the custom house. Were this permission granted, those who accepted of it should be obliged to give bond for the payment and to put their goods under the lock and key of the officer by the way of additional security. And then they should be allowed to dispose of their effects and to pay the duties gradually according as they could find purchasers or as they wanted to remove such and such parcels, etc. . . . to their own private warehouses. By these means every merchant could extend his trade and credit . . . . because he would need to make no reserves of cash or credit for prompt payments at the custom house; every merchant also could buy when and where and as much as he pleased on speculation and sustain no loss of interest on that money which must now be advanced to pay the duties . . . .

[1] *Instruct. for Trav.*, p. 41.

In short, this single regulation would go a great way towards making Great Britain a magazine and storehouse for other countries, and render her ports free." [1]

The particular additional taxes he suggests are all to be levied according to his general principle that a good tax discourages vice, idleness and extravagance. In the *Instructions for Travellers,* he simply catalogues what he considers to be the proper subjects for added taxation:

"Taxes ought to be laid on dogs, on saddle horses, when exceeding two in number; on livery servants, on all places of public resort and diversion, such as public rooms, music gardens, playhouses, etc., also on booths and stands for country wakes, cricket matches, and horseracing, stages for mountebanks, cudgel-playing, etc., moreover on fives-places, and ball-courts, billiard tables, shuffleboards, skittle alleys, bowling greens, and cock-pits. Also capitation taxes should be levied on itinerant players, lottery men, showmen, jugglers, ballad-singers and indeed on all others of whatever class or denomination, whose very trades and professions have a natural tendency and whose personal interest it is to make other people profuse, extravagant and idle. Lastly the stamp duty might very properly be extended to take in printed songs, novels, romance, music, plays and such like articles of mere amusement, to be stamped in the same manner as almanacs are. Now it is obvious that such taxes as these are so far from impoverishing that they must necessarily enrich every state where they take place." [1]

Tucker's exceeding great faith in the efficacy of state

[1] *Instruct. for Trav.*, p. 42. Tucker was an advocate of this warehousing system from the very first of his published economic works. See *Essay on Trade, 3rd ed.*, pp. 108 and 122-126, for a more detailed presentation of this scheme.

action in general, and of taxes in particular, is well shown by his closing sentences on this topic:

"And therefore, let it be laid down as an infallible rule, that in proportion as this system of taxation or its contrary doth prevail in any state throughout the world, in the same proportion doth industry or idleness, plenty or want, riches or beggary prevails likewise. And in short, the course of nature is fixed and cannot be altered." [1]

In the third edition [2] of his *Essay on Trade,* Tucker elaborated more fully his thought as to new British taxes. In his earlier statement he includes two special taxes not mentioned above, a tax upon bachelors and a "double turnpike tax upon all who travel on Sundays—a modish and reigning vice." The tax upon bachelors is evidently an outgrowth of his idea that Great Britain needed a larger population. It is rather surprising that he should omit this from the list of desirable new taxes given in the *Instructions.* As was shown in the chapter upon population, he, throughout his life, advocated plans to increase the British population. There is nothing to indicate that he deliberately omitted the bachelor tax [3] from the *Instructions'* list.

Tucker once proposed a single tax upon luxuries. His statement, introducing the fully elaborated plan, well illustrates the practical man. He says that his proposals, the

[1] *Instruct. for Trav.*, pp. 42–43.

[2] *Essay on Trade, Appendix, 3rd ed.*, pp. 127–139. A similar list occurs in *Manifold Causes Inc. Poor*, pp. 16–20.

[3] This bachelor tax was first proposed by Tucker in 1751 in *Spiritous Liquors;* again in 1753 in the *Appendix* to the *3rd Ed. of the Essay on Trade.* Altho omitted in the list of desirable taxes in *Instruct. for Trav.*, it was advocated again in *Manifold Causes Inc. of Poor*, pp. 16–17 (1760). In this latter (p. 20) occurs, again, the Sunday-driving tax omitted also from the *Instructions* list.

taxes on bachelors, dogs, saddle-horses, etc., previous to this single-tax plan,

"were aimed to change the present system as little as possible, I did not propose some of the above mentioned alterations as what appeared to me the very best which could be devised; but the best in our present circumstances and the likeliest to succeed. For I am convinced that what I am going to offer is, in itself, a much more effectual remedy, if our constitution is strong enough to admit the application of it." [1]

After presenting the plan, he says of it:

"This is alright but it will never do; it is too honest."

The single-tax plan [1] is too elaborately developed to be given here. The general plan is to take certain luxuries as standards for estimating, and listing for taxation, all incomes, *e. g.*, all persons keeping two coaches and six for their use shall be listed as having incomes of £8,000; those using silver service at the table as having incomes of £4,000; those keeping one coach and six as having £2,000; and so on, down to those having pictures, or more than one mirror, etc., whose incomes listed for taxation shall be £25. Tucker suggests that if each taxpayer were required to pay on each item that he listed at the rate set by the costliest luxury that he consumed, the system would then be the "most excellent sumptuary law that ever was desired."

The scheme for levying the tax is ingenious. Parties are to list themselves voluntarily for the first year; and, since the larger the amount listed the lower the rate would need to be to raise needed revenue, neighbors can be depended

[1] This "Plan for raising one only tax on the consumers of luxuries" is given in the *Essay on Trade, 3rd edition*, pp. 148–168.

upon to report those who live above their listed rating. The tax is to be laid on the first year without removing others, and these others are then to be gradually removed as the single tax becomes adequate as a revenue-raiser.

An argument, in an illustrative case, that this tax would be less of a burden to a given taxpayer than the more expensively collected direct and indirect taxes then in use, completes the presentation of this taxation scheme by which "sunshine of commerce and plenty would be diffused equally." It is to be borne in mind that Tucker offers this single tax on luxury as an ideal only. He presents it merely as *addenda* to the 1753 edition of the *Essay on Trade,* and nowhere later refers to it. The taxation plan that appeared feasible and practically desirable to him is outlined above.

Tucker makes it very clear that his intent, in his practicable plans, is not to advocate taxation upon consumption in general, but to advocate the raising of taxes by such levies as will discourage idle, vain and extravagant consumption. He states this position most clearly in a letter to historian Hume, written in 1769. Since this letter gives his mature theory of taxes, in a summary made by himself, for the correction of both Hume and Turgot, in their misapprehensions of his taxation system, it is worthy of presentation here entire, as being perhaps the most important declaration upon the subject of taxes to be found in any of his writings:

"I beg leave to observe that both you and Mr. Turgot have greaty mistaken my meaning, that I am a friend to taxes upon 'consummation' in general. I mean no such thing. On the contrary my system is, that every country throughout the universe, ought to endeavor to render industry very cheap and idleness very dear; and that therefore it ought to encourage all kinds of occupations tending to promote the former, by freeing them from all shackles and restraints and more especially, excepting them from taxations and impositions as much as possible. Whereas, it ought, on the other hand, to put a check upon those which subsist themselves by the idleness, drunkenness, extravagance, etc., of other people by subjecting them to discouragements, and by loading them with judicious taxes. And, were this the place for a dissertation of this nature, I think I could prove with an evidence not easily to be resisted, that taxes of this sort will always enrich a nation, instead of impoverishing it; nay that they will, in their consequences, and as the vulgar say, in the long run, multiply the number employed in those very occupations which they seemed intended at first sight to destroy or to starve.

"But to keep within the bounds of a letter, I would only ask you a plain, simple, question, viz., would you wish that there was no tax upon spiritous liquors? Would you choose, if you had the option that the good people of England should get drunk for a penny rather than that it should cost them six pence? and, suppose that they will procure a *quantum sufficit* of this liquor at some price or other, which is better for the public that they should be compelled to work twelve hours before they can procure their intoxicating draught, or be able to purchase it by the labor of only one hour?

"You see my dear sir, that I leave Christianity and a future state entirely out of the question; for I would not affright you with any apprehensions that I was going to write a sermon. And yet, I think that you must agree with me, that the hand of the diligent, considering only the present state of things, is the only hand which can make rich in a national view and that idleness, drunkenness, and extravagance of every kind must make poor." [1]

[1] *Letters of Eminent Persons addressed to David Hume, etc.* (edited by J. H. Burton, Edinburgh and London, 1899), pp. 176 and 177.

III. Taxation Miscellany

There are scattered observations respecting taxes in Tucker's works which indicate that, had he developed his taxation treatise as designed in the plan for the great work, he would have given a quite complete survey of the subject.

a. ABILITY-TO-PAY CANON

Lying back of both his practical and his theoretical taxation systems, as outlined above, is the criterion, ability to pay. He expressly states this as the test for equitable taxes in his *Tract III,* where he says, that whether or not a given tax is excessive "must depend upon the relative poverty and inability of those who are to pay it." [1]

b. INCIDENCE

In his discussion of the union between England and Ireland, he raises the question of incidence by inquiring whether any of the English taxes "really fall on the laboring poor." [2] In answering this question, he observes that both customs duties and excises are borne by the final consumer.

c. COLLECTION

In his plan as outlined in the "skeleton," [3] Tucker was to devote an entire section to a consideration of "regulations for the most frugal methods of collecting the revenue, and the most serviceable to trade and industry." He nowhere fulfils this promise, but, in connection with special-tax plans [4] he is suggesting, he states what appears to him to be

[1] *Four Tracts,* p. 123.

[2] *Union or Separation* p. 6. The discussion of incidence referred to occupies pp. 6–10.

[3] See *Appendix* of this volume.

[4] See *Manifold Causes Inc. Poor,* pp. 22 and 23, and *Essay on Trade, 3rd ed.,* pp. 158 seq.

the wisest way to collect the particular tax being considered. He notes "the expensive manner of collecting our customs," etc.,[1] and writes to M. Necker:

"The inequality of taxes and host of collectors within your kingdom Englishmen cannot understand."[2]

d. DISTINGUISHES HIGH FROM HEAVY TAX

Tucker distinguishes between a high tax and a heavy tax:

"High taxes are one thing and heavy taxes are another. And it is as evident as any proposition in Euclid that a kingdom many be beggared by a tax that produces no more than 50,000£ a year and enriched by another that produces 5,000,-000 £. In short if taxes are so laid on as to check or stop the circulation of industry and labor, how can that kingdom be rich? But if they tend to promote and encourage it, how can such a kingdom be poor?"[3]

e. SMUGGLING

Plans for preventing smuggling are developed several times in Tucker's works, most fully in *Spirituous Liquors.*[4] They include the incorporation of the islands of Guernsey, Jersey and Man under the British crown, establishment of king's warehouses for French wines and tobacco, and reorganization of the coast patrols and of methods for paying customs officials. There is never a hint to abolish duties, and thus destroy incentive to smuggle.

[1] *Essay on Trade*, p. 43.

[2] *Cui Bono*, p. 29.

[3] *2nd Lett. on Naturalization*, pp. 13-14. Similar statement with argument and illustration by supposing a single tax of £20 per year upon every plow and vehicle: *Treat. on Gov't*, pp. 79-80.

[4] *Spirit. Liq.*, pp. 16-21.

f. LOTTERY

To secure funds for erecting cottages, in his scheme for reclaiming waste lands, by placing militia upon them, Tucker proposes " a guinea lottery, one-half to go to the adventurers in prizes and the other half to cottagers." But he does not consider the lottery an ideal way to raise taxes, as is proven by his apology for suggesting such a plan:

" I would wish to apologize for having recourse to any scheme whose principles cannot be defended and whose example is so contagious. The only excuse I can make is this: That it having been found, by long experience, that men and women are become so corrupt that they will gamble under one denomination or another in spite of all our laws—therefore the best use that can be made of this national infatuation is to draw good out of evil and to turn this general insanity into a public benefit." [1]

g. NATIONAL DEBT

There are but two finance topics, aside from taxation, of which Tucker treats. One, the plan for issuing small national bonds to induce small savings, has already been presented in the chapter upon money; the other is the national debt in general. Tucker makes two points with reference to the public debt: (*a*) It should not be allowed to increase indefinitely. (*b*) The burden of a national debt is relative to the wealth of the country. These positions are taken in " State of the Nation," where he suggests a comparison of the national debt of 1759 with that of 1777:

" great it (the debt) undoubtedly is—by much too great to be suffered to accummulate any farther if it can be possibly avoided. But, comparatively speaking, it is not so great at

[1] *Reflections on Wools*, pp. 38–39.

present as it was in the year 1759. For if the nation is now much richer, then it follows that we may be much better able to bear an equal or a greater load of national debt . . . . But nevertheless . . . I do not offer . . . any apology . . . or encouragement for running any farther into debt if we can possibly avoid it."

PART III

SOURCES, INFLUENCE AND CONCLUSIONS

CHAPTER I

SOURCES OF TUCKER'S THOUGHT

THE sources from which Tucker obtained his economic facts and ideas were of three kinds: I. Previous economic writers. II. Parliamentary reports and state papers, statutes, histories, and special collections of economic data. III. His own observations and original thought upon the economic relations of men and things.

I. DEBT TO OTHER WRITERS

Tucker was acquainted with the work of the leading writers preceding his author-day. He quotes or refers to William Petty, Josiah Child, Joshua Gee, Harrington, Mandeville, Berkeley, Ustariz, and Montesquieu. He does not mention Sir Dudley North. It does not appear that any of these writers, with the exception of Montesquieu, exercised any direct influence upon Tucker which is worth noticing.

Petty is merely referred to as having believed that England could sustain a larger population.[1] Gee is criticized because he was despondent, and alleged so great a balance

[1] *Reflect. Nat. For. Prot.*, Part ii, p. 18.

of trade against Great Britain "that for sixty years past, according to his figures, we should not have had a shilling, . . . yet we have lavished £150,000,000 on useless wars." [1] Harrington is referred to as a writer of moderate ability, who, "himself a gentleman," maintained that only gentlemen were fit to rule, and "proceeded to discover a gentleman ancestor for his darling megaleter, Oliver Cromwell." [2] Mandeville's *Fable* is characterized as an "absurdity." [3] The one idea from Berkeley which seems to have remained with Tucker is his query whether a man might not be proprietor of twenty square miles in America and yet be in want for a dinner.[4] It is not improbable that Tucker may have adopted from Berkeley his frequent use of the query [5] form of presenting an argument. Ustariz is mentioned in two [6] of Tucker's works, and from his treatise Tucker secured many of the facts relative to Spanish history and economic conditions, which he used illustratively in his writings.

Josiah Child is oftener referred to than any of the above-mentioned authors, and his works found favor in Tucker's eyes. In *Instructions for Travellers,*[7] he recommends Child's treatise on trade as the leading work under his division on

[1] *Cui Bono*, p. 74.

[2] *Letters to Shelburne*, pp. 88–91.

[3] *Essay on Trade, 3rd ed.*, p. 130.

[4] This query is twice referred to: *Four Tracts* pp. 64 and 216.

[5] The whole of *Reflect. Nat. For. Prot.*, Part ii, is in this *Querist* style.

[6] *Reflect. Nat. For. Prot.*, Part i, p. 61, and *Elements*, p. 148, both mention *The Theory and Practise of Commerce*, by "Don Geronimo Ustariz, one of the lords of trade to his Catholic Majesty of Spain." The work of Ustariz is a critical commentary upon the commercial history and conditions of European countries, closing with a practical program for revivifying Spanish industry and trade. It makes no attempt at scientific exposition of general economic principles.

[7] pp. 5 and 9.

"Commerce and Taxes." Child is quoted with approval [1] several times, but Tucker's knowledge of human nature leads him to explain why Child made an exception of the East India Company when he was advocating open trade. "Sir Josiah, himself, was the chairman of that company, and his brother the chief governor abroad." [2] Since Tucker approves Child's writings so generally, and ranks them so highly in advising others as to their reading, it seems reasonable to suppose that Tucker learned much from Child. But Tucker has left a direct statement to the contrary. In the *Elements* [3] he criticizes Child's claim that the East India Company was necessary to maintain forts. He prefaces this criticism with the remark:

"Sir Josiah Child (with whom the writer of these sheets had the honor to agree in every other commercial point, before he had read his book) etc."

This is express testimony that Tucker had worked out his thought-system without any assistance from Child.

Tucker probably learned from Montesquieu that environment is a most important factor in explaining human institutions. *L'Esprit de Lois* is recommended [4] by Tucker as one of the three works on "Ethics, Civil Law, and Government in General," which his traveler should study. His comment is: "The Spirit of Laws by Mr. de Montesquieu is

[1] See *Essay on Trade*, pp. ix and x, and *Reflect. Nat. For. Prot.*, Part ii, p. 14.

[2] *Reflect. on Turkey Trade*, p. 5.

[3] *Elements*, p. 95. Tucker here again notes that Child was "Chairman and director of the company at home, and his brother, John Child, was their governor abroad."

[4] *Instruct. for Trav.*, p. 5.

superior to all eulogiums whatever." [1] The entire *Instructions for Travellers* is framed according to the Montesquieu idea. The young traveler is first advised to keep before himself such questions as how far the looks, numbers, behaviour, clothing, food, dwelling, agriculture, manufacture, arts and sciences are due to soil and climate, to the peculiar genius and inventions of the people, to the spirit of the constitution, and to religious principles.[2] The remainder of the work consists of illustrative queries and answers concerning British people and conditions. Montesquieu is to be credited with influencing the development of Tucker's historic sense.

Tucker was also in touch with at least two contemporary writers who might have influenced him in his economic productions. They were Hume and Turgot. Rightly to estimate their influence, it must be remembered that Tucker had developed substantially his whole system of economic thought by the close of his economic decade, in 1758. There is no evidence that prior to 1758 Tucker had been acquainted with either of the men in any way. The correspondence with Hume did not begin until 1758, and that with Turgot not until 1770.[3] There is nothing to show that Hume's political essays (1752) influenced Tucker in any way. He had expressed his thought upon the trade balance and upon the philosophy of exchange in the *Essay on Trade* [4] (1749), so that he did not derive these from Hume's essays. It is possible that Hume's discussion of the jealousy of trade between nations may have stimulated Tucker, to some extent,

[1] *Instruct. for Trav.*, p. 7. See *Elements*, p. 101, for the only exception Tucker takes to any of Montesquieu's ideas. He there denies the allegation that Oriental people do not desire English wares.

[2] *Instruct. for Trav.*, p. 10.

[3] See *ante*, pp. 32, 33 and 67, for data as to these correspondences.

[4] *Essay on Trade*, *Introduction*, pp. v and vi.

towards his own later amplification of this theme. Beyond this mere possibility, neither Hume nor Turgot had opportunity to impress their thought upon Tucker until after he had worked out his system of economic thought to substantial completeness.

Two facts make it certain that the Physiocratic school had no influence[1] in shaping Tucker's economic thought: (1) the *Elements*, containing Tucker's entire economic thought, at least in full outline, was printed in 1755, the year in which Cantillon's *Essai sur le Commerce*, the first of the Physiocratic works, was published; (2) Tucker did not read French readily,[2] and therefore could not have carried on extensive correspondences with Frenchmen, nor could he have read French manuscripts prior to 1755.

Tucker does not mention either James Steuart or Adam Smith. The *Wealth of Nations* appeared after his economic work was done. There is nothing in any of his writings to indicate that he knew anything about this great work.

There is but one topic of any length and importance, in all of Tucker's writings, which he has taken almost bodily from the writings of another man. This is a plan for a single tax, taken from an anonymous pamphlet.[3] He presents this plan simply for its interest as an ideal tax-system,

[1] It is extremely unlikely that the plagiarized portions of Cantillon's *Essai* which appeared in Postlethwayt's *Universal Dictionary of Trade and Commerce* (1751, 1st ed.), exercised any influence upon Tucker.

[2] In his letter to Tucker, dated Dec. 10, 1773, Turgot apologizes for writing in French saying that English is difficult for him and that a mutual friend, Mr. Bostock, may translate the letter for Tucker. See Turgot, *Oeuvres* (Paris, 1810), vol. ix, p. 370.

[3] *An Essay on the Causes and Decline of Foreign Trade*, London, 1744. Printed for J. Brotherton. Quoted by Tucker in *Essay on Trade*, *3rd ed.*, pp. 124, 131, 133 and 148 to 168.

and he frankly acknowledges his debt and gives full credit [1] to the pamphlet.

The practical plan for taxation which Tucker advocates is very different from this ideal plan. This practical plan, which he proposed and consistently advocated as a practical system, was original with himself. He testifies directly upon this point. In the *Elements* he asks for the criticisms and suggestions of friends,[2] saying that he cannot hope to succeed, in the remainder of his planned work, without their aid,

> " especially that relating to taxes . . . . For indeed the reasons on the moral tendency and commericial use of proper taxes have never yet been exhibited to the public; or if they have, the author hath not been so happy as to meet with them; and therefore, since he must consider them as a *new system*, he would be the more desirous of producing it finished and complete etc." [3]

The evident conclusion from this consideration of the influence which economic writers, precedent and contemporary, had upon Tucker, is that he was very slightly indebted to them. A general impression left from reading the works of such writers may have given him his mercantilism and may have inspired his opposition to privileged companies; more probably it tended, as was the undoubted case with reference to Josiah Child's writings, to confirm him in views which he had culled from current thought or had worked out for himself. But whatever debt he may have

[1] See *Essay on Trade*, pp. 148 *et seq*, for this plan, and p. 149 for explicit acknowledgment of the source: "The scheme is taken out of a quarto pamphlet which would do honor to any man, etc."

[2] It will be remembered that only 50 or 60 copies of this first rough draft and outline of Tucker's great work were privately printed and circulated among friends for criticism, etc.

[3] *Elements*, p. 169.

owed, possibly, with reference to trade thought, his systematization of economics, with all of its expressed connotations, his emphasis upon self-interest, his taxation theories, his opposition to colonies, were clearly his own contributions. He appears to have been unusually independent of earlier writers. He certainly believed his system of economic thought to be original. In the *Advertisement* of the *Elements* he apologizes to the reader for his elaboration of every point, saying:

"as his manner of treating the subject is entirely new, he is obliged to be more explicit in setting it forth. For in a new system, everything must be proved, etc."

II. Reports, Statutes, &c.

Attention has already been called [1] to the fact that Tucker made frequent use of first-hand materials. A few examples may be here mentioned. When making his attack upon the privileged companies, he quoted freely from a report in the "3d of James I," by Sir Edward Sandys, giving reasons for destroying trade monopolies. The quotations and comments upon this report occupy twelve quarto pages,[2] the abstracts from the report serving as texts from which Tucker developes an entire argument against privileged companies.

There are many citations to such sources as *Journals of the House of Commons*, Townshend's *Historical Collections*, British Statutes, and the *British Merchant*.[3]

Tucker's warehouse scheme was adopted by him from a

[1] See *ante*, pp. 40, 41 and 95 to 103.

[2] *Elements*, pp. 155 to 167.

[3] He characterizes the *British Merchant* as a "Book . . . which will be remembered as long as any regard for commerce or love of our country shall remain." *Reflect. Nat. For. Prot.*, Part i, p. 55.

proposal for warehouses made by Sir Robert Walpole. Tucker commends the plan frankly as "Walpole's 'excise scheme.'"[1]

These are but illustrations. Tucker's works are replete with references to statutes, to parliamentary records, to reports of special commissions, to historical documents, and to historical collections. It is evident that he preferred to study records of facts and speeches, or documents, bearing directly upon public problems, rather than the opinions and speculations of economic writers.

III. Personal Observation.

Tucker's own personal observations furnished him much material and suggested to him much of his best thought. Bristol was a working laboratory in economics for him. He studied human nature very observantly; that he was habitually introspective is proven by his many statements of aims and interests. His analyses of wants and of self-interest, and his conclusion that self-interest is the supreme economic motive, are direct results of his study of human nature. The life of his works is born of reflection upon the facts of commercial and industrial life and of human nature, which he observed. Tucker was essentially a constructive student of life in his own world and in the world of history; he was not an echo author, who simply recast the ideas of other writers.

[1] *Elements*, p. 148.

CHAPTER II

INFLUENCE

TUCKER has not exercised much influence upon the development of economic thought. Two leading reasons may be given in explanation: I. Most of his writings were controversial pamphlets dealing with current questions. II. His more ambitious essays in the realms of economic science were never published.

I. CONTROVERSIAL PAMPHLETS

Tucker won recognition as an able advocate for a general naturalization law, for abolition of privileged trading companies, and for a peace policy. His reputation as an economic writer has been largely due to his pamphlets upon these themes.

The popular aversion to foreigners, the power of custom, and the strength of the London chartered companies, rendered almost fruitless the efforts, in the decade from 1750 to 1760, for naturalization and for destruction of trading monopolies; but the tracts and speeches of that decade strengthened the movement towards freedom in British industrial and commercial life, and contributed appreciably toward the ultimate success of that movement. As the leading English pamphleteer in favor of freedom, in that ten years, Tucker had direct influence upon practical legislation, and both direct and indirect influence upon the development of the freedom idea; but it is doubtful if any later British economic writer of any consequence has been appreciably influenced in his thought-system by any of these mid-century pamphlets of Tucker. This is to be expected. That tracts, devoted to championing or to attacking particular bills or particular companies, under particular conditions, should be buried with their kind and their generation is most natural. If any live, it will be more probable that they live rather as landmarks than as means of inspiration. So it has been with these naturalization and anti-monopoly tracts of Tucker. They have been sometimes quoted, but have been quoted usually simply as good illustrations of the advance thought of their day.

Tucker's American tracts are political rather than economic. Their leading thesis is that Great Britain should cast off her ungrateful American colonies. It is true that the basic arguments, *viz.*, that war is ruinous to trade, and that goodness and cheapness of a nation's wares, and not its political relations, win markets for it, are economic; but the political conclusion looms larger than the economic premises.

What is true of the earlier pamphlets is true of these. They undoubtedly had their share of influence in reconciling the British mind to separation; but what direct influence upon the course of scientific thought-development is reasonably to be expected from a series of *Tracts* and *Letters* upon the subject-matter of a closed controversy? Their very titles, *Tracts* and *Letters*, and their avowedly controversial and apparently political character, have failed to attract the economic student, even if they have not caused him deliberately to pass by these writings.

II. Tucker's Scientific Works Unknown

Tucker's *Elements of Commerce* and his *Instructions for Travellers* were never published. They give his leading thoughts upon economics. In main part, they are not controversial, but impartially scientific in character. They contain some advances upon current ideas, and probably would have contributed to an earlier and a better systematization of economic thought if they had been published. Their titles, and their scientific and avowedly economic character, would have attracted attention among economic writers. The fact is, that they do not appear to have been known, except by the friends to whom Tucker sent them for criticism. Among these friends there seems to have been no one who won reputation as an economic writer. This distribution of the few privately printed copies of each of the above works was made in the years 1755 and 1757. Each friend was requested to return his volume, with marginal comments, to Tucker, within a few months. Since this request was probably respected, it is exceedingly doubtful if any of the leading economic writers of the seventy-five years following 1755 ever read either the *Elements* or the *Instructions,* for Tucker never prosecuted the work any further, and had no reason for redistributing these first drafts. They probably remained in his hands for the forty years following, and then perished in the irreverent ridding up after his death.

That these works were unknown to economic writers of the half century immediately following 1755 seems the more probable when it is considered that, despite the patient and painstaking research in the field of the history of economics, during the past two generations, there is very little now known, among economists, of either of these works. So far as the writer has been able to learn, there are but three copies of each of these works extant.[1] The meagerness of

[1] The British Museum Library has a copy each of the *Elements* and the *Instructions;* the New York Public Library (Astor division) has a copy of the *Elements* with a number of marginal notes in Tucker's own

knowledge of these works is most strikingly evidenced by the fact that writers of histories of economics do not mention them. McCulloch, in his *Literature of Political Economy*, does not even list the *Instructions* among Tucker's works, and he says of the *Elements*, that its principles are identical with those of Tucker's other writings, and that the " theory of taxation is not touched upon." The facts are, that the *Elements* is the only one of Tucker's writings that clearly attempts to present a science of economics, and that its closing pages outline Tucker's taxation theory. Neither Blanqui, in his *History of Political Economy*, nor Cossa, in his *Introduction to Political Economy*, mentions either the *Elements* or the *Instructions*. Ingram, in his *History of Political Economy*, mentions neither of these works, and dismisses Tucker with the statement that his " works (are) deficient in permanent interest."

Influence on English Economics

The above facts and reasons show why Tucker had little or no direct influence upon the development of English economics, as it is to be traced through the masters. Biographers for encyclopædiæ have insisted upon repeating the tale that Tucker was a commercial writer of some merit. Occasionally an economist has read one of Tucker's tracts and has selected a quotation for later use. Quotations from Tucker have been noticeably more frequent in the recent years of developing interest in the study of the history of economic thought. It is notable, however, that neither James Anderson, in his tracts, nor Adam Smith, in his

hand; and Professor Edwin R. A. Seligman of Columbia University, has a copy of the *Instructions* in his extensive and valuable private library of economics and political science. Professor H. S. Foxwell of Cambridge, England, has a copy of each of these works in his rich collection of eighteenth century English pamphlets.

Wealth of Nations, make any reference to Tucker or to his works, while Malthus has one[1] passing reference only, in his *Essay*. Tucker does not appear to have influenced these men, and in the course of its real development since 1770, English economic thought has taken the treatises of Anderson, Smith and Malthus as starting-points. The reasonable conclusion appears to be that Tucker's *direct* influence in the evolution of English economic thought is nearly negligible.

On the other hand, Tucker must be accredited with a considerable *indirect* influence upon the development of British economics. Through his advocacy of economic freedom in relatively ephemeral, but, at the time, highly influential,[2] tracts, published intermittently during fifty years, through his sermons and conversations,[3] and through his correspondences,[4] Tucker undoubtedly helped to create and to ex-

[1] *Essay on Population, 3rd ed.*, vol. ii, p. 441, barely refers to Tucker's opinion that friendly societies should be voluntary.

[2] The tract *Reflect. on Expediency of Opening Trade to Turkey*, written by Tucker in 1753, aroused action against the Turkey Trading Company. Voluntary subscriptions were raised in Bristol and Liverpool to war against this company, and petitions were sent in from many places. June 24, 1754, Parliament, in response, opened the Turkey trade to any citizen of Great Britain on payment of £20. See *Appendix to 2nd Edition* of this tract (1755) for Tucker's account of this movement against the Turkey trading monopoly.

[3] Tucker's letter of May 11, 1755, commends to Dr. Birch a young nobleman Mr. Combes, and a young clergyman, his stepson, Mr. Woodward, and says that these young men are pupils of his, in a sense, and agree with him upon all commercial topics. See Birch Mss. (4319, vol. xx, p. 818) in British Mus. Library.

[4] Tucker's correspondences and conversations with Lord Hardwicke, Townshend and Nugent [with the latter of whom he was intimate for many years] evidence his probable influence upon British politicians; his correspondences with Hume and Kames evidence his probable influence on British men of letters; his correspondences and conversations with Dr. Birch and Dr. Forster evidence his probable influence upon the British clergy.

tend the demand for larger commercial and industrial freedom. He helped to prepare the British mind for a readier reception of the teachings of a *Wealth of Nations*. Inasmuch as he helped to shape the British commercial mind from 1750 until 1785, and the later writings of others were but expressions of this mind, he may be said to have indirectly influenced later British writers.

Influence on the Physiocrats

Tucker exercised a measure of direct influence upon Turgot and upon the Physiocrats.

The direct correspondence between Tucker and Turgot did not begin until 1770; but years before this Turgot had translated two of Tucker's tracts. He was but twenty-six years old when he translated the first one, a tract on *Naturalization*, and it is altogether probable that Tucker's thought aided in shaping the young man's economic ideas.

Turgot's first letter to Tucker, in 1770, does not directly acknowledge any such influence, although it is very complimentary in tone. Turgot states that he had translated, some years before, Tucker's *Naturalization of Foreign Protestants, Part II*,[1] and his tract, *The Case of Going to War for the Sake of Trade*.[2] He sends Tucker a copy of his *Reflections*, &c., as a part " of the homage a translator owes to his author." He says the *Reflections* will bring to Tucker no new idea, for they have the same ideas of the principles of liberty and of the important economic aims. He credits Tucker with being the only author in a nation which allows freedom of the press, who " perceived the advantage of free

[1] *Questions Importantes sur le Commerce, etc.*, 1755. See *Biographie Universelle*, vol. xlii, p. 240.

[2] 1765. See *Nouvelle Biographie Générale*, vol. xlv, p. 691.

trade, and had not been seduced by the puerility and hopeful illusion of exclusive commerce." [1]

Tucker's direct influence upon the Physiocratic school is unquestionable. Besides these two tracts translated by Turgot, Frenchmen had a chance to read the essence of Tucker's *Essay on Trade,* in their own language, and prior to the beginning of the physiocratic publications. In 1754 Plumard d'Angeul brought out his *Remarques sur les Avantages et les Désavantages de la France et de la Grande Bretagne par rapport au Commerce,* &c. This is, in large part, a free paraphrase [2] of Tucker's *Essay on Trade.* Mr. Henry Higgs notes that this tract of Plumard d'Angeul "was constantly present to Quesnay's mind in writing the article *Fermiers,* and was quoted," and that Gournay recommends Tucker as an economic writer of merit.[3]

[1] See *Oeuvres de Turgot* (Paris, 1810), vol. ix, pp. 366–375, for two letters to Tucker. The above statements are taken from the letter dated Sept. 12, 1770.

[2] An English translation appeared in London in the same year (1754) entitled *Remarks on the Advantages and Disadvantages of France and Great Britain with Respect to Commerce.* It purported to be written by John Nickolls. In the preface the author makes the following express acknowledgment of his indebtedness to Tucker: "I hope that Mr. Josiah Tucker, a worthy clergyman of Bristol and at the same time an eminent patriot, will without offence see some of his ideas amongst mine. I borrowed from his essay upon Commerce the title which I have given to these remarks; I have taken from it almost word for word my first seven paragraphs by way of necessary introduction to my work; in short, he it was, who inspired me with the resolution of travelling and of making observations; and I pay to him homage of the fruits thereof with pleasure and gratitude." Tucker in his *Instructions* recommends to his traveler this volume. He says of it: "This tract is in a great measure a translation of my *Essay on Trade* and other commercial pieces. But as the author is a native of France, viz., the Marquis D'Angeul, tho appearing under the borrowed name of an Englishman, Sir John Nickolls, he was capable of making great improvements on my plan, etc." *Instruct. for Trav.*, p. 9.

[3] See *The Physiocrats* (pp. 15, 31, 67), by Mr. Henry Higgs.

Aside from these French translations of Tucker, it must be remembered that Tucker's *Essay on Trade* had passed to its third edition in 1753, and that his tracts on spirituous liquors, on naturalization, and on the trade with Turkey, had all been published by the year 1753. Those of the Physiocrats who could read English thus had opportunity to be influenced by seven different economic tracts, written and published by Tucker at least two years prior to the appearance of the first Physiocratic work. These facts make a clear case that Tucker exercised a measurable influence upon the Physiocratic school, rather than that he was a satellite of theirs, as Blanqui seems to imply.[1]

[1] See *History of Political Economy*, p. 364, where Blanqui says that Tucker "belonged to the shade of Gournay."

CHAPTER III

CONCLUSIONS

Two theses may now be stated:

I. *Josiah Tucker deserves a creditable rank among English economic writers. He should receive more consideration than he has heretofore been given when English economists are being treated.*

He was the first English writer to attempt to present a scientific system of economics. He was the first to approach economics as a psychologist: he began with a study of human wants and made self-interest the central economic thread. Tucker, the scientific economic theorist, is far more interesting than Tucker the pamphleteer, far more deserving of credit, and far less known.

It seems unnecessary, after the extended presentation of Tucker's economic system in *Part II,* to make an elaborate argument here: the review of his works in *Part II* substantiates this first thesis. In simple summary of the more striking parts of Tucker's economic thought, it may be noted that he saw clearly and presented well:

(1) The possibility of a science of economics.

(2) That self-interest is the supreme economic motive.

(3) That an analysis of human wants is a proper starting-point for a study of economics.

(4) The relation of economics to ethics.

(5) That in economic reasoning due allowance must be made for the natural and the social environment.

(6) The evils of monopolies generally, and of chartered trading companies in particular.

(7) That the Navigation Act was an objectionable monopoly.

(8) The philosophy of exchange.

(9) The advantages of machinery.

(10) That slave labor is uneconomic.

(11) The infant-industry argument.

(12) The advantages of enclosure of commons.

(13) The national disadvantages from distant colonies.

(14) The conduct-regulating function of taxes.

(15) The error of the bullionist.

(16) The error of usury laws.

(17) The error of trade jealousy between nations.

(18) The economic condemnation of war.

II. *Tucker's writings illustrate the fact that the ideas developed in the Wealth of Nations were Zeitgeist thoughts.*

Smith did not influence Tucker in any way. It is extremely unlikely that Smith ever saw either the *Elements* or the *Instructions*, and there is no reason to believe that he had ever given any attention to Tucker's controversial pamphlets. Considering that these two writers had little or no direct influence upon one another, it is of interest to note the large number of points upon which they agree. Among such common points are:

(1) Discussion of the advantages of a division of labor.

(2) A labor theory of value.

(3) Cosmopolitanism.

(4) Insistence that both agriculture and manufacture should be developed and encouraged.

(5) Approval of education of common people in charity schools.

(6) Admission that exclusive companies may be justified in initiating a trade.

(7) Opposition to the particular trading companies then in existence.

(8) Opposition to the Apprenticeship Act.

(9) Opposition to the bullionist view.

(10) Advocacy of the warehouse scheme.

(11) Approval of a union between Great Britain and Ireland.

(12) Argument that a high tax is not necessarily a heavy tax.

(13) Objection to the existent taxes on salt, soap, candles and leather.

(14) Approval of fixed tax upon land.

(15) Advocacy of ability-to-pay tax criterion.

The fact that Tucker did not anywhere fully elaborate his views upon taxes and upon money and banking, lessens the number of common points that may be shown in their thought.

Tucker and Smith disagree in a number of points, and not always to Smith's advantage, *e. g.*, Tucker opposed the Navigation Act, consistently applying his anti-monopoly principle. The chief point upon which they disagree is the proper extent of trade freedom. Tucker was a mercantilist. Adam Smith's pre-eminent contribution was a clear argument for full trade freedom. They appear to be far apart in their thought upon this subject; but it is interesting to observe that, although Tucker fell short in his practical policy, he was far on the way toward the full freedom-of-trade conclusion. Probably, had not the chartered companies of London so aroused him as an outport citizen that he gave his best efforts towards the abolition of company privileges, he would have taken the full step and advocated trade freedom in the modern sense. The many suggestions, illustrations, and even complete arguments, that lead irresistibly to free trade, to be found in Tucker's works,[1] make it seem

[1] See *ante*, pp. 158 to 160, for these suggestions and arguments.

passing strange that he did not, with his finely logical mind, arrive at that general conclusion. But the very fact that a reader expresses wonder that Tucker did not become a full free-trader, is proof that he had in hand the materials out of which the full free-trade thought is made. In other words, the fact indicates that the time was fully ripe for the free-trader. There was needed a mind similar to Tucker's in its historical grip and its logical acumen, but unthwarted by distractions in the shape of current problems of large local interest which called for only half-way free-trade measures fully to remedy them. Such a mind, so calmly environed, would take the final step and present the world an invincible free-trade argument. This mind and this environment were Adam Smith's. So the very point upon which Smith at first thought seems so far in advance of Tucker, proves, carefully considered, to be only a further illustration of the second thesis, viz., that Tucker's economic writings are evidence that the ideas marshalled in the *Wealth of Nations* were in the air. The seeming leap from the modified mercantilism of Tucker's writings to the full free trade of Smith resolves itself into a final very short, but very essential, step taken by Smith.

APPENDIX

SKELETON OF TUCKER'S GREAT WORK*[1]

Advertisement.

A preliminary discourse setting forth the natural disposition, or instinctive inclination, of mankind towards commerce.

The Elements of Commerce and Theory of Taxes.[2]

INTRODUCTION.

PART I.[3] CONTAINING CERTAIN POLITIES FOR INCREASING THE NUMBER OF PEOPLE.

CHAPTER I. A polity for the encouragement of the married state.

CHAPTER II. A polity for the admission of wealthy and industrious foreigners.

[1] When *Mss.* marginal notes by Tucker are referred to in footnotes to this skeleton, the references are to the Copy of the *Elements* in the New York Public Library (Astor division).

[2] Mss. note by Tucker changes this title to read, "*The Moral and Political Theory of Trade and Taxes.*"

[3] A *Mss.* note changes this *Part I* to *Book I.*

CHAPTER III. Other polities for increasing the number of people.

PART II. CONTAINING CERTAIN POLITIES FOR THE EXTENSION AND IMPROVEMENT OF COMMERCE.

CHAPTER I. Certain polities for encouraging and improving husbandry.

Sec. I. A polity for dividing large estates.

Sec. II. A polity for enclosing commons and common fields.

Sec. III. A polity for changing tithes into glebe.

Sec. IV. A polity for increasing buildings in low, fenny or marshy ground, and rendering them healthy.

Sec. V. A polity for creating a plenty of timber.

Sec. VI. A polity for registering the title-deeds of houses and landed estates.

CHAPTER II. Certain polities for the increase and improvements of manufactures.

Sec. I. A polity for opening such exclusive companies as relate principally to our home trade, or domestic commerce.

Sec. II. A polity for opening those exclusive companies which relate to foreign trade.

An Appendix to the first and second sections of the chapter on Manufactures.

Outline theory of taxes.[1]

Sec. III. A polity for improving our colonies, and

[1] All of the *Skeleton* that precedes this point is an outline of what in full first draft composes the *Elements* as this volume was privately printed and circulated among Tucker's friends. All of the *Skeleton* that follows is the outline which he intended later to have fully developed.

extending the trade between them and the mother country, to their mutual advantage.

Sec. IV. A polity for making all ports free and easing trade of several burdens.

Sec. V. A polity for suppressing smuggling.

Sec. VI. A polity for a sure and expeditious manning of the fleet without pressing.

Sec. VII. A polity for making good roads, navigable rivers, and canals.[1]

Sec. VIII. A polity for establishing a uniformity of weights and measures throughout the kingdom.

Sec. IX. A polity for a perfect incorporation with Ireland.[2]

CHAPTER III. On coin and credit as the mediums of commerce.

Sec. I. On the nature and circulation of human industry.

Sec. II. On the rise and origin, the use and necessity, of some medium, deposit, or certificate whereby the exchange of the produce of one man's labor may be facilitated for that of another—and that this medium, deposit, or certificate is what we call money.

[1] In N. Y. Public Library (Astor division) copy of the *Elements* occurs a marginal note, written in Tucker's own hand, under this section: "A canal a public road in times of peace, a fortification in times of war."

[2] Marginal note in Tucker's hand suggests additions of:

A polity for defensive strength and security at home. By land enlisting regulars for 5 years; then disbanding them and incorporating with the militia of each county. Independent companies of light horse. Every sergeant and corporal as well as superior officer on horse or foot to be capable of searching for and seizing upon *run* goods imported, in the same manner as custom house officer or excise man. By sea, 12 stations; 3 ships at each station. These to be applied likewise to prevent smuggling.

A polity for civilizing "ye" Indians and preserving peace in "ye" colonies.

Sec. III. On the true meaning of the relative terms, market-price and values of commodities, cheapness, dearness, scarcity, plenty, &c., &c.

Sec. IV. The reasons assigned why gold and silver are found preferable to other metals for the purposes of making them into money; and how far a paper certificate may as truly become money as pieces of the metals of gold and silver.

Sec. V. What is intrinsic in these metals and what is more properly relative, viz.: the intrinsics of gold and silver are size, weight, and fineness; the relatives are the several proportions of the weight and fineness of the coins in one country compared with those of another; and from these comparisons results that imaginary coin, or medium between the two, called the par of exchange. After this comparison with foreign coins, whether gold or silver, there is a secondary, or domestic, comparison, which has a universal influence, though little attended to, viz., the domestic proportion between gold and silver, whether set higher or lower than it is in other countries.

Sec. VI. On the doctrine of exchanges and the nature of banking, illustrated by familiar ideas taken from common life and then applied.

Sec. VII. Reasons for increasing the quantity of metal money and the polities for so doing.[1]

Sec. VIII. Reasons for changing a considerable part

[1] Tucker's marginal *Mss*. note: "The proprietors of plate the only horders—a polity proposed for melting down plate. Permission given the universities and all public companies to convert such plate as they deem useless into money. The colleges in the universities to lay out this money in augmenting small livings in their gift, building or repairing parsonage houses—companies in mending high roads, building bridges, widening narrow passes, etc."

of the dead national debt into circulating certificates or paper money; and a scheme proposed whereby every man in the kingdom may receive interest every moment for his money and become his own banker; so that the national debt shall become the most advantageous institution to commerce, manufactures, agriculture and general industry that ever existed.

PART III. A SYSTEM OF POLITIES FOR THE PRESERVATION AND IMPROVEMENT OF GOOD MORALS.

DISSERTATION I. On the connection and entire harmony between national commerce, good morals, and good government, that they all promote each other; nay, that they are but parts of one general scheme, in the designs of Providence, though considered by us as separate and distinct, and sometimes as unconnected.

DISSERTATION II. That as commerce must be under the guidance of good morals, the rules of good morals are, therefore, applied to regulate these artificial wants of mankind which are the bases of commerce. And these reasonings illustrated by plain facts and examples. Polities proposed.

Sec. I. Proved, that all the former polities relating to the increase of mankind, Part I, are useful to good morals.

Sec. II. Proved, that all the former polities relating to national industry and the right employment of time, Part II, are productive of the same effect.

Sec. III. A polity for superintending all public places of expense, pleasure and diversion.

Sec. IV. A polity for securing those trades to the female sex which are fittest for their condition.

Sec. V. A polity for preventing the present bad effects of electioneering.[1]

Sec. VI. A polity for preventing national perjury.

Sec. VII. A polity for clearing the streets of street-walkers, for the well-regulating of jails and Bridewells, and for making executions less frequent, but more decent and solemn.

Sec. VIII. An annual survey and register of inhabitants.

PART IV. A SYSTEM OF TAXES PREVENTIVE OF IDLENESS, EXTRAVAGANCE, &C., PROMOTIVE OF GOOD MORALS, AND PRODUCTIVE OF NATIONAL INDUSTRY, WEALTH AND PLENTY.

Sec. I. A dissertation on the nature, reason and use of taxes.

Sec. II. Rules for judging whether any tax proposed is bad, innocent, or good. These principles applied to our present system, viz.:

[1] *Mss.* note by Tucker:

"All freedoms of towns corporate to remain untouched any farther than they are affected by some of the preceding polities. But in regard to the election of members of Parliament, confine that wholly to landed property. The reason to be given afterwards. The Quantum to be £6 per annum, the same qualification as that for jurymen. The consequence of this regulation would be, that lands of £4 or £5 per year value would be better cultivated in order to be worth £6. That houses within cities or towns corporate would become very desirable and objects of great attention. That every tradesman capable of purchasing a house would be sure of buying one, in order to be of the rank of voters. Thus, the freeholds in cities and towns corporate would be greatly multiplied, and as these houses for the most part would be occupied by their owners, old houses would be rebuilt, new ones erected, and all made to wear a better face than they now do. In order to avoid collusion, the house or lands entitling to a freehold must have been rated to the land tax."

Sec. III. Such taxes as ought to be continued *in statu quo*.

Sec. IV. Such as ought to be augmented.

Sec. V. Such new taxes as ought to be laid on.

Sec. VI. Such as ought to be lessened.

Sec. VII. Such as ought to be totally abolished.

Sec. VIII. Such bounties, drawbacks, or premiums as ought to be added, increased, lessened, withdrawn.

Sec. IX. Regulations for the most frugal methods of collecting the revenue, and the most serviceable to trade and industry.

PART V.[1] MISCELLANEOUS REFLECTIONS AND OBSERVATIONS.

Sec. I. Such vulgar errors exposed relating to trade as were not particularly confuted in the foregoing treatise.[2]

[1] *Mss.* note of Tucker changes this to read *Book V.*

[2] *Mss.* marginal notes by Tucker give a list of the errors he desired to confute: "1. Vulgar Error: That money is riches, and that mere spending of money in a country is a good thing for that country. 2. Do. (i. e. Vulgar Error): That rival nations cannot all flourish at the same time; that poor nations will draw away trade from rich; that low wages create cheap manufactures. 3. Do: That slavery is necessary in the colonies. 4. Do: That colonies are essentially necessary to trade. 5. Do: That companies of trade at home and of merchant adventurers abroad were originally necessary, tho' allowed to be not so now. 6. Do: That the principles of commerce can only be understood by commercial people. [In the *Essay on Trade*, *Preface*, p. x, Tucker says that the person of liberal education "is better fitted for the study of the *Science* than the merchant himself, because his mind is freer from the prejudice of self-interest and therefore more open to conviction in things relating to the general good."] 7. Do: That luxuries are beneficial to trade. 8. Do: That we ought to imitate the antient Greeks and Romans (see Lit. Liv. Lib. I, 59, Romanos homines, etc.). On the contrary the Romans under their little petty kings when the Roman territory was not half as big as Yorkshire, were richer than the inhabi-

Sec. II. Rules for judging of the increase or decrease of trade in general, and of any branch of it in particular.

Sec. III. Rules for setting up any new branch of trade, merchandise, or manufacture.

Sec. IV. General directions to travelers, whether through our own or in foreign countries, viz.: what questions to ask, relating to civil, religious, or commercial liberty; the tenure of lands, different holdings and jurisdictions, nature of governments, courts of justice, tendency of taxes, and the like; and what inferences to make from the respective answers; how to judge of the genius of a people from their political constitution, and *vice versa;* how to account for the decay or improvement of trade, manufactures, agriculture, husbandry, &c.; of the increase or diminution of the numbers of people; also a true method of finding out the comparative riches or poverty of the state or country through which you travel. [*Instructions for Travellers* developed this plan.]

Sec. V. The whole science and systems of commerce reduced into a series of short maxims or aphorisms. The conclusion.

tants of Rome under Augustus Caesar—Proof. Money got by conquest is like money got by privateering—Proof. 9. Do: For the populousness of antient Judea."

BIBLIOGRAPHY

I. TUCKER'S WORKS[1]

1. Queries and Arguments Addressed to Mr. Whitefield Concerning Methodism.

An article published in the *London Mag.*, vol. iii (1739), pp. 340–343.

2. / A Brief / History / Of the / Principles / of / Methodism / Wherein / The Rise and Progress, together with / the Causes of the several Varia- / tions, Divisions, and present In / consistencies of this Sect are attempted to be traced out, and / accounted for. / By Josiah Tucker M. A. Vicar of All Saints, / and one of the Minor Canons of the College / of Bristol. / Oxford, / Printed for James Fletcher: and sold by S. Rivington in / St. Paul's Church yard, London: and the Booksellers at / Bristol. MDCCXLII. / 8° 51 pp.

3. / A Calm Address to all Parties in Religion / concerning Disaffection to the present Govern / ment.

A tract first published in 1745. "A New Edition Corrected and Enlarged" appeared as an *Appendix to Part II of Reflect. on Nat. For. Prot.* pp. 49–68 in 1752.

4. / Hospitals and Infirmaries, considered as / Schools of Christian Education for the adult / Poor and as Means conducive towards a / National Reformation in the Common People. / A / Sermon / Preached in the / Parish-Church / Of / St. James in Bristol, / Before / The Contributors to the Support / of the Bristol Infirmary, at their Anniversary / Meeting, held the 18th of March, 1745. / By Josiah Tucker, A. M. / Vicar of All Saints, in Bristol. / Published by the Desire of the Subscribers for the / Perusal of the Patients of the said Infirmary. / London: / Printed for William Cassley, Bookseller / in Bristol. MDCCXLVI. / 8° pp. 66–89 of *Six Sermons*.

Reprinted as *Sermon VI* of the *Six Sermons* and of the *Seventeen Sermons*.

[1] Endeavor has been made to give, in lists I and III of this Bibliography, an exhaustive bibliography of Tucker's works, so far as they can be well authenticated, and of his correspondences. It is perhaps too much to hope that the attempt has been wholly successful. See *ante*, pp. 48 to 70, for further bibliographical comment than is given in the following list of Tucker's Works.

5. / Two / Dissertations / On certain Passages of / Holy Scripture / Viz, the First / on Luke xiv, 12, 13, 14. / And the Second / on Rom. xiii, 1, 2, 3, 4. / Wherein the Cavils and Objections of the Late / Mr. Chubb, in the First Volume of his / Posthumous Works, viz., *Remarks on the Scriptures*, are particularly considered and refuted / By Josiah Tucker, A. M. / Vicar of *All Saints* in *Bristol*, / London, / Printed for T. Trye, near *Gray's Inn Gate*, in Holborn, / and Sold by J. Fletcher in Oxford, Mr. W. / Thurlborne in Cambridge, Mess Leak and / Frederick at Bath, and by the Book / sellers at Bristol. MDCCXLIX. / [Price one Shilling.] / 8° 59 pp.

6. A / Brief Essay / On The / Advantages and Disadvantages / which Respectively Attend / France / And / Great Britain, / With Regard To / Trade / By Josiah Tucker, D. D. / Dean of Gloucester / London: / Printed for John Stockdale, / Opposite Burlington-House, Piccadilly. / MDCCLXXXVII. / xvi+53 pp.

This is the *5th Edition* of the *Essay*. 1st Edition, 1749; 2d, 1750; 3d with an appendix enlarging it to 168 pp, 1753; 4th Edition, Glasgow, 1756. The "3d Edition corrected" is reprinted in McCulloch's *Tracts*, 1859. Reviewed in *Monthly Rev.*, Vol. lxxvii (1787).

7. / An Impartial / Inquiry / Into The / Benefits and Damages / Arising to the Nation from the Present / very great Use of Low Priced / Spiritous Liquors / With / Proper Estimates thereupon, and some / Considerations humbly offered for preventing / the Introduction of Foreign Spirits not paying / the Duties. / By J. T. of Bristol. / Author of the Brief Essay on the Advantages / and Disadvantages which respectively attend / France and Great Britain, with regard to Trade. / London. / Printed for T. Trye, near Gray's Inn Gate. / Holborn, 1751. / [Price Six-Pence] / 8°, 33 pp.

8. / Reflections / On The / Expediency of a Law / For The / Naturalization / Of / Foreign Protestants / In Two Parts / Part I / Containing Historical Remarks on the / Disposition and Behaviour of the Natives of / This Island, in regard to Foreigners; occasioned / by the Rejection of the late Naturalization Bill. / By Josiah Tucker, M. A. / Rector of St. Stephen's in Bristol, / And / Chaplain to the Right Reverend the / Lord Bishop of Bristol. / London: / Printed for T. Trye, near Gray's Inn Gate, Holborn. / MDCCLI. / [Price One Shilling] / 8° vii + 72 pp.

Reviewed in *Monthly Rev.*, vol. v (Dec., 1751), p. 523.

9. / Reflections / On The / Expediency of a Law / For The / Naturalization / Of Foreign Protestants: / In Two Parts / Part II / Containing Important Queries Relating to Com / merce,—The Employment of the Poor;—The / Landed and National Interest,—

Taxes of All / Kinds, particularly the Poor Tax,—The real / Interest of Tradesmen,—Reformation of Mo / rals,—Constitution both in Church and State, / The Duties of Humanity, and the Principles of / the Christian Religion. / By Josiah Tucker, M. A. / Rector of St. Stephen's in Bristol, / And / Chaplain to the Right Reverend the / Lord Bishop of Bristol, / London: / Printed for T. Trye, near Gray's Inn Gate, Holborn, / MDCCLII. / 8° xv + 68 pp.

Reviewed in *Monthly Rev.*, vol. vi (Apr., 1752), p. 265.

10. / Reflections / On The / Expediency / Of / Opening the Trade / To / Turkey. / Humbly offer'd to Publick Consideration. / By a Sincere Well-wisher to the Trade and / Prosperity of Great Britain. / Tros Tyriusque mihi nullo Discrimine agetur. Virg. / Printed / For T. Trye, Near Gray's Inn-Gate In / Holborn, London. MDCCLIII / [Price Three Pence] / 8° 22 pp.

A 2d Edition was published in 1755, to which a 12 pp. *Appendix* was added. Reviewed in *Monthly Rev.*, vol. viii (Feb., 1753), p. 147.

11. / An Earnest and Affectionate / Address / to the / Common People / of / England / Concerning their / Usual Recreations / on / Shrove Tuesday / London / Printed for J. F. and C. Rivington Book / Sellers to the Society For Promoting / Christian Knowledge, N° 62, St. Paul's / Churchyard, 1787. / [Price 4s. per Hundred to give away]/. 12°, 6 pp.

A Second Edition.

The first edition of this tract was first written in 1753 or earlier. It is advertised T. Trye's edition of *Reflections on Expediency of Opening the Trade to Turkey, 1753.*

12. / A / Letter / To A / Friend / Concerning / Naturalizations: Shewing, / I What Naturalization is *not;* / II What it *is;* / III What are the Motives for the present Cla- / mours against the Bill passed last Sessions for / enabling the Parliament to naturalize such Jews, / as they shall approve of. / IV Setting forth the Nature of this Affair consi / dered in a Religious Light. / V Proposing a Scheme for the Prevention of all / future Naturalizations, by explaining, how the / same Ends may be obtained in a Way much / more efficacious and altogether Popular. / With a Hint relating to the *Orphan* Fund in the / City of *London.* / By Josiah Tucker, M. A. / Rector of St. Stephen's in Bristol / And / Chaplain to the Right Rev. the Lord Bishop of Bristol. / London: / Printed for Thomas Trye, near Gray's Inn Gate, / Holborn. MDCCLIII / [Price, Sixpence] /

A "Second Edition, corrected" the same year. A complete *MSS.* of this *Letter* is in the Library Brit. Museum, *MSS.* 4207, 2. Not in Tucker's hand, but marginal notes are. Reviewed in *Monthly Review*, vol. iv (Oct., 1753), p. 317.

13. A Second / Letter / To A / Friend / Concerning / Naturalizations: / Wherein / The Reasons are given why the Jews were an- / tiently considered as the immediate Vassals / and absolute property of the Crown; but / are now in a State of Liberty and / Freedom like other Subjects. / To which are added, / The Opinions of the most eminent Lawyers, toge / ther with Proofs and Argument drawn from divers important Facts and Statutes of the / Realm relating to the same Subject. / By Josiah Tucker, A. M. / Rector of St. Stephen's in Bristol, / And / Chaplain to the Right Rev., the Lord Bishop of Bristol. / London / Printed for Thomas Trye, near Gray's Inn Gate / Holborn. MDCCLIII / [Price Six pence] / 8° 44 pp.

14. A full and true Account of many, barbarous, bloody and inhuman Murders, &c. 1753.

A reply to charges of *London Evening Post* that Jews crucified infants, &c. Tucker mentions this article in a letter to Dr. Thos. Birch, Sept. 20, 1753, and says it is to appear in the *General Evening Post*. See British Museum Library MSS. 4319, vol. xx, 818.

15. REASONS against chusing Mr. Nugent.

A Folio tract of one page, dated at Bristol, Mar. 23, 1754. One of the election tracts. See Library Brit. Museum, *MSS*, 4319, vol. xx, 818.

16. / Reasons / for preferring Sir —— /

A Bristol Election tract dated Mar. 29, 1754. Sir John Phillips was Mr. Nugent's opponent in this election. See Library Brit. Museum, *MSS*, 4319, vol. xx, 818.

17. / Great News from Rome! / Being / The Pope's Bull in favor of the High / Flyer, against N——t, the Heretic. / Translated into English for the Benefit of the Gentlemen of W. L——n C——b. /

A Bristol election tract of 1754. A Pretended Excommunication of Nugent addressed to a political club, the White Lion Club. In a letter to Dr. Birch of Mar. 30, 1754, Tucker says that he sent the above tract and a similar one in the guise of *A Letter from King James*. The latter is not preserved in the *Birch MSS*, which see, for the above, Library Brit. Museum, *MSS*, 4319, vol. xx, 818.

18. A Solemn and Earnest Appeal to the Worthy and Loyal Citizens of Bristol. Apr. 2, 1754, Bristol.

A tract in the Bristol Election Controversy, advocating Nugent's cause. See *Birch MSS*, British Museum Library, *MSS*, 4319, vol. xx, 818.

19. / A full Answer to a fallacious Apology, / detecting the many gross Prevarications in the said Per / formance, and / Vindicating the Character of an eminent Gentleman from being the / Author of it. /

A Bristol Election Tract, 1754.

See Library Brit. Museum, *MSS*, 4319, vol. xx, 818. Also printed in the *Bristol Weekly Intelligencer* of Saturday, Apr. 13, 1754.

20. The Mountains in Labor, / To The / Worthy Electors / Of / Bristol / Folio, 3pp. Bristol, 1754.

One of the tracts of the Bristol Election of 1754. See Library Brit. Museum, *MSS*, 4319, vol. xx, 818.

21. The "Challenge about Jasen."

A newspaper article referred to by Tucker in a letter to Dr. Thos. Birch, dated Oct. 30, 1754. See British Museum Library *MSS*, 4319, vol. xx, 818.

22. / The / Important Question / Concerning // Invasions / A Sea War // Raising the Militia // And Paying / Subsidies for Foreign Troops; / Fairly and impartially stated on both Sides, / And / Humbly referred to the Judgement of the Public. / Being a new Edition of the Papers first published in the Evening Advertiser. / London. / Printed for R. Griffiths, at the Dunciad in / Paternoster Row. MDCCLV. / 8°, 64 pp.

This tract was listed as anonymous in the British Museum Library. It was identified, by the present writer, as Tucker's, from an acknowledgment of its authorship, made by him in a letter of Dec. 6, 1755, written to Dr. C. N. Forster. See Brit. Mus. Library, *MSS*, 11275.

23. / The / Elements of Commerce / And / Theory of Taxes. / Folio, 175 pp.

Privately printed. Dated July 10, 1755, at Bristol. Fifty or sixty copies were sent to friends with the request that they be returned with critical notes on the wide margins left for that purpose. The work is very rare. Only three copies are extant, so far as the present writer can learn. One of these is in the British Museum Library; one is in the New York Public Library, Astor Division; and one is in Professor H. S. Foxwell's Collection of Economic Works.

24. / The / Case / of the / Importation / of / Bar Iron / from our own / Colonies of North America; / Humbly recommended to the Conside / ration of the present Parliament by / the Iron Manufacturers of / Great Britain. / London / Printed for Thomas Trye; near Gray's Inn Gate, Holborn / MDCCLVI / [Price sixpence.] / 8°, 29 pp.

25. / A Short and Familiar Way of explaining the important Doctrine of / *Justification* and the Points dependent on it, agreeably to Scrip / ture, and the Church of England. /

A Tract addressed "To the Inhabitants of the Parish of St. Stephen in the City of Bristol . . . by their faithful pastor, Josiah Tucker. Date sometime prior to 1757. See Library Brit. Museum, *MSS*, 4319, vol. xx, 818.

26. / Instructions / For / Travellers / 1757. / 4°, 64 pp.

Only 50 or 60 copies were privately printed and circulated among friends with request that they be returned to Tucker with criticisms on the wide margins left for that purpose. The book is very rare now. So far as the writer can learn there are but three copies of it —one in the British Museum Library; one in the private library of Professor Edwin R. A. Seligman, in New York City, and one in the library of Professor H. S. Foxwell in Cambridge, Eng.

27. / The / Manifold Causes / Of the Increase of the / Poor / Distinctly set forth; / Together With / A Set of Proposals for removing and preventing some of / the Principal Evils, and for lessening Others. / 4°, vi + 42 pp.

The title page has no date, no name and no place; but the *Advertisement* is signed *Josiah Tucker*, and dated *May 26, 1760*, at *Glocester*.

28. / Improvements and Savings in Inland Na / vigations exemplified on the River / Stroud, in the County of Gloucester. /

An article published in { *Gent's Mag.*, vol. xxx (Apr., 1760), pp. 167–168. *Annual Reg.*, vol. iii (Apr., 1760), pp. 142–144. *London Mag.*, vol. xxix (Apr., 1760), pp. 192–194.

29. / The / Case / Of / Going to War / For the Sake of / Procuring Enlarging, or Securing / Of / Trade, / Considered in a New Light. / Being / A Fragment of a greater Work. / London: / Printed For R. And J. Dodsley, In Pall-Mall; And / L. Hawes, W. Clarke And R. Collins, At The / Red Lion, In Pater-Noster-Row. / MDCCLXIII. / 12°, 59 pp.

This was republished as *Tract II* of the *Four Tracts*.

30. / A / Sermon / Preached in the Parish-Church of / Christ-Church, London, / On *Wednesday*, May the 7th, 1766: / Being The Time of the Yearly Meeting of the Children Educated in the Charity / Schools, and in and about the Cities of *London* / and Westminster. / By Josiah Tucker, D. D. / Dean of Glocester. / *Published at the Request of the Gentlemen Concerned* / *in the said Charity* / To which is annexed / An Account of / The Society for promoting Christian Knowledge. / London: / Printed by J. and W. Oliver, Printers To The Said Society, in Bartholomew-Close; and Sold by / John Rivington, Bookseller, at the *Bible* and / *Crown* in *St. Paul's Churchyard*. / MDCCLXVI. / 4° 132 pp.

31. / An / Apology / For The / Present Church of *England*, / As by Law Established / Occasioned By A Petition / Said to be preparing by / Certain Clergymen, and Others, / To be laid before Parliament, / For / Abolishing Subscriptions, / In a Letter to one of the Petitioners. / By Josiah Tucker, D. D. / Dean of Glocester. / Glocester / Printed By R. Raikes. / MDCCLXXII. / 8°, 61 pp.

A second edition with very slight additions and corrections was published the same year. Title page same as above except that "said to be preparing by certain clergymen and others to be" is omitted and "The Second Edition, corrected" precedes "Josiah." Reviewed in *Monthly Rev.*, vol. xlvi (Feb., 1772), pp. 157–161, and in *London Mag.*, vol. xli (Feb., 1772), pp. 85–86.

32. / Six / Sermons / On / Important Subjects. / By Josiah Tucker, D. D. / Dean of Gloucester: / And Rector of St. Stephen, Bristol. / Bristol: / Printed by S. Farley, in *Castle Green*; and / Sold by her; the Booksellers in Bristol and Bath; / and by S. Bladon, in Paternoster Row, London. / MDCCLXXII. / [Price One Shilling and Six-pence] / 12°, viii + 91 pp.

These were republished as the first six sermons of the *Seventeen Sermons*. Reviewed in *Monthly Rev.*, xlviii (Jan., 1773), pp. 59 to 63.

33. / Letters / To The / Rev. Dr. Kippis, / Occasioned By His / Treatise / Entitled, / *A Vindication of the Protestant Dissenting / Ministers*, / With Regard To / Their late Application to Parliament. / By Josiah Tucker, D. D. / Dean of Glocester / Glocester / Printed By R. Raikes: / And Sold By / S. Bladon, In Pater-Noster-Row, London. / MDCCLXXIII. / 8° 135 pp.

Reviewed in *Monthly Rev.*, vol. xlviii (Mar., 1773), pp. 185–192.

34. / Religious Intolerance / No Part Of The / General Plan / Either Of The / Mosaic, or Christian Dispensation, / Proved By / Scriptural Inferences and Deductions / After A / Method Entirely New. / By Josiah Tucker, D. D. / Dean of Glocester. / Glocester: / Printed by R. Raikes. / And Sold In London By / J. Rivington, In St. Paul's Church-Yard; T. Cadell, / In The Strand; and J. Walter, Near Charing- / Cross. / MDCCLXXIV. / 8vo, 55 pp.

Reviewed in *London Mag.*, vol xliii (1774), p, 242.

35. / A / Brief and Dispassionate View / Of The / Difficulties / Attending The / Trinitarian, Arian, and Socinian Systems: / Occasioned By The / Fierce Controversies now on Foot in divers Parts of the / Kingdom respecting those Subjects: / And Designed To Assist / Candid, Humble, and Modest Inquirers in their / Searches after Gospel Truths. / By Josiah Tucker, D. D. / Dean of Glocester. / Glocester: / Printed by R. Raikes / MDCCLXXIV. / [Price Three Pence] / 8°, 23 pp.

Republished in 1776 as an *Appendix* to *Seventeen Sermons*. Reviewed in *Monthly Rev.*, vol. l (Feb., 1774), p. 413; *Gent's Mag.*, vol. xliv (1774), p. 211; and in *London Mag.*, vol. xliii (1774), p. 243.

36. / Four Tracts / Together With / Two Sermons, / On Political and Commercial / Subjects. / By Josiah Tucker, D. D. / Dean of Glocester. / Glocester: / Printed By R. Raikes. / And Sold By / J.

Rivington, In St. Paul's Churchyard, London. / MDCCLXXIV. / 8°, 216 + 35 pp.

2d Edition, 1775.
3d Edition, 1776. Sold by T. Cadell, xv + 224 pp.
Tract V is sometimes bound with the 3d Edition.
The *Two Sermons* appear as *Sermons VII and VIII* of *Seventeen Sermons*.

Reviewed in { *Monthly Rev.*, vol. l (Feb., 1774), pp. 129–136. *Gent's Mag.*, vol. xliv (1774), pp. 29–30, 78–81 and 126–129; vol xlvi (1776), pp. 413–415.

37. / A / Review / Of / Lord Vis. Clare's Conduct / As / Representative / Of / Bristol. / Virtutem incolumem odimus, / Sublatum ex oculis quaerimus invidi, / By Josiah Tucker, D. D. / Dean of Glocester, and Rector of St. Stephen's in Bristol. / Glocester: / Printed By R. Raikes; / And Sold By / T. Cadell, in London; / And / T. Cadell, in Bristol. / [Price Two-Pence.] / 12°, 34 pp.

An acknowledgment of the *Merchants' Testimonial* by Lord Clare, quoted at the close, is dated Jan. 30, 1775. The pamphlet has no date, but was issued in 1775.

38. / A / Letter / To / Edmund Burke, Esq; / Member of Parliament For The / City of Bristol, / And Agent For The Colony Of New York &c / In Answer To / His Printed Speech; / Said To Be Spoken In The House Of Commons / On The Twenty Second Of March, 1775. / By Josiah Tucker D. D. / Dean of Glocester / Glocester / Printed by R Raikes; / And Sold By / T. Cadell, In The Strand, London / MDCCLXXV, / [Price One Shilling.] 8°, 58 pp.

A "Second Edition, Corrected," was published in the same year.
Reviewed in *Monthly Rev.*, vol. liii (Aug., 1775), p. 180.

39. / Seventeen Sermons / On Some Of The / Most Important Points / On / Natural and Revealed Religion, / Respecting The / Happiness Both Of The Present, And Of / A Future Life. / Together With An / Appendix, / Containing A / Brief And Dispassionate View Of The / Several Difficulties Respectively Attending The / Orthodox, Arian and Socinian Systems / In Regard To / The Holy Trinity. / By Josiah Tucker, D. D. / Dean of Glocester; / Printed by R. Raikes; / And Sold By J. Rivington, In St. Paul's Churchyard, London, / MDCCLXXVI. / 8°, ix + 351 pp.

Reviewed in *Monthly Rev.*, vol. lvi (Apr., 1777), pp. 253–256.

40. / The True / Interest of Britain / Set Forth in Regard / To The / Colonies; / And the only Means of / Living in Peace and Harmony with Them, / Including Five different Plans, for effecting this desirable / Event. / By Jos. Tucker, D. D. Dean of Glocester. / Author of the Essay on the Advantages and Disadvantages / which respectively attend France and Great Britain, with / regard to Trade. /

To which is added by the Printer, a few more Words / on the Freedom of the Press in America. / Philadelphia; / Printed and Sold, by Robert Bell, in Third Street, / MDCCLXXVI. / 8° 66 pp + 4 pp on Press Freedom.

This is *Tract IV* of the ***Four Tracts.***

41. Address to the Public in favour of Dr. Campbell's Sermon. June 1778.

Proof page in British Museum Library. See *add. Mss.*, 5825. f. 159. b.

42. The State of the Nation in 1777 Compared with the State of the Nation in the famous year of Conquest and Glory, 1759. By the Dean of Gloucester.

Written in 1778.

A proof sheet in British Mus. Library *Mss.* See *Mss.* 34414, f. 568.

43. / Dean Tucker's / Reflections / On The / Terrors / Of / Invasion / Re-Published By / A Friend to His Country. / London: / Printed For Edmund Lloyd, / Harley Street. / 1806 / 8°, 15 pp.

First published by Tucker in 1779. Mentioned July 31, 1779, *Gent's Mag.*, vol. xlix, p. 375.

44. Further Thoughts on the Present Posture of Affairs. October, 1779.

Signed "Cassandra." Proof sheet in British Museum Library. See *Add. MSS.*, 34. 416, f 409.

45. / Dispassionate Thoughts / On The / American War / Addressed To The / Moderate of All Parties / In the Multitude of Counsellors there is Safety. / Solomon, London. / Printed for J. Wilkie, No. 71, St. Paul's / Church Yard. / MDCCLXXX / [Price One Shilling] / 8°, 36 pp.

46. The Dean of Gloucester's Thoughts [adapted] / to the Enquiries not set on Foot] hum- / bly submitted to the serious Considerations / of Lords and Gentlemen in Town and / Country. Gloucester Feb. 22, 1780.

Signed "Cassandra." Printed in *Gent's Mag.*, vol. l, pp. 132–133.

47. Proposals for a General Pacifi- / cation. / By the Dean of Gloucester. /

Signed "Cassandra." Printed *Gent's Mag.*, vol. l (1780), pp. 221, 222. Published also in ***Second Edition of Cui Bono?*** (1782) as an ***appendix.***

48. / A / Treatise / Concerning / Civil Government / In / Three Parts / Part I / The Notions of Mr. Locke And His Followers, / Concerning The Origin, Extent, And End / Of Civil Government, / Examined And Confuted. / Part II / The True Basis of Civil Government Set / Forth And Ascertained; Also Objections / Answered: Different Forms Compared; And / Improvements Suggested. /

Part III. / England's Former Gothic Constitution Cen- / sured And Exposed; Cavils Refuted; And / Authorities Produced; Also The Scripture / Doctrine Concerning The Obedience Due To / Governors Vindicated And Illustrated. / By Josiah Tucker D. D. / Dean of Glocester. / London; / Printed for T. Cadell, In The Strand. / MDCCLXXXI / 8° v + 428 pp.

49. / Cui Bono? / Or An / Inquiry / What / Benefits Can Arise / Either To The / English Or The Americans, / The French, Spaniards Or Dutch, / From The / Greatest Victories or Successes, / In The / Present War? / Being A / Series of Letters, / Addressed to Monsieur Necker, / Late Controller General of the Finances of France. / By Josiah Tucker, D. D. / Dean of Glocester. / Glocester: / Printed By R. Raikes: / For T. Cadell In the Strand: / Sold Also By Evans and Hazell, / In Glocester: / MDCCLXXXI. / 8°, 141 pp.

2d Edition, "corrected," Glocester, 1782.

3d Edition, with "Proposal for a General Pacification" as an Appendix, London, 1782.

A French translation was published in 1782: *Cui Bono, Ou Examen quel avantages les Anglais etc., . . . traduit de l'Anglais, Londres, 1782.* Reviewed *Gent's Mag.*, vol. lii (1782), pp. 82, 83.

50. Addenda to

/ A / Sermon / Preached At The / Cathedral Church of Glocester / Upon The / Anniversary of The Restoration, / And Published At The Request Of The Dean And / Chapter And Other Clergy Of That Church, / By the Rev. Thomas Stock, A. M. / Head Master Of The Grammar School At Gloucester; / And Late Fellow of Pembroke College, Oxford. / Glocester. / Printed by R. Raikes. / MDCCLXXXII: / 12°, Sermon 29 pp. Addenda 14 pp.

The Addenda, written by Tucker, contain "an historical detail of the Political Affairs of this Country during the Grand Rebellion."

51. / Reflections / On The / Present Low Price / Of / Coarse Wools, / Its Immediate Causes, / And / Its Probable Remedies. / By / Josiah Tucker, D. D. / Dean of Gloucester. / Tros Tyriusque Mihi Nullo Discrimine Habetur. / London: / Printed for T. Cadell, In The Strand. / MDCCLXXXII / [Price One Shilling] / 8° 46 pp.

Reviewed in *New Rev.*, vol. i (1782), p. 44, and in *Monthly Rev.*, vol. lxvi (Mar., 1782), pp. 228–230.

52. / Four Letters / On Important / National Subjects, Addressed to the Right Honourable / The Earl of Shelburne, / His Majesty's First Lord Commissioner / Of The Treasury. / By Josiah Tucker, D. D. / Dean of Glocester / London: / Printed by R. Raikes / for T. Cadel, In The Strand. / MDCCLXXXIII / . 8° vii + 120 pp.

A second edition, in same year, with only minor alterations—also, in same year, a *Dublin* edition "Printed by R. Marchbank, for W. & H. Whitestone, W. Wilson and P. Byrne." An evident typographical blunder made the date on the title page of the *London 2nd Edition* read "MDCCLXXIII." This edition seems to be more common. This title-page error has led most bibliographers to list this tract as of 1773. See Bibliography by Mr. Paul Leicester Ford in *Journal Pol. Econ.*, vol. ii, p. 330–337, and Bibliography by Mr. Leslie Stephens in *Dict. Nat. Biog.* article on Tucker. The error is patent from the title page itself, for the Earl of Shelburne was not "First Lord of the Treasury" until 1782–83. Again there is internal evidence for Tucker mentions in the tract that the Americans have declared independence.

Reviewed in *New Rev.*, vol. iii (1783), p. 44.

53. Subjects for Dissertations and Premiums, to be offered to the Graduate Students of the Universities of England and Scotland.

Written in December, 1784. Published as an *Appendix to Reflections on the Present Matters in Dispute Between Great Britain and Ireland* (1785), pp. 35–41. Republished in *European Magazine*, vol. vi, pp. 17–18 (Jan., 1792).

54. / A Sequel to / Sir William Jones' Pamphlet / on the / Principles of Government, / in a / Dialogue between a Freeholder / in the / County of Denhigh and the / Dean of Gloucester. / Gloucester / Printed for R. Raikes, / and sold by / T. Cadell, in the Strand, London: / Evans & Hazell, Gloucester. / MDCCLXXXIV / [Price six pence] 8° v + 29 pp.

Reviewed in *Monthly Rev.*, vol. lxxi (Dec., 1784), p. 474. The reviewer says: "Let the 'political deans' chew each other."

55. To the Philological Society: "Dean Tucker's Opinion on the Present most interesting Disputes."

Published in { *The Europ. Mag. and Lon. Rev.*, vol. v (1784), pp. 220, 221. *Gent's Mag.*, vol. liv (1784), p. 202, 203. }

56. / Reflections / On The / Present Matters In Dispute / Between / Great Britain and Ireland; / And On The / Means of converting these Articles into / Mutual Benefits to both Kingdoms. / By Josiah Tucker, D. D. / Dean of Gloucester. / Dublin: / Printed for Messrs. Wilson, White and Byrne. / MDCCLXXXV. / 8° 34 pp.

Appendix (pp. 35 to 41) contains the *Subjects for Dissertations*, etc.

57. / Union Or Separation / Written Some Years Since / By The Rev. Dr. Tucker, / Dean Of Gloucester, / And / Now First Published / In / This Tract / Upon The Same Subject. / By The Rev. Dr. Clarke, / Secretary For The Library And Chaplain To / His Royal Highness The Prince of Wales / [In this work the great Objections urged at a Meeting of / the Irish Bar are distinctly considered and confuted.] / "Tros Tyriusque Mihi Nullo Discrimine Habetur." / London / Sold By J. Hatchard & J. Wright, In / Piccadilly; Clarke,

New Bond / Street; and Rivington, St. / Paul's Church Yard. / 1799. / 8° ii + 83 pp.

Clarke had submitted queries to Tucker in 1785 and received then the answers here printed. There was an Irish edition of the above, title page exactly like the above except that it begins " / Dean Tucker's / Arguments / On The / Propriety Of An," etc., and ends, "/ Dublin: / Printed For J. Milliken, 32 Grafton Street, / 1799. "

58. / Thoughts / On / War, / Political, Commercial, Religious / And / Satyrical / By Josiah Tucker, / Dean of Gloucester, / William Law M. A. / And / Jonathan Swift, / Dean of St. Patricks / London / Printed In The Year MDCCXCIII / By Darton And Harvey, Grace Church Street / 8°, 54 pp.

37 pp. contain Tucker's *Prevention of Wars*, from his *The Case of Going to War*, etc.

59. / Arguments / For And Against An / Union / Between / Great Britain And Ireland / Considered; / To which Is Prefixed A / Proposal On The Same Subject, / By Josiah Tucker, D. D. / Dean of Gloucester / London / Reprinted for John Stockdale, Piccadilly. / 1798. / 8°, 31 pp.

pp. 2 to 4 give Tucker's argument against the plea that Ireland would run away with English trade if incorporated.

II. REPLIES[1] TO TUCKER'S WORKS.

1. / The / Principles / Of A / Methodist / By John Wesley, M. A. / Fellow of Lincoln College, Oxford, / Occasioned by a late Pamphlet, intitled, A Brief History / of the Principles of Methodism / The Second Edition / Bristol: / Printed by Felix Farley, in Castle-Green, and sold / at the New School in the Horse Fair: Also at the / Foundry, near Upper Moorfields, and by T. Trye at Gray's Inn Gate, London; likewise by R. Aken- / Head, on the Tyne Bridge, Newcastle. 1746 / [Price two pence] / 12° 23 pp.

A 3rd edition, "London, 1796," with no changes.
A reply to Tucker's *A Brief History of the Principles of Methodism*.

2. / Remarks / On The / Reverend Mr. Tucker's / Letter / on / Naturalizations. / In Two Letters to a Friend. / . . . . / London: / Printed for E. Withers in Fleet Street, 1753 / Price Six pence / 8° 32 pp.

3. Remarks on a paper entituled, Im / provements and savings in inland / navigations, exemplified on the ri / ver Stroud in the County of Glou / cester, by the Dean of Gloucester /

This is an article published in the *Annual Register*, vol. iii (1760),

[1] There is no pretence that the following is at all an exhaustive list of the tracts Tucker's pamphlets inspired. There are probably many others in the unwieldy mass of 18th century pamphlets. Omissions in these title pages, indicated by . . . . . are simply Latin mottoes.

pp. 144-148, and in the *London Mag.*, vol. xxix (1760), pp. 351-354. The article is dated from Gloucester, May 29, 1760, and is signed Ferd. Stratford.

4. / The / Scripture The Only Test / As Well As / The Only Rule / Of / Christian Faith / Maintained in a / Letter / To / The Rev. Dr. Tucker / Dean of Glocester. / . . . / London / Printed for Benj. White, at Horace's Head, in Fleet Street. / MDCCLXXII. / 8° 41 pp.

5. / A / Letter / To The / Rev. Dr. Josiah Tucker, / Dean of Gloucester: / Occasioned / By his Apology for the present Church / of England, as by Law established, &c. / Wherein / Every Material Article is Examined: / And / The Plan of the Petitioning Clergy, and others, / is fully vindicated, upon the Principles of Christianity, / all Protestant Churches, / and the Church of England / in particular. / By a Petitioning Clergyman. / London: / Printed for the Author and J. Walder, and sold by / Mr. Buckland, in Pater-Noster-Row; and Mr. Lamte- / rett, in Clift, Lewes; and may be had of most other / Booksellers in Town and Country. MDCCLXXIII / [Price One Shilling] / 8° 57 pp.

6. / A / Letter to Doctor Tucker / On His / Proposal of a Separation / Between / Great Britain / And Her / American Colonies. / London. Printed for T. Becket, Corner of the Adelphi, Strand / MDCCLXXIV / 8° 36 pp.

7. / Some / Reasons / For Approving / Of The / Dean of Gloucester's Plan, / Of / Separating From The Colonies: / With / A Proposal / For A Further Improvement / . . . / London: / Printed for N. Conant, Successor to / Mr. Whiston, in Fleet Street. / MDCCLXXV. / 8°, 32 pp.

An ironical tract.

8. A / Letter / To The Reverend / Josiah Tucker, D. D. / Dean of Glocester, / In Answer to / His Humble Address and Earnest Appeal &c / With A / Postscript, In Which / The present War against America / Is Shewn to be / The Effect / not of the Causes Assigned by Him and Others, / But of A Fixed / Plan of Administration, / Founded in System. / The Landed opposed to the Commercial / Interest of the State. / Being as the Means in order to the End. / By Samuel Estwick, LL. D. Assistant Agent, for the Island of Barbadoes / . . . / London / Printed for J Almon, opposite Burlington House, Piccadilly, / MDCCLXXVI. / 8°, 125 pp.

9. America—addressed to the Rev. Dean Tucker.

A poem, ridiculing Tucker's separation scheme, said to have been written by Mr. Soame Jenyns. Published in *Annual Register*, vol. xix (1776), pp. 204, 205.

A ludicrous blunder occurs in Joseph Stratford's biography of Tucker in his *Gloucestershire Biographical Notes* (p. 135). Jenyns, in the above poem, in humorous metaphor, credits Tucker with having invented a spring for freeing runaway horses from the vehicle to which they are attached. The hit at Tucker's plan for separating from the fractious colonies is obvious, but Stratford quotes the poem and stolidly credits Tucker with inventive mechanical genius.

10. / Plain Truth / Or A / Letter / To The Author Of / Dispassionate Thoughts / On The / American War / In Which / The Principles and Arguments of that Author / are refuted and the necessity of carrying on that / War clearly demonstrated. / By the Author of Letters to a Nobleman on the / Conduct of the American War; and of Cool / Thoughts on the Consequences of American Independence. / London: / Printed for G. Wilkie, in St. Paul's Churchyard; / and R. Faulder, in Bond Street. / MDCCLXXX. / 8° vii + 76 pp.

11. / A / Dissertation / On The / National Assemblies / Under The / Saxon and Norman / Governments / With / A Postcript addressed to the Dean of Gloucester. / By James Ibbetson, Esq. / Barrister At Law / . . . / London, Printed for R. Faulder, Bond Street. / MDCCLXXXI. / 4° 45 pp.

    A four-page "Poscript" to Tucker.

12. / A / Vindication / of the / Political Principles / of / Mr Locke: / In Answer To The Objections Of / The Rev. Dr. Tucker / Dean of Gloucester. / By Joseph Towers, LL. D. / . . . / London / Printed for G. Robinson, Pater Noster Row / MDCCLXXXII. / 8° 113 pp.

13. / An / Union / of / England and Ireland / Proved To Be / Practicable and equally Beneficial to each / Kingdom / With / Supplementary Observations / Relative To The / Absentees of Ireland. / . . . / To which is added / A Collateral Reply to the Dean of Gloucester's Advice to the Irish to trade / with Foreign in Preference to the British / Colonies. / By John Williams, Esq. / Late of Merton College, Oxon. / Author of Constitutional Guide &c &c / London / Sold by G. Kearsley Fleet Street. 1787. / 8°, 50 pp.

    Pages 22 to 42 inclusive are directed to Tucker.

III. TUCKER'S CORRESPONDENCES.

1. Correspondence With Lord Townshend.

    Six letters by Tucker, ranging in dates from March 12, 1752, to March, 1753. Four replies to Tucker by Lord Townshend are printed with these letters of Tucker. The correspondence dealt freely with economic themes, such as the bounty on corn, infant industries and taxes. In the letter of June 1, 1752, occurs the first reference, by Tucker, to his "great work" which he had then under way.

    These letters are published with *MSS.* Marquis of Townshend, in

Eleventh Annual Report Hist. MSS. Commission of Great Britain, Appendix, Part iv, pp. 371 to 379 and 382. See Sessional Reports, 1887, vol. xlvii, pp. as above.

2. Letters to Rev. Dr. Birch.

Forty-three letters, ranging in dates from July 19, 1752, to February 18, 1764. The letters are, like those of the Foster *MSS.*, largely personal and private in their contents. The Bristol elections of 1754 and 1756 and the conditions at Gloucester after Tucker had accepted the Deanship, are described. A number of proof sheets of political pamphlets by Tucker accompany these letters.
See Library Brit. Museum, *MSS* 4319, vol. xx, 818.

3. Letters to Dr. C. N. Forster.

Thirty-eight letters, dating from October 8, 1752, to October 24, 1757. These letters deal mainly with private business matters, Tucker having acted as agent for some property in Bristol, owned by Foster. The Bristol elections of 1754 and 1756 are described.
See Library Brit. Museum, *Add. MSS.*, 11275.

4. Letters to Lord Hardwicke (Philip, Earl of Hardwicke).

Six letters, dating from March 13, 1756, to January 3, 1761. These letters are mainly concerning the Bristol elections of 1756 and Tucker's standing in Gloucester in 1760 and 1761.
See Library Brit. Museum, *MSS.* 35692, f. 130–134–143.

5. Letters to Nugent. (The Honorable Robert Nugent.)

Three letters dated, respectively, August 25, 26 and 31, 1756. All tell about the Bristol elections. A draft of an address to King George, drawn up by Tucker for Bristol subjects, accompanies these letters. All were forwarded to the Duke of Newcastle by Nugent, and were thus preserved in the Newcastle *MSS.*
See Library Brit. Museum, *Add. MSS.* 32867, pp. 127, 195, 197.

6. Letters to David Hume.

I. Dated March, 1758. A reply to Hume's letter to Lord Kames, dated March 4, 1758. These letters discuss the relative trading strength of rich and poor nations. Tucker's letter contains the outline of thought afterwards expanded into *Tract I* of the *Four Tracts*. Tucker claims to have converted Hume to his theory through this correspondence of 1758. (See *Preface* to *Four Tracts.*) Both of these letters are printed in Clarke's *Survey of the Strength ana Opulence of Great Britain* (1799), pp. 20–27.

II. Dated January 16, 1769. Subject, Taxes. This letter is reprinted in full in this volume, see pp. 207 and 208. It was first published in *Letters of Eminent Persons Addressed to David Hume, etc.*, pp. 176–177. J. H. Burton, Editor, Edinburgh and London, 1849.

7. Letter to the Duke of Newcastle.

Dated June 25, 1758. Acknowledges his preferment to Deanery of Gloucester.
See Library Brit. Museum *Add. MSS.*, 32, 881, f. 74.

8. Letters to Lord Kames.

I. Dated July 6, 1758—on comparative advantages for manufactures of a poor and a rich country.

II. Dated October 18, 1761 — on charitable eollections and on the "great work."

III. Dated December 10, 1763—on the "great work" and on the visit to Ireland.

IV. Dated December 26, 1763—on the *Elements of Criticism*, etc.

V. Dated February 15, 1764—on Tucker's writings and literary and other occupations.

VI. Dated June 16, 1782—on Locke's political ideas and on errors in conduct of American affairs.

VII. Dated June 24, 1782—on socage and the Saxon government.

These letters were printed as a few selected from the many written during the long correspondence with Lord Kames—a continuous exchange of letters from 1758 until the death of Lord Kames in 1782. These selected letters are published in vol. iii, pp. 157–183 of *Memoirs of the Life and Writings of the Hon. Henry Home of Kames*, by Hon. Alex. Fraser Tytler.

9. Letters from Turgot.

Two, dated September 12, 1770 and December 10, 1773. The content of these letters was outlined on pp. 226 and 227. They are printed in Œvres de M. Turgot (Paris, 1810), vol. ix, pp. 366–375.

10. Letter to William Seward, Esq.

Dated October 29, 1790. This letter refers to the colonial policy of Great Britain, to the Subscription Controversy, to the American Revolution and to Tucker's approaching "last stage of all."

See Library Brit. Museum, *Add. MSS*, 5419.

IV. REFERENCES[1] UPON TUCKER'S LIFE.

1. *Alumni Oxonienses*.

See vol. of 1715–1886 for Tucker's record.

2. *Anecdotes of Distinguished Persons*, etc. 4th ed. 4 vols. London, 1798. By W. Seward.

See *Preface* of vol. i and last anecdote of vol. ii. Seward introduces this anecdote of Tucker as the only exception to his general rule not to deal with living characters. In excuse for this exception, he says, "a man like Dr. Tucker *omni major eulogio* should be also *omni exceptione major*." [See *Preface*, vol. i.]

3. *Biographie Universelle*. Vol. xlii, p. 240.

[1] There is no definitive biography of Tucker. Of the numerous brief sketches of his life and writings, those in Palgrave's *Dictionary of Pol. Econ.* and in the *Dict. of Nat'l Biography* are the most acceptable. The obituary biographies in the magazines, current at the time of Tucker's death, with Seward's and Nichol's *Anecdotes*, are the chief sources of most of the *Dictionary* and *Encyclopædia* biographies which are not simply re-hashes of preceding *Dictionary* and *Encyclopædia* sketches.

Tucker's own letters, especially those to Forster, to Birch and to Kames, supply biographical material. His will is recorded at Somersett House in London; but it is not autobiographical; it simply bequeaths his all to his widow. His controversial works and occasional sermons indicate where his interests lay at different periods of his life. There are a few direct biographical references in his works, notably in the *Preface* to his *Four Tracts*.

4. *Chalmer's Biographical Dictionary*. Revised edition. London, 1816, Vol. xxx, pp. 59–63.

5. *Dictionary of National Biography*.
Tucker's life is written and his writings estimated by Mr. Leslie Stephen.

6. *Dictionary of Political Economy*. R. H. I. Palgrave, editor. Vol. iii, pp. 588, 589.

7. *English Thought in the Eighteenth Century*. By Leslie Stephen. Vol. ii, pp. 216, 217, 301–304.

8. *Gloucestershire Biographical Notes*. By Joseph Stratford. Gloucester, 1887.
Pp. 129 to 136, inclusive, treat of Tucker's life.

9. *Handwörterbuch Der Staatswissenschaft*. By J. Conrad and others. Vol. vii, pp. 230 and 231.

10. *History of England in the Eighteenth Century*. By Wm. E. H. Lecky. London, 1878. Vol. iii, p. 388.

11. *Imperial Dictionary of Universal Biography*. John Francis Waller, Editor. Vol. iii.
Sketch of Tucker's life by Rev. John Eadie.

12. *Journal of Political Economy*. Vol. ii, pp. 330–347.
An article "Josiah Tucker and His Writings," by Paul Leicester Ford.

13. *Letters From A Late Eminent Prelate To One Of His Friends*. 2d ed. London, 1809. Pp. 403, 443, 444 and 452.
Bishop William Warburton's caustic references to Dean Tucker.

14. Bishop Thomas Newton's *Life Written by Himself*. Vol. ii of *Lives of Eminent English Divines*. London, 1816. Pp. 107–108.

15. *Literary Anecdotes of the 18th Century*. By John Nichols. Vol. iii, p. 428 and vol. ix, p. 295.
An engraving of Tucker in vol. ix, p. 295.

16. *Nouvelle Biographie Genérale*. Vol. xlv, p. 691.

17. *Public Characters of 1798–1799*. 4th edition. Pp. 162–174.

18. *The Annals of Bristol in the Eighteenth Century* (1893). By John Latimer. Pp. 117, 118, 238, 283, 284, 289, 318, 319, 322, 329, 435, 462 and 473.

19. *The Annual Register*. Vol. xl, p. 232.
A statement of Burke's attitude towards Tucker.
Vol. xli (1799), pp. 350–354.
An obituary biography.

20. *The European Magazine.* Vol. i (1782), p. 35.
Uncomplimentary criticism of Tucker.
Vol. xxxvi, pp. 291–293.
An obituary biography. Reproduction of a portrait of Tucker on p. 290.

21. *The Gentleman's Magazine.* Vol. lxxxvi (1799), pp. 1000–1003.
Obituary biography.

22. *The Georgian Era.* Vol. i, pp. 502–503.
Tucker's memoir classed with that of churchmen.

23. *The History of Bristol.* By John Corry and John Evans. Bristol, 1816.
Vol. ii tells the story of Bristol in the Eighteenth Century.

24. *The Life of William Warburton, D. D.* By John Selby Watson. London, 1863. Pp. 496 and 603.

25. *The Monthly Magazine.* Vol. viii (1799), pp. 912–914.
An obituary biography.

26. *The Penny Cyclopædia.* London, 1843. Vol. xxv, pp. 338–341.
An appreciative biography.

VITA

The writer of this dissertation was born at Defiance, Ohio, on June 9th, 1873. He was graduated from the public school at Delphos, Ohio, in 1890, and entered Ohio Wesleyan University in 1891. He was graduated from this University in 1896, and received the B. A. degree. In 1898, for special work in History, he received the M. A. degree from this same University.

In 1899 he entered Columbia University, and registered with Political Economy and Finance as his major subject, and with Sociology and Statistics and European History as his minor subjects. In these courses he attended lectures under Professors John B. Clark, Franklin H. Giddings, James Harvey Robinson, Edwin R. A. Seligman, Richmond Mayo-Smith, and William M. Sloane.

He held the following honor-appointments under the Columbia University Faculty of Political Science: Scholar in Economics, 1900–1901; Alternate Fellow in Economics, 1901–02; Fellow in Economics, 1902–03.

In 1896 he was elected Tutor in Mathematics in Ohio Wesleyan University, and served there three years. In the summer sessions of 1900 and 1901 he delivered courses of lectures at Ohio Wesleyan University upon Political Economy. In January, 1901, he was elected Tutor in Philosophy in the College of the City of New York, and in December of 1902 he was advanced to be Instructor in Philosophy in the same College, which position he now holds. In this capacity he gives the Political Science courses of the College of the City of New York.

Bei Fragen zur Produktsicherheit wenden Sie sich bitte an:
If you have any questions regarding product safety,
please contact:

Walter de Gruyter GmbH
Genthiner Straße 13
10785 Berlin
productsafety@degruyterbrill.com